Free Traders

Elites, Democracy, and the Rise of Globalization

MALCOLM FAIRBROTHER

OXFORD
UNIVERSITY PRESS

OXFORD
UNIVERSITY PRESS

Oxford University Press is a department of the University of Oxford. It furthers
the University's objective of excellence in research, scholarship, and education
by publishing worldwide. Oxford is a registered trade mark of Oxford University
Press in the UK and certain other countries.

Published in the United States of America by Oxford University Press
198 Madison Avenue, New York, NY 10016, United States of America.

© Oxford University Press 2020

Library of Congress Cataloging-in-Publication Data
Names: Fairbrother, Malcolm, author.
Title: Free traders : elites, democracy, and the rise of globalization / Malcolm Fairbrother.
Description: New York : Oxford University Press, [2019] |
Includes bibliographical references and index.
Identifiers: LCCN 2019012351 | ISBN 9780190635459 (hardback) |
ISBN 9780190635466 (pbk.) | ISBN 9780190635473 (updf) |
ISBN 9780190635480 (epub) | ISBN 9780190635497 (online)
Subjects: LCSH: Free trade—Government policy—United States—History. |
Free trade—Government policy—Canada—History. |
Free trade—Government policy—Mexico—History. | Globalization—History.
Classification: LCC HF1756 .F25 2019 | DDC 382/.71097—dc23
LC record available at https://lccn.loc.gov/2019012351

1 3 5 7 9 8 6 4 2

Paperback printed by Marquis, Canada
Hardback printed by Bridgeport National Bindery, Inc., United States of America

Free Traders

CONTENTS

FIGURES

PREFACE

Politics is not just about interests; it's also about ideas. This book is about the peculiar ideas that gave us the global economy we have today.

These ideas helped hold together coalitions of elites who pushed through the policies and international agreements that made globalization happen. Without these coalitions, free traders would have struggled to get their way, given the public's doubts and the frequent civil society opposition to globalization. The ideas motivating free traders bear striking similarities to the mercantilist ideology that dominated economic thinking in early modern Europe. Surprisingly, then, ideas that economists rejected long ago remain central to international economic policymaking today. Maybe even more surprisingly, scholars have not noticed the contradiction; instead, many have exaggerated globalization's legitimacy by saying its rise since the 1980s has been based on mainstream academic economics.

The book tells the story of globalization from the perspective of North America in the late twentieth century. It uses case studies of how Canada, Mexico, and the United States proposed, negotiated, and ratified two free trade agreements that substantially opened and integrated their economies. On the basis of more than a hundred interviews and analyses of materials from archives in all three countries, the book provides a new history of the political origins of the bilateral Canada-US and the trilateral North American Free Trade Agreements (CUFTA and NAFTA). Building on prior work in sociology, political science, economics, and history, this comparative-historical analysis examines the rise of globalization in the sense of growing international trade and investment, plus states' adoption of new commitments in a range of other areas addressed by recent trade agreements. These include most notably, and controversially, investor and intellectual property rights.

The book shows that these agreements have had little to do with the preferences of the median voter, or the incentives of democracy. There have been systematic differences in the politics of globalization in developed and developing countries, but in both contexts governments have had to buy off businesspeople who were skeptical of free trade, using favorable and often protectionist content in the agreements they negotiate. This domestic cooptation has pitted nations against nations, and helps explain the mercantilist character of international trade negotiations.

The prevalence of mercantilist ideas matters not just because of their consequences for free trade. Mercantilism also shapes domestic political conflicts. People who believe that nations compete are less likely to protect the environment, or to support ordinary workers and the poor. They also blame globalization for problems not of its making; the very ideas used to sell it have also sowed the seeds of the current backlash against it.

ACKNOWLEDGMENTS

My work on this book began an embarrassingly long time ago, in a grad school far, far away. The project took me to Mexico City, Ottawa, and Washington, DC, and to archives across North America. It followed me, on and off, as I moved to England and then on to Sweden. During many years of work, I accumulated many debts.

First, I have above all been the beneficiary of lots of love and support from my family—my parents, siblings, their partners, and many nieces and nephews. I feel fortunate to have them all in my life. I was also lucky to get as much time as I did with my English grandparents, and my uncle.

Next, I would like to thank my advisers at the University of California, Berkeley: Peter Evans, Michael Burawoy, Marion Fourcade, and Richard Walker. I thank them all for their input and patience. I should also mention that Fred Block generously served as a kind of bonus committee member, from his vantage point at UC Davis.

Also in my years at Berkeley, and during fieldwork back and forth across North America, I was supported by a great many friends—too many for me to name them all. Among those to whom I am particularly grateful, I should mention Ofer Sharone, Ana Villalobos, Manuel Vallee, Simone Pulver, Basak Kus, Isaac Martin, Keyvan Kashkooli, and Eréndira Rueda. Away from the university, the friendship of Eric Greene and Vanessa Ramirez, and the support and inspiration of the BZC and CZM communities made a big difference. Tom Medvetz stands apart, not only as a good friend (and flatmate on two separate occasions), but also someone who shaped my thinking a great deal over the years.

My fieldwork would not have been possible without the warm welcome I received at a number of academic institutions: the Centro de Investigaciones sobre América del Norte at the Universidad Nacional Autónoma de México; the Centre on North American Politics and Society at Carleton University in Ottawa;, and the Center for Latin American Studies at Georgetown University in Washington,

DC. The libraries of the Colegio de México, Centro de Investigación y Docencia Económicas, George Washington University, and Concordia University also gave me access to their collections.

As I developed the ideas and arguments that appear here, I received thoughtful feedback from many individuals and audiences. Nitsan Chorev's input stands out: at a crucial moment, she gave me detailed comments on a long paper, and let me know that I needed to up my game; in hindsight, it was just what I needed to hear at that time. I also benefited from feedback and conversations about my study at the Institute for Qualitative and Multi-Method Research at Arizona State University. More recently, this book's main arguments have benefited from the comments of anonymous Oxford University Press reviewers who read both the book proposal and the full manuscript. American University's North American Research Initiative has been a congenial community within which to discuss issues of regional cooperation and integration.

In 2007 I moved to England, and thus began ten years in the School of Geographical Sciences at Bristol University, with many wonderful colleagues. Four in particular stand out: Kelvyn Jones, Jeff Henderson, Adam Dixon, and Sean Fox. Every young academic should be so lucky as to have smart and caring mentors like Kelvyn and Jeff, and blindly loyal cheerleaders like Adam and Sean. Near the end of my time at Bristol, I benefited from a year's sabbatical funded by the university's Institute for Advanced Studies. That year not only gave me much-needed time to work on this and several other projects, but I got to know two academic hosts at institutions abroad—Diana Zavala-Rojas and Cristiano Vezzoni—who became excellent friends, and supported me through some challenging times.

A postdoctoral fellowship at UC San Diego's Center for U.S.-Mexican Studies helped get me through the awkward period between finishing my PhD and landing a permanent academic post. A small grant from the British Academy enabled additional archival research that made the case studies here far more robust.

I am indebted to my interviewees, for giving me their time and considered answers to my questions. Many of these people would surely disagree with large parts of this book, but they still influenced my thinking a great deal. I am also very grateful for the work and assistance of the many archivists who helped me locate relevant materials.

I gratefully acknowledge permission to reuse some material previously published in three articles (in the *American Journal of Sociology, Review of International Political Economy,* and *Politics & Society*) plus a book chapter in *Hegemonic Transitions, the State and Crisis in Neoliberal Capitalism* (published by Routledge).

In 2017 I moved to Sweden, and since then I have benefited from the support of many new colleagues. Stefan Svallfors, Gustaf Arrhenius, and Sverker Jagers are all exemplary scholars who have given me valuable advice and new opportunities. Jan Mewes and Mo and Erin Eger were big reasons I moved to Umeå in the first place. Maureen also provided helpful feedback on some chapters at a late stage, as did Per Wisselgren and Anna Baranowska-Rataj on Chapter 1 long before. Umeå University and the Institute for Futures Studies have given me time to think and write; I do not take that for granted.

Finally, thanks above all to my wife Ava for coming into my life at just the right time (bringing the rest of the remarkable Hassens, plus a small dog, along for the ride). Since then she has not let me take myself too seriously, and without her good-humored support I doubt I would have been able to finish this book. One day in 2018 when I was moaning about how the "new NAFTA" keeps changing and so how can I stop writing about the old, she started singing the chorus of the music to "The NeverEnding Story." That's the kind of thing she does to keep me going.

CHRONOLOGY

1973   Canada and Mexico both introduce restrictive foreign investment laws.

1980   Canada and Mexico reject the idea of North American integration.
Mexico decides not to join GATT, after negotiating an accession protocol.

1982   Severe international recession.
Mexico briefly defaults on its foreign debt.

1984   Progressive Conservative government of Brian Mulroney elected in Canada.

1985   Canada formally requests to negotiate free trade with the United States.

1986   CUFTA negotiations begin.
Mexico joins GATT.

1987   CUFTA negotiations end.

1988   Mulroney Tories re-elected in Canada, on a platform to enact CUFTA.
Carlos Salinas de Gortari becomes president of Mexico.
George H. W. Bush elected US president.

1989   CUFTA goes into effect.

1990   Mexico approaches the United States about negotiating a free trade agreement.
Canada requests to participate, and the United States and Mexico agree.

1991   Start of NAFTA negotiations.

1992   End of NAFTA negotiations.
Bill Clinton elected US president.

1993   Negotiations on labor and environmental side-agreements.
Each country ratifies NAFTA.
Liberal government of Jean Chrétien elected in Canada.

1994   NAFTA goes into effect.

1

Explaining the Rise of Globalization

Democracy legitimates.

Everything else being equal, in today's world it is harder to criticize or to question something that is democratic. In almost all the world's nations, democracy is now such a powerful ideal commanding such widespread loyalty that even most dictators say their countries are democracies; it would be awkward to admit otherwise, if not self-destructive. It matters whether or not a government and its actions are perceived as democratic. And that is true even though the meaning of democracy is highly malleable. If asked to define it, many people would say something about abstract principles like freedom, accountability, inclusion, rule by the people, the popular will. A lot of social science takes a narrower, more practical view and defines countries as democracies as long as they hold free and fair elections on a regular basis. Other scholars say the only real proof of democracy is when competitive elections actually change the government.

Whatever the definition, there are certainly a lot of social scientists working to identify democracy's causes and consequences. And given the legitimacy attached to democracy, anything they identify as a cause or a consequence immediately itself becomes more legitimate. This book is about one of the most significant global trends of the last thirty years, and something whose relationship with democracy—and therefore whose legitimacy—has been debated during all of that time: globalization, in the sense of expanding international trade and foreign direct investment.

Globalization, in this sense, may feel a little abstract; but some comparisons with the past can make it more concrete. It used to be that consumers who wanted to buy something made in another country had to pay a hefty premium to do so—when they could get goods and services from abroad at all. Firms that wanted to invest in a foreign country and establish some kind of operation there were often turned away, or allowed access only to specific economic sectors. In the late 1980s, though, this sort of national segmentation in economic life started to fall away. And governments chose to make it happen. Before that, they had been skeptical about the merits of allowing most cross-border flows of goods, services, and capital; suddenly they changed their minds and decided that these were actually good things. In some cases, they even decided to negotiate international agreements limiting their own freedom to restrict international trade and investment. This book asks why the priorities of so many policymakers around the world changed so much compared to before—and what, if anything, that change of priorities had to do with democracy.

One of the reasons for thinking there might be a relationship is that just when many countries were opening up their economies—in the late 1980s and through the 1990s—many were also transitioning to democracy. Statistical analyses, discussed further below, find the two variables are correlated: countries that transitioned to democracy have opened their economies more than countries that did not. There is little debate that the correlation is real, but what is more contentious is that those scholars who emphasize the correlation tend to go further and claim the statistical relationship is *causal*. Their argument is that democracy makes governments accountable to voters, and the majority of voters stand to benefit from freer trade and investment.[1] Under authoritarian regimes, on the other hand, this school of thought holds that powerful social elites—business owners, executives, and professionals—stand to lose out from globalization, and so they use their privileged access to politicians to override the will and interests of the majority. If this theory, which I will call "liberal," is correct, the rising democracy of many nations in recent decades may well have been the most important factor behind the ascent of globalization.

Does this theory matter? It is certainly an influential perspective in the literature on globalization. But outside of academia, it is also consistent with informal suggestions by many advocates and commentators that globalization possesses the legitimacy of democracy—maybe even that political and economic liberalization are mutually reinforcing freedoms.[2] If in some sense globalization rests on democratic political foundations, and/or reflects the will of ordinary people rather than a narrow elite, then its legitimacy is harder to question.

And yet one of the striking qualities of the academic literature on globalization is its encompassing studies at complete variance with each other. While the liberal scholars take globalization's benefits for the many as a given, others see them as a fiction. This second group of scholars—whom I call "critics"—argue that instead of encouraging the rise of globalization, democracy was if anything an impediment to it. In defending this view, critics argue that trade negotiators meet behind closed doors and only disclose the outcomes of their work when they present agreements for final ratification, by which time few opportunities

---

[1] Eichengreen and Leblang 2008; Liu and Ornelas 2014; Mansfield and Milner 2012; Mukherjee 2016; Pandya 2014.

[2] Friedman 1999; Micklethwait and Wooldridge 2000; Moore 1999.

for amendments remain. Only select parties, therefore, get their voices heard in such negotiations. Once international agreements are enacted, moreover, critics point out that they tie governments' hands. For these reasons, the critics say that globalization rests on undemocratic foundations.[3] They argue that the real force behind the rise of globalization in the last thirty years has been the rich and powerful: business executives, owners, and corporate professionals.[4] Amazingly, these kinds of economic elites are just the people that the liberal perspective says were *opposed* to globalization.

In short, contradictory views of the relationship between democracy and globalization map onto similarly contradictory assumptions about globalization's effects. Some scholars believe in its benevolence and attribute its political success to the will of the majority; others believe in its malignance and point to the preferences of a privileged minority. Some see the displacement of elites, others their dominance. Globalization's foundations, then, are as contested as its consequences.

The stark divide between the liberal and critical literatures reflects that they barely talk to or even acknowledge each other, much less try to reconcile their differences. This mutual ignorance, if not disdain, is unfortunate. The proliferation of parallel research programs engaging separately with many of the same topics and problems is not efficient or intellectually productive. My objective in this book is to bring the diverse literatures on globalization together, especially since, I will argue, each community of scholars possesses insights the other needs to hear. Above all, the two literatures disagree about the role of business. From the democracy-based, liberal perspective, there is little chance of a nation's businesspeople uniting in support of free trade. International integration inevitably represents more of a threat than an opportunity to many firms and industries, such that their owners and managers should not want it. If this is correct, economic elites cannot cohere enough to support globalization, as a group. Still, by the logic of the economic model underlying the democracy-based arguments, if the private sector *were* to lobby for globalization, it would be more likely to do so in developed rather than developing countries. And, for the most part, that is what this book shows to be the case. Economic elites have provided strong, often proactive support for globalization initiatives in richer countries; in poorer ones they have tended to be more lukewarm, passive, and divided. In these latter contexts, instead of private sector preferences, states' decisions to pursue globalization have reflected the changing worldviews of political elites themselves. Since the 1980s, there has been a marked increase in the number

---

[3] See, e.g., Bermingham 2014; Mirowski 2013; Scholte 2005; Polanyi-Levitt 2012.

[4] E.g., Duménil and Lévy 2004; Dreiling and Darves 2011, 2016; Harvey 2005; Kotz 2015; Panitch and Gindin 2012; Sklair 2002; Robinson 2014.

of politicians and senior bureaucrats in developing countries holding advanced degrees in neoclassical economics—training that makes them firm believers in liberal trade and investment policies. Supporting the thrust of the critical literature, then, this book shows that globalization has been a project of elites—but two different kinds in two different contexts.

Both the liberal and the critical perspectives, then, get it partly right and partly wrong. The former is correct in expecting that the private sector will be riven by conflicts of interest with respect to freer trade and investment. It is clear that many industries *are* skeptical, because governments routinely have to buy off their opposition, by providing concessions like long transition periods and antiliberal protections against imports from third countries. The critical literature rightly emphasizes the near-unanimous support for globalization that these concessions generate, but it fails to acknowledge that unanimity is the result of a process. The liberal literature, in contrast, recognizes these concessions, but expects them not to work nearly as well as they do. According to the trade models the liberal perspective adopts, protection for one industry imposes offsetting costs on others and so should generate no net additional support. But it does.

If most people derive few (or negative) benefits, to what do critics say globalization owes its seeming popularity? Much of the literature suggests that politicians and the public have welcomed liberal trade and investment policies because they have come to believe economists' ideas. The liberal literature also suggests, albeit more implicitly, that policymakers think like economists. On this point, oddly, the liberal and critical literatures therefore actually agree. But here both perspectives are incorrect. Unless they are themselves trained in economics, politicians subscribe much more to a kind of folk economics, far removed from the trade theory of economists, based on the lived experience of businesspeople. In other words, the private sector is so powerful that its worldview dominates the public and political spheres. It is not the technical ideas of economists that influence policy, as many economists themselves remark (and bemoan). Ironically, then, in this sense the critical literature *under*estimates the power of business and exaggerates the legitimacy of globalization's intellectual foundations. The substance of the public advocacy for globalization, the character of international trade negotiations, and many of the contents of the resulting agreements do not derive much from economic science. One telling feature of globalization (and one that economists find especially perplexing) is its pervasive "mercantilism." That is, not unlike European powers in the sixteenth to eighteenth centuries, nations seek access to foreign export markets and only grudgingly concede import access to their own. Many people find nothing surprising about this. But, from economists' point of view, it is actually perverse: they say instead that countries stand to gain from opening up their own markets no matter whether any other country does. So while the mercantilist ideas of early modern Europe have long since been discredited in mainstream economics, that is not true elsewhere. To most people, the mercantilist worldview makes much more sense. And that is particularly so for businesspeople, as mercantilism extrapolates the situations of individual firms to those of whole countries.[5]

Overall then, this book sides with the core of the critical perspective, though it also shows that elite-based explanations of globalization have come to the right general answer for the wrong specific reasons. Critical accounts provide misleading or at least partial explanations of why elites support globalization, and the liberal literature helps resolve these problems—even if it substantially underestimates the power and influence of elites.

In examining globalization in the forms of trade and direct investment, this book focuses on the kinds of international agreements that states have used to liberalize these two things. Such agreements have often incorporated commitments in other areas—notably investor and intellectual property rights, which I will describe in future chapters. The arguments I elaborate apply specifically to these forms of globalization, and not to many others—such as international financial integration, increasing migration, and expanding flows of information across borders. These forms of globalization differ in being less driven by changes in public policy.[6] Policy changes have not been the only reason why trade and investment have grown so much, but the evidence suggests they have made more of a difference than anything else.[7]

I test arguments about the rise of globalization by assessing their consistency with the experiences of three specific country cases: Canada, Mexico, and the United States. The book considers how these countries proposed, negotiated, and ratified two agreements that substantially opened and integrated their economies after being enacted in 1989 and 1994—see Figure 1.1. These were historically important agreements: the bilateral Canada-US and trilateral North

---

[5] These folk mercantilist ideas are little related to the structuralist or developmentalist ideas of serious economists who believe in the merits of industrial policies or the protection of infant industries. For these purposes, some economists think some restrictions on trade and investment can be beneficial (particularly for developing countries); but that is not the same as rejecting the very idea of comparative advantage. Ha-Joon Chang is one well-known development economist, for example, who argues for the merits of selective liberalization at most; but he acknowledges the concept and analytical usefulness of comparative advantage (see Chang 2013). Mercantilism, as I use the term here, means a crude set of ideas that few if any serious economists embrace today.

[6] Garrett 2000.

[7] Baier and Bergstrand 2001, 2007; Büthe and Milner 2008; Goldstein, Rivers, and Tomz 2007; Neumayer and Spess 2005. The decline of war among nations in recent decades has also been a contributing factor, as well as the development of new communication and transportation technologies (e.g., Findlay and O'Rourke 2009).

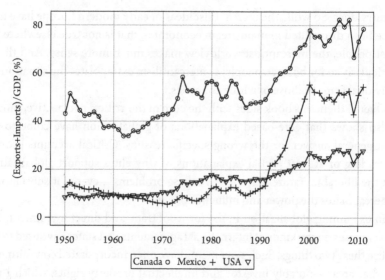

Figure 1.1 Trade Openness, 1950–2011. Source: Penn World Table 8.0.

American Free Trade Agreements (CUFTA and NAFTA) set precedents that changed the world of international economic relations. At the time of NAFTA's creation, no other agreement had established such deep ties among countries at such different levels of development as the United States and Canada, on the one hand, and Mexico on the other. For these reasons alone, the origins of North American free trade—these two agreements taken together—are worth understanding. But for the purposes of this book, these three countries are especially valuable as cases given the diversity of their circumstances and experiences. They arrived at North American free trade in distinct ways, though those ways were typical given the types of countries they are.

The US government was enthusiastic about free trade throughout the post–World War II period, including on a regional basis in North America. That CUFTA and NAFTA were only negotiated near the end of the twentieth century was not due to a lack of earlier interest on the part of the United States, but of Canada and Mexico, who rejected proposals for broad-based regional integration. Their economies have always been dwarfed by that of their much larger neighbor, and for a long time their governments sought to keep their distance in order to manage the risk—as they saw it—of American domination. There were striking parallels in their experiences. In 1973 both Canada and Mexico passed nationalist, restrictive foreign investment laws. In 1980 they issued a joint statement rejecting many American politicians' proposals for continental economic integration. And yet within ten years the governments of both countries would recant. Canada agreed to negotiate free trade with the United States in 1985, Mexico in 1990. Consistent with the experiences of most developed and developing countries elsewhere, Canada's decision followed a change of priorities on the part of business, and Mexico's the ascendance of neoclassical economists inside the state. When opponents threatened to derail free trade, the national business communities in Canada and the United States campaigned aggressively in favor. Parts of Mexican business did too, but in that country the state had to work harder to cultivate support from others. In all three countries, economists endorsed the goal of regional free trade, lending it intellectual legitimacy, though the ideas motivating their endorsements resonated little outside their own circles.

This book describes these decisions, and tells the stories of the people who made them, identifying the barriers they had to overcome in order for free trade to become a reality in North America. It uses this material to assess existing theories of the ascendency of globalization, and to correct and complement them with new insights about that ascendancy. The next section of this chapter elaborates these arguments, explaining how existing theories of globalization are useful in some ways but inadequate in others.

Democracy, Elites, and Globalization

It's easy to forget what the world was like before globalization. It was in the early 1990s that observers began remarking on a "rush to free trade," as Dani Rodrik put it in 1994. The changes are especially stark in the developing world. By one measure, only 37 out of 140 countries were open to international markets in 1980, and of those 37 only 15 were developing countries.[8] By 2000, the world had changed dramatically; 103 countries were open. Meanwhile, trade expanded further in the already "open" developed world, such as through European integration, the Uruguay Round of the General Agreement on Tariffs and Trade (GATT), the relaxation of barriers to imports in Australia and Japan, and the negotiation of free trade in North America. Foreign direct investment (FDI) and the multinationalization of production also expanded dramatically, from less than 5 percent of gross domestic product (GDP) globally in 1980 to more than 30 percent by the end of the 2000s—see Figure 1.2.

But these trends don't represent all of globalization. Trade and investment have been liberalized largely through the negotiation of international agreements whose contents also address other matters—most notably,

---

[8] The data set, described and made available in Wacziarg and Welch (2008), is an updated and refined version of one generated originally by Sachs and Warner (1995).

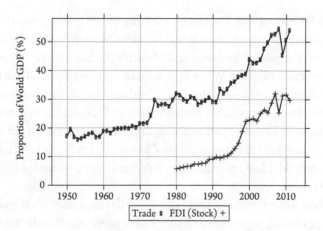

Figure 1.2 Trade and FDI as Shares of World GDP, 1951–2014. Sources: Penn World Table 9.0; UNCTAD.

intellectual property rights and investor rights, including quasi-judicial systems for resolving conflicts with host country governments.[9] This book shows that this content—governance provisions favorable to investors—has been central to the rise of globalization. In this sense, to examine only quantifiable rises in trade and investment as shares of GDP would miss one of globalization's crucial features. Similarly, some might object that initiatives like CUFTA and NAFTA are not "real globalization," since they are regional and preferential rather than global and nondiscriminatory. From economists' point of view, regional and preferential agreements distort trade flows, inefficiently diverting countries' economic relationships toward parties to such agreements at the expense of nonparties.[10] In this strict sense, it is true that regional agreements are not a pure form of globalization. Dismissing them, though, would require obtusely overlooking how much of all international economic integration has been organized on a bilateral or regional basis.[11] This book treats the regional, partial character of globalization (plus the governance content of globalizing agreements) as a feature to explain, not a deviation from some idealized form of integration that is in reality the exception and not the rule.

Having defined globalization for the purposes of this book, I will now summarize the main approaches previously used to explain it. I begin with the liberal literature.

[9] McBride 2006; Shadlen 2005.

[10] Baldwin 1997; Bhagwati 2008.

[11] Duina 2006; Fligstein and Merand 2002.

Democracy and the Power of Public Opinion

The common thread running through the liberal literature is its adoption of economists' view that restrictions on trade and investment are generally costly and undesirable. Statistical research in this literature finds that democracy has been associated with international economic liberalism in recent decades,[12] a period when many countries have transitioned to more politically liberal regimes.[13] Compared to countries with authoritarian governments that have survived, those that have turned democratic have experienced larger increases in trade flows, tariff reductions, and more liberalization of nontariff barriers to trade.[14] Similar results hold for direct investment.[15] If democracy is taken somewhat more abstractly to be relative equality of power in society, there is other evidence for the proposition that democracy and economic openness are associated. For example, postcommunist countries with more fragmented state power have tended to liberalize trade more than similar states where power has been more centralized—and this holds even for nondemocratic countries.[16] In short, there appears to be strong statistical evidence for the theory, though some questions remain about the relationship's robustness, and the possibility that democracy is partly a consequence, not just a cause, of globalization.[17]

Theoretically, the liberal view is that political democracy discourages restrictions on trade and investment because democracy grants political power to a wider share of the population, making the policy preferences of the majority more influential. Most people should have favorable views of freer trade and investment, because they stand to gain from them.[18] That is, governments pursue globalization because it is popular, and justifiably so. Under authoritarianism, in contrast, the generalized interest of the many is pushed aside by the special interests of the privileged few, who stand to lose out from openness. This expectation derives from the Heckscher-Ohlin-Samuelson model of trade ("HOS"), according to which a country's relatively abundant factors of production stand

[12] Studies do not generally specify exactly what they mean by democracy. Instead, they just work empirically with measures of it from large data sets like Polity IV or Freedom House, which concentrate on procedural and institutional criteria like the holding of elections, constraints on the executive, or the protection of political rights. The assumption is that these things ensure that policy reflects the preferences of the median voter, at least to some significant degree.

[13] See, e.g., Lindberg et al. 2014; Wejnert 2005.

[14] Henisz and Mansfield 2006; Dutt and Mitra 2002; Eichengreen and Leblang 2008; Mansfield, Milner, and Rosendorff 2002; Milner and Mukherjee 2009.

[15] Pandya 2014.

[16] Frye and Mansfield 2003.

[17] Bell and Jones 2014; Kono 2006; Bak and Moon 2016; Eichengreen and Leblang 2008; Li and Reuveny 2003; Rudra 2005.

[18] Milner and Kubota 2005; Mansfield and Milner 2012.

to gain from international economic integration, and scarce factors do not.[19] A scarce factor, by virtue of its being scarce, commands a high price in the status quo situation of economic closure, whereas international integration makes it less scarce and so undermines its power in the marketplace. In developing countries integrating with wealthier ones, labor and particularly low-skilled labor are the relatively abundant factors, while in the wealthier nations capital and highly skilled labor are abundant. Given this view of different people's interests, and the rational choice expectation that preferences reflect interests, HOS predicts that capital owners and higher-skilled workers in poorer countries will prefer economic closure, while lower-skilled workers will support opening. There is therefore reason to expect more liberalism in developing countries where public policies are more accountable to majority opinion; autarky is likelier under conditions of nondemocracy, where political rulers cater to privileged, well-connected elites—who are often capital owners and highly skilled professionals. Governments' responsiveness to the will of the median voter, and the threat of electoral punishment, therefore drives the liberalization of trade and direct investment.[20]

But despite this perspective's compelling theory, and the statistical evidence consistent with it, there are reasons to be skeptical that the correlations it emphasizes are really evidence of a causal relationship.

First, it assumes that public opinion supports globalization.[21] But the empirical evidence is far from clear. Schneider summarizes simply: "One prevalent assumption is that the public at large comprises consumers who benefit from lower prices and should therefore have strong preferences for free trade and regional integration. This assumption is unwarranted."[22] In much the same way, the economist Larue argues that "the public is clueless about the welfare costs of trade protection."[23] The third wave of the World Values Survey, for example, asked nationally representative samples of respondents in fifty-two countries in the mid-1990s: "Do you think it is better if: (A) goods made in other countries can be imported and sold here if people want to buy them, or (B) there should be stricter limits on selling foreign goods here, to protect the jobs of people in

---

[19] Leamer (2012: 15) explains that the basic idea behind the model is that "trade across space is a consequence of the uneven geographical distribution of the world's productive resources." See also Watson 1993.

[20] Busch and Mansfield 2010; Mukherjee 2016; Pandya 2014. Ironically, some early advocates of "market reforms" expected them to prove so unpopular that they would have to be implemented in undemocratic ways (see Schneider 2004). Over time, advocates have grown less concerned about contradictions between economic and political liberalism.

[21] E.g., Baccini 2012; Mukherjee 2016; see O'Rourke and Sinnott 2001.

[22] Schneider 2017: 233.

[23] Larue 2018: 11.

this country?" In only eight countries did more respondents answer A than B.[24] On the other hand, there are certainly also surveys that find substantial support for trade and investment liberalization. Surveys by the Pew Global Attitudes Project, for example, have found that majorities everywhere think "growing trade and business ties" with other countries are a good or very good thing for their countries.[25] These seemingly contradictory results are probably reconcilable given the effects of question wording, order, and framing. Survey experiments show that people possess different attitudes about trade depending on how the issues are presented.[26] Trade issues have very low salience for the public; voters are little aware of how their elected representatives voted on recent trade legis-lation, and seldom use the ballot box to hold politicians accountable for those votes.[27] Research suggests that voters possess strong biases against trade and/or take their cues directly from elites.[28]

Second, arguments about the consequences of political democracy for policy outcomes follow from the HOS trade model described above. Economic elites in poorer countries should favor autarky, while the majority should be more pro-trade, and the opposite should hold in richer countries. Do the available survey data support these predictions? Systematic measurements of the policy preferences of capital owners and high income-earners specifically are rare. But many studies at least consider the highly educated—owners of exceptional human capital. Within single capital-abundant countries there is indeed a strong positive correlation between various measures of skill and support for freer trade, as HOS would predict.[29] And cross-nationally, the more capital-abundant the country, the greater the impact of a worker's skill on support for freer trade, another finding consistent with HOS.[30] Contrary to expectations, however, there is no *negative* correlation between skill and pro-trade sentiment in poorer countries: skill correlates with support for freer trade even in countries where HOS predicts it should not.[31] And analyses of individual-level survey data belie a Heckscher-Ohlin-Samuelson-based model of people's policy preferences in other ways too. Some studies find that, rather than HOS, policy preferences and

---

[24] Economists might point out that this is a misleading question to ask, since trade actually has little impact on employment. Still, people's responses are indicative about their views and policy preferences irrespective of whether the ideas underlying them are valid.

[25] Stokes 2018.

[26] Ardanaz, Murillo, and Pinto 2013; Hiscox 2006.

[27] Guisinger 2009; Medrano and Braun 2012; Mendelsohn and Wolfe 2001.

[28] Caplan 2007; Achen and Bartels 2016. Even in Europe, where regional integration has gone so far, ordinary citizens have never been very enthusiastic about it (Gabel 1998; Haller 2008).

[29] Blonigen 2011; Hainmueller and Hiscox 2006; Scheve and Slaughter 2001.

[30] Mayda and Rodrik 2005.

[31] Kleinberg and Fordham 2010; Margalit 2012; Medrano and Braun 2012.

political cleavages follow the logic of a different model, known as Ricardo-Viner, in which the interests of capital and labor are consistent within industries and contradictory across them.[32] Cross-sectionally, preferences are tied to consumption, not just positions in the labor market, and net of many other controls lower-income earners are less supportive of freer trade.[33] Moreover, education appears to affect people's trade policy preferences by shaping their broader worldviews rather than their human capital.[34] Perhaps even more importantly, setting aside the survey data, the distributional implications of HOS in the real world have not been proven correct in recent decades.[35] It is not clear then that the theory captures the key interests at stake.

Third, while the liberal, democracy-centered theory's implications are clear for and have been extensively tested in developing country contexts, this is less true for richer countries. Only countries experiencing significant changes over time in the level of democracy are useful for investigating the relationship with globalization longitudinally, and few wealthy countries have recently transitioned to democracy. But the liberal theory implies that in wealthier—more capital-abundant and labor-scarce—nations, the benefits of opening will flow disproportionately to capital owners rather than workers. Yet because the median voter remains a worker with middling human capital, the theory suggests that public opinion on trade should at best be lukewarm. If democracy makes policymakers accountable to the preferences of the majority, and the majority of voters in richer countries have ambiguous interests with respect to trade, then HOS provides little reason to expect liberalization in such nations to derive from the democratic accountability of politicians to the electorate. Consistent with this implication, while democracies and wealthier countries tend to be more open than nondemocracies and poorer countries, the interaction between these conditions is associated with greater trade barriers.[36]

All in all, there is little evidence that the public has clear and strong preferences with respect to trade and investment policies, or that voters tend to think much about these issues when it comes time to vote. What preferences people do possess are only partly reflective of the trade model underlying arguments about the influence of democracy. The mechanisms translating (putative) majority interests into policy also remain unclear, as advocates of the liberal approach themselves concede.[37] The liberal literature has provided very few case studies,

[32] Hicks, Milner, and Tingley 2014; Hiscox 2001.

[33] Blonigen 2011; Mayda and Rodrik 2005; Baker 2005.

[34] Hainmueller and Hiscox 2006.

[35] Goldberg and Pavcnik 2007.

[36] Tavares 2008.

[37] Milner and Mukherjee 2009: 178; see also Guisinger 2009: 554; Eichengreen and Leblang 2008: 320.

which might otherwise help identify such mechanisms. Mansfield and Milner use secondary sources in a discussion of regional economic integration following democratization in southern Africa and South America, but they provide no clear evidence that politicians were significantly motivated by mass public opinion. At least in South America they even note that "business was largely in favor."[38] The liberal literature argues that democratization contributes to globalization by liberating policy from the preferences of economic elites with an interest in autarky; that business *supported* globalization makes it unclear why democratization therefore even mattered. Overall, the theory that globalization rests on foundations of democracy and public opinion suffers from a deficit of evidence for the causal processes it presumes.

I should note before concluding this discussion that, while I call this literature "liberal," the label is in some ways not ideal. In North America, "liberals" are left-leaning, concerned about social inequalities and the pathologies of free markets, and many social scientists associate the left with criticism of globalization. For Europeans, "liberals" believe in free markets, express reservations about social democracy, and fall to the right of center politically. The label "neoliberalism" has been closely associated with the rise of globalization, and the literature on neoliberalism links trade and investment liberalization to other kinds of free market policies—attitudes to which do not all necessarily line up. (Supporters of free trade are not necessarily advocates of tax cuts or welfare state retrenchment.) Survey research finds that public preferences about globalization are not much different between people who identify as right versus left, in the typical country (Edwards 2006); in the United States, for example, Democrats are more supportive of free trade than Republicans (Miller 2009). The democracy-based literature is "liberal" in its positive view of free markets and free politics, and its opposition to conservative or populist nationalism.

Moving on, the alternative to the liberal perspective is a critical one, according to which globalization has been a project of elites. The next subsection outlines the claims of existing studies in this second literature, and how this book both uses and modifies them. I develop this discussion in three parts, each one concluding with a corrective to existing studies.

The Roles of Elites in Diverse Pathways to Globalization

Critics regard the motor force behind globalization as the agendas and actions of elites, in the sense of people possessing exceptionally large amounts of some valued resource—money, authority over a bureaucracy, control of policy, or

---

[38] Mansfield and Milner 2012: 54; see also Kingstone 2001.

technical/intellectual expertise. This work often takes globalization as part of a broader shift to neoliberal, or free market, policies in recent decades.[39] The emphasis on the agendas and actions of the few, rather than the preferences and interests of the many, sets this second literature at odds with the first. Not all accounts argue explicitly that democracy has been antithetical or at least an impediment to globalization.[40] But all these arguments clearly diverge from the liberal view that globalization derives in large part from the rising power of public preferences, and the disempowerment of a previously privileged minority. While the liberal literature expects business and corporate professionals to favor autarky (at least in developing countries), many of this second group of studies see them as natural advocates of economic openness and integration.

Characterizing the elite-based literature is complicated by the fact that it comprises several distinct variants. Some do not emphasize (1) business as an important agent of globalization, but point instead to the influence of (2) international financial institutions and creditors (and their staff), (3) economists, and/or (4) technocrats. So the critical literature provides not just one type of elite-based explanation, but four. This diversity reflects an important reality of the comparative politics of globalization: each argument applies to some types of countries, but not all. Considering the types of cases on the basis of which each argument has been based, it is clear that two different combinations of elites have pursued globalization.[41] In the discussion that follows, then, I review each of the four types of elite-based explanations of globalization, and then propose how the elites they discuss can each occupy a place in a two-pathway model of globalization.

First, arguments focusing on the private sector hold that the policies behind globalization have been the product of proactive lobbying and campaigning by business, especially big business and multinational firms specifically.[42] Most such studies suggest that business wins from globalization at the expense of others; neoliberal agreements and policies suppress wage and benefit demands by labor and entrench pro-business governance measures in areas like investor and intellectual property rights.[43] As when pursuing any kind of agenda favorable to business as a whole, the private sector can achieve the globalization policies it

[39] For useful discussions see Boas and Gans-Morse 2009; Mudge 2008.

[40] Though some do, such as Crouch 2011, 2016; Harvey 2005, 2007; Mirowski 2013; Sklair 2002; Streeck 2014, 2017.

[41] See also Fairbrother 2008, 2014.

[42] Carroll 2004; Cox 2012; Kotz 2015; Harvey 2005; Panitch and Gindin 2012; Robinson 2014; Rupert 2000; Sklair 2002; Van Apeldoorn 2000.

[43] Gill 1995; see Bartley 2018 for a discussion.

wants by funding think tanks that will conduct and disseminate the results of supportive studies.[44]

A second set of studies stress instead the power of well-resourced international financial institutions—the World Bank and International Monetary Fund—and private creditors.[45] Developing states grow dependent on the international financial institutions (IFIs) because of debt or balance-of-payments crises, and cannot repay private creditors without financial assistance. When that happens, the IFIs can ask for the policies they want in return for this assistance—policies that are typically liberal and conducive to economic opening and integration, given the professional backgrounds of the IFIs' staff and the interests of their funders.[46] In another variant of this argument, dependence on the IFIs shifts the balance of power in domestic politics and gives an advantage to actors sympathetic to liberal policies.[47] Political actors with the training and connections that allow them to negotiate with a state's foreign creditors gain an advantage domestically in competing for policymaking control, and as a consequence are eventually empowered to implement market-oriented policy revolutions as an inside job.[48] A final variant suggests that the influence of the IFIs can be intellectual: financial dependence makes it harder for states to ignore the abundance of IFI-generated reports and studies advocating economic liberalism.[49] Some work then suggests that the IFIs are only really influential in combination with willing domestic collaborators.[50]

A third approach suggests that economists, as recognized technical authorities, can use the force of their expertise to convince political elites and/or the general public to become favorable to neoliberal policies.[51] Like other experts, their power derives from the legitimacy ascribed to the superior, scientific knowledge they possess.[52] As recognized experts, their voices carry the weight of technical-intellectual credibility, helping to legitimate policy agendas.[53] Consequently, while economists in universities and think tanks may have neither formal authority over policymaking nor exceptional financial resources, they can still exercise significant influence over policy.[54] Their written reports, oral testimony,

---

[44] Carroll and Shaw 2001; Domhoff 2010.

[45] Park, Jang, and Lee 2007; Peet 2007; Woods 2006.

[46] Babb 2007, 2009.

[47] E.g., Nelson 2014, 2017; Schneider 1998; Teichman 2004.

[48] Babb 2001.

[49] Broad 2006.

[50] Pop-Eleches 2009.

[51] Bockman 2011; Christensen 2017; Jones 2012; Rupert 2000; Sheppard 2005.

[52] Centeno and Silva 1998: 4.

[53] See Campbell 2002: 31; Adler and Haas 1992; Centeno and Cohen 2012.

[54] Bockman and Eyal 2002; Helgadóttir 2016; Montecinos and Markoff 2001; Mirowski and Plehwe 2009; Mirowski 2013.

and statements in the media can make policies more politically attractive to politicians and the public, and therefore more feasible or likely. Consistent with these arguments, the higher the number of American-trained economists in a country, the greater the likelihood of trade liberalization.[55] Surveys also show that economists strongly prefer liberal trade policies.[56] At least among US-based economists, there is possibly no policy around which preferences are more unified than low tariffs.[57] In industrial democracies, the strength of economists' support for free trade has been consistently strong since the Great Depression. Support among developing country economists has been much more variable, though as developing country economists have become more similar to their developed country counterparts (i.e., more neoclassical), their policy preferences have converged.[58] This shift could help explain why developing countries' international economic policies have become more liberal over time.

A fourth and final elite-based argument looks again at economists, but this time within rather than outside the state.[59] "Technocrats" are state actors with formal authority over policymaking, which allows their preferences to exercise significant direct influence over key outcomes. What distinguishes technocrats from other politicians is their prior academic training and possession of recognized credentials in economics. Such training makes them intellectually committed to liberal trade and investment policies, to a much greater degree than other politicians would be, given specified levels of support versus opposition by the general public and relevant interest groups. Non-technocratic politicians may therefore bend with the political winds on trade, with interest group pressures exogenously determining their policy priorities. In contrast, technocrats' own biographies condition their policy preferences, leading them to enact and promote systematically different policies than would other potential occupants of the same political or bureaucratic posts. Policy outcomes therefore vary with the educational backgrounds of relevant office-holders; as the composition of state office-holders changes, so do policies. Unlike economists in universities and think tanks, moreover, technocrats have direct, formal authority over policy. Having economists in top government posts therefore, for example, increases the probability of a country liberalizing its capital account.[60]

[55] Weymouth and Macpherson 2012.

[56] Blendon et al. 1997; Frey et al. 1984.

[57] Klein and Stern 2007.

[58] Coats 1997; Babb 2001; Montecinos and Markoff 2001; Fernández-Kelly 2007.

[59] For discussions see Centeno 1993; Dargent 2014; Domínguez 1997; Markoff and Montecinos 1993; Montecinos and Markoff 2009.

[60] Chwieroth 2007. Some scholars who *supported* globalization (and free market policies more generally) used to talk about countries where a "handful of heroes," in the sense of well-placed

These four different explanations of globalization are in a sense competitors. Arguments about the power of technocrats, for example, suggest that occupants of top posts in the state have sufficient power to impose their policy preferences on the societies they govern; in this view, states must have substantial autonomy. On the other hand, arguments about the power of business suggest that states are weak, dominated by the projects of others. Similarly, if globalization is an external imposition by international financial actors, then domestic elites of any kind cannot be a very important impetus.

The liberal literature, however, points to a resolution. As discussed earlier, the Heckscher-Ohlin-Samuelson model implies that capital owners in developing countries receive fewer benefits from international trade and investment compared to capital owners in developed countries. Developing country governments are therefore less likely to embrace globalization because of proactive lobbying by the national business community. Consistent with this expectation, the critical literature includes an abundance of case studies where developed countries have liberalized trade and investment pursuant to private sector mobilization.[61] On the other hand, many other studies note instances in which developing country states have opened their economies under little pressure from domestic business, but substantial influence from abroad, or under the guidance of technocrats whose policy preferences largely dovetail with those foreign influences.[62] Rather than denying the importance of any of the four types of elites emphasized in the critical literature, then, I propose to recognize contextual differences in their relevance: globalization has been business-led in developed countries, and state-led in developing ones.[63] In both, academic economists have provided legitimacy, though that has only been a significant change over time in developing countries, where until recently economists were much more skeptical about the benefits of liberal trade and investment policies. Also unlike in developed countries, the rise of globalization in developing countries has been tied to the striking growth of economists in the top ranks of the public sector, and to the influence of international finance.[64] While globalization is an elite project, then, it is not necessarily a corporate project.

---

technocrats, pursued free market policies even in the face of political opposition (Harberger 1993). Not all arguments about elites' pursuit of globalization from the top down are critical.

[61] E.g., Dreiling and Darves 2011, 2016; Harvey 2005; Kotz 2015; Levitt 2006; McBride 2001; Rupert 2000; Saad-Filho and Johnston 2005; Sandholtz and Zysman 1989; Sklair 2001.

[62] Babb 2001; Dargent 2014; Geddes 1995; Haggard and Kaufman 1992; Mukherji 2013.

[63] The literature on the politics of trade policy comprises studies emphasizing either pressure from outside interest groups or the agendas of actors inside the state (e.g., Hanson 1998). Prior studies have not recognized that these two approaches apply to different kinds of countries.

[64] Fourcade 2006; Montecinos and Markoff 2009.

All of these elite-based arguments presume that politicians' policy decisions do not much reflect voters' preferences—policies are little influenced by electoral pressures and incentives or by majority opinion. Therein lies the tension with democracy, and with the liberal literature on globalization. The arguments making up the critical literature partake of a long tradition of social science that sees the preferences of powerful minorities overriding those of the majority, even within the context of modern political democracy.[65] Historically, this kind of perspective struggled for recognition in mainstream social science. In recent years, however, that has changed, at least in the United States. Studies show that policy dilemmas in America are settled far more often in accordance with the preferences of economic elites and organizations allied to them than with the preferences of the median voter and more mass-based organizations.[66] This income-based policy bias would seem strong evidence of elites' power, especially since, with respect to trade policy, high-income earners are much more liberal than poorer Americans.[67]

Economists and Their Ideas

Much of the critical literature is so negative about globalization that it assumes businesspeople have pursued it in order to roll back public-interest reforms to capitalism: labor and environmental laws, redistributive taxes, social spending, and so on. How then, according to this perspective, have elites won public acquiescence to globalization? Virtually any account of politics wherein a minority rules at the expense of the majority points to some kind of intellectual or ideological dimension to their domination, including the need for minority rule to obscure itself.[68] Some set of ideas must serve to frame an elite agenda as beneficial to a much broader class of people. With respect to globalization, many previous studies point to the ideas of economists in universities and related organizations as those that persuade nonelites to adopt preferences for globalization. Given economists' strong support for free trade and their status as the recognized experts in this policy domain, the argument is that the ideas to which economists subscribe also shape the thinking of policymakers and serve to legitimate globalization to the public.[69]

---

[65] Domhoff 2010.

[66] Bartels 2008; Gilens 2012; Gilens and Page 2014.

[67] Gilens 2009.

[68] Wacquant 1996. In recent times, one such strategy has been efforts to shape public opinion using seemingly independent agents like think tanks (Carroll and Shaw 2001; Domhoff 2010; Medvetz 2012; Smith 2000).

[69] See, e.g., Harvey 2005; Levitt 2006; Mirowski 2013; Plehwe et al., 2006; Rupert 2000; Scholte 2005; Sheppard 2005.

The claim that noneconomists embrace economists' ideas stretches beyond the argument, outlined earlier, that economists influence policy because of their intellectual authority and credentials. In that view, endorsements matter, but not the ideas motivating the endorsers. In this case, economists provide not just endorsements, but also the substantive ideas that shape how people see the world and the policies they support. And critics of globalization are not alone in ascribing this level of influence to economists' ideas. Implicitly, much liberal political economy literature makes the same suggestion in assuming that politicians act rationally according to interests as defined by neoclassical models.[70] For example, a widely cited 1995 paper by Grossman and Helpman suggests that voters and policymakers balance pressures from special interests against concerns about the welfare of voters, from a neoclassical perspective. Some liberal studies also suggest explicitly that changes in policy over time are hard to explain without reference to changes in policymakers' core ideas about trade.[71] The thesis that neoclassical economics has substantial impact on policy outcomes therefore spans the liberal-critical divide.

But if economists' ideas have been a major motive behind politicians' pursuit of globalization, someone should tell the economists. The Nobel Prize–winning economist Paul Krugman has been saying for decades that core neoclassical ideas about trade are very marginal outside of economics, and often misunderstood— including by politicians and businesspeople.[72] The neoclassical perspective holds that the freedom to trade and invest across national borders allows economies to reap the gains of specialization, giving consumers access to the best goods and services at the best prices, and raising people's standards of living. For economists, trade is about mutually beneficial exchange, where every nation comes out ahead. Yet the focus of much rhetoric in the political and media spheres is about competition, conveying a sense of the zero sum, that exports are in some sense good, while imports are not. Advocates use arguments about exports (and the jobs based on producing them) to promote freer trade, while opponents emphasize how much imports will increase too.[73] And not just the rhetoric, but the logic of international trade negotiations is difficult to explain from a neoclassical point of view. Trade negotiations are strongly mercantilist, a quality that means they are clearly at odds with neoclassical theory.[74] Much the

---

[70] See Baldwin 1996.

[71] See Milner 1999.

[72] Krugman 1996, 1997; Samuelson 1969. Economists have certainly not always had their way; famously, in 1930, more than a thousand petitioned in vain for US president Hoover not to pass the Smoot-Hawley bill that substantially raised American tariffs (*New York Times* 1930). In Britain, two-thirds of a sample of 164 economists recommended that the country join the Eurozone, and 364 told Margaret Thatcher's government not to impose austerity in 1981.

[73] Ethier 2004: 306.

[74] Bhagwati 1988; Ethier 2007; Regan 2015.

same holds for their outcomes—the contents of the agreements as negotiated—and indeed the very fact that negotiations are needed at all.

Insofar as economists' ideas were to diffuse and influence the minds of policymakers—leading politicians and bureaucrats to see international economic issues in the same way as economists—globalization might represent the fulfillment of economists' visions and ideals. This book shows, though, that agreements like NAFTA do not embody economists' policy ideals. Their contents diverge in many ways from economists' vision of "free trade," and the ideas that motivate politicians to pursue agreements like NAFTA derive much less from the formal theories of economists than from the informal, and quite distinct, folk ideas of businesspeople.[75]

Since economists play a number of different roles in this book, to the point where readers may be confused, I will recap: First, I cite economists as commentators and researchers, like myself, on the politics of globalization. Second, they are the source of the models and trade theory on the basis of which political scientists have constructed their own theories of globalization. Third, economists' models and theory also represent a worldview that motivated some of NAFTA's creators (though not many, as previously explained). Fourth, economists are political actors in the story I tell, whether as technocrats or public intellectuals.

The Formation of Business

The liberal literature expects business to be divided with respect to the liberalization of policies on trade and investment, while the critical literature sees business as largely unified in support. This disagreement reflects a broader debate in the political economy literature. Some scholars question the political power of business generally, because they believe that firms' owners and managers are seldom sufficiently unified so as to act collectively.[76] From this perspective, the rule of business should be impossible, as policy dilemmas should divide elites themselves.[77] Empirically, some research suggests that firms' stances on globalization are indeed far from homogenous.[78] But other studies—even some

[75] Except where politicians are themselves economists.

[76] E.g., Hart 2004.

[77] Smith (2000) argues that the kinds of policy debates around which business is most united are also those most likely to engage the public; those are policy debates on which public opinion is most relevant and business least certain to get what it wants. Business exercises more influence, Smith claims, with respect to policies of interest just to specific sectors or firms; but these issues are less likely to exercise the public.

[78] Bombardini and Trebbi 2012; Hiscox 2001, 2002.

from the liberal literature—point to many instances where national business communities have campaigned for globalization with striking unanimity.[79]

For critics, private sector influence figures large in most explanations of globalization's rise, and that influence presumes a high degree of consensus. But despite the centrality of business unity, the critical literature is vague about its character and foundations.[80] Some argue that the ties linking businesspeople to each other across national borders are strong and dense enough such that it is legitimate to talk of a transnational capitalist class.[81] In this view, "business" supports globalization everywhere because of a broad commonality of interests. But why then are international trade negotiations so contentious? There should be nothing for representatives of different nations to disagree about. The notion of a nationless, seamless world of business ties is difficult to reconcile with the realities of international negotiations, wherein negotiators strongly disagree with each other, and their contradictory priorities are derived at least partly from the preferences of their nations' business communities. Evidence from network studies also suggests that while transnational ties are growing among national business communities, important divisions remain.[82]

A second possible reason why critics might say trade negotiations are contentious is that the interests of capital divide along national lines. But then, if globalization benefits capital in some countries but not others, business in some contexts should be opposed—yet the critical literature identifies no such cases. The third possibility, and the only realistic one, is that some business segments within a given country win from globalization, while others lose: so business interests are heterogeneous. But acknowledging this fact brings the critical perspective closer to the liberal one, and raises the same question: Given the private sector conflicts of interest, how is unified business advocacy for globalization possible? Why do the business sectors that stand to lose out fail to object? Despite placing business advocacy at the heart of its explanation, the critical literature ultimately has little to say about this question.

The answer I develop in this book draws on classically sociological approaches to collective actor formation. There is no doubt, from any theoretical perspective, that some segments of each country's national business community have much to gain from globalization—particularly, most perspectives agree, large or multinational firms. Though the liberal view is that globalization's benefits

---

[79] E.g., Beaulieu and Magee 2004.

[80] Studies focused on the power and campaigning of businesspeople also provide little explanation of variation over time in private sector support for globalization in any given country. If business rules, and business always wins from globalization, why was globalization formerly so much scarcer?

[81] E.g., Robinson 2014; Sklair 2001.

[82] Carroll 2010; see also Block 2001.

to these firms come to some extent at a cost to others, the more mercantilist perspective of businesspeople in practice de-emphasizes such trade-offs. This makes it easier for advocates to frame globalization as a project in the interests of business and the nation as a whole. In this ideational context, then, the state further organizes business support materially in the course of specific international negotiations. Trade negotiators give industries a choice: accept the principle of a new agreement and receive favorable terms and conditions, or resist and risk suffering ones that are painful. Given these options, and in the face of (mercantilist) campaigning by leaders in the national business community, many industries that might otherwise object do not. This strategic interaction between the state and the private sector also helps explain why trade negotiations are so contentious, and nonsensical from the perspective of mainstream economists. In order to make trade liberalization politically viable, negotiators seek to please domestic industries, by providing antiliberal content—long transition periods and protections against imports from abroad. The mercantilist character of international trade negotiations constructs business support helpful for the political viability of free trade at home, but at the cost of fostering resentment abroad.

The book therefore shows that the rise of globalization in the late twentieth century was a project of identifiable groups of elites, whose preference for globalization prevailed in the face of public skepticism or at least ambivalence. In showing this, the book meets a classic test of Robert Dahl, one of the twentieth century's most influential political scientists. Dahl famously rejected the elite theory of his time, as expounded by C. Wright Mills in his 1956 book *The Power Elite*. In a rebuttal, Dahl identified three criteria for a "ruling elite" thesis to be validated: a ruling elite must be (1) a well-defined group whose (2) distinct preferences (3) regularly prevail in situations of political conflict.[83] Dahl's test was meant for theories of elite domination in society generally, but it can also provide a useful framework for studying political outcomes in specific areas, as with respect to globalization. The question is whether states have consistently enacted policies for globalization at times when identifiable groups of elites were seeking globalization, while other constituencies were opposed.

Studying the Rise of Globalization

This section outlines the approach and methods I use in this book to explain the rise of globalization. Consistent with the preceding arguments, one distinguishing feature of the book is its taking people's subjective motives and ideas

---

[83] Dahl 1958.

as important explanations of political outcomes. Not all contemporary political research does so. Many political economy studies adopt rational choice assumptions, wherein actors' behaviors are "explained" insofar as they approximate the strategic pursuit of interests as some outside observer defines them. This kind of approximation is then taken as validation of the theory or model from which the researcher deduced those objective interests, and any correspondence between those interests and actual behavior is not generally considered very interesting. In contrast to this approach, there are also studies that emphasize how actors' interests with respect to many political dilemmas are not so obvious, and that even when researchers do consider those interests unambiguous, the actors themselves may see things differently. The ideas (worldviews, norms, beliefs about causal relationships, etc.) to which people subscribe can shape preferences and behaviors net of any interests that researchers may ascribe to them.[84]

Attending to ideas comes, admittedly, at the cost of reduced parsimony. Friedman articulated the merit of a simpler, rational choice approach to social life as follows:

> A hypothesis is important if it "explains" much by little, that is, if it abstracts the common and crucial elements from the mass of complex and detailed circumstances surrounding the phenomena to be explained and permits valid predictions on the basis of them alone. To be important, therefore, a hypothesis must be descriptively false in its assumptions.[85]

Friedman was not alone in holding to his kind of view. Other celebrated (and Nobel Prize–winning) economists, like Samuelson and Vickery, said much the same.[86]

Consistent with their manifesto, many social scientists aspire to explain outcomes of interest without making reference to what the people they study actually *think*. This ambition underlies most work in economics, and a lot of research in other social sciences too—including with respect to politics, and the politics of trade policy.[87] Their view is that interests alone, deduced a priori, are enough; subjective ideas, concerns, and worldviews are not worth worrying about, since they add complexity for no explanatory gain. And yet Friedman himself noted that the question remains whether such parsimonious theories,

---

[84] Blyth 2002; Campbell and Pedersen 2014; Centeno and Cohen 2012; Goldstein and Keohane 1993; Jacobs 2015; Lindvall 2009; Woll 2008.

[85] Friedman 1953.

[86] Samuelson 1939: 205; Vickery 1964: 5.

[87] E.g., Feenstra 2016; Grossman 2016.

with their intentionally unrealistic assumptions, actually "work," in the sense that they predict relevant outcomes. In practice, sometimes they do and sometimes they don't. Fukuyama says they are "correct about 80 percent of the time," a share that seems more or less consistent with, for example, Ostrom—another Nobel laureate.[88] People are neither inevitably selfish, nor inevitably rational, as demonstrated by the lab experiments of behavioral economics. Rational actors might decide not to spend time and resources acquiring all the information necessary for them to act rationally.[89]

As explained above, my claim in this book is that the liberal and critical literatures both fail to explain important characteristics of globalization's rise. This is in part because these literatures' interest-based arguments overlook the economic ideas shaping the decisions and behaviors of key actors. The liberal perspective struggles to explain why so many businesspeople support liberalization, for example, and why trade negotiations are so mercantilist. The critical literature has little to say about why so many businesspeople support free trade (especially given that this fact is historically variable), and why trade negotiations are so contentious. Rather than elaborating a purely interest-based model of political action a priori, the book investigates political action empirically and inductively and seeks to identify the underlying motives and worldviews to which relevant actors subscribed—irrespective of whether those ideas make any sense to outside observations in academic circles.

A second reason the book attends to actors' ideas is methodological. Competing theories, explicitly or implicitly, posit distinct motives and concerns that politicians should possess when making the key decisions leading to the rise of globalization. And ideas are causal mechanisms that lend themselves well to case-based empirical testing. Liberals argue that politicians have fostered globalization because they believed their electoral fortunes would best be served by doing so, given the nature of majority opinion. Critics counter that politicians have been motivated by some mix of loyalties to, persuasion by, and powerlessness before other kinds of elites. These two perspectives therefore imply different things about politicians' perspectives on their decisions. Moreover, since the goal is to explain change over time, contrasts between key actors' views and preferences at different moments are revealing about the political economic circumstances whose transformation made a difference.

The book adopts a qualitative, case-based approach, combining controlled comparisons across nations and time with process tracing within each case.[90] Testing whether there are mechanisms that plausibly link either democracy

---

[88] Fukuyama 1995; Ostrom 2003. See also Simon 1995.
[89] Posner 1997: 1553.
[90] Jacobs 2015; Mahoney 1999; Slater and Ziblatt 2013.

and public opinion, or elite agendas and actions, to relevant policy outcomes stands in contrast to the approach used by the democracy-based literature. The latter has been based almost exclusively on statistical models fitted to observational, often longitudinal, country-level data. The correlational results of such studies are certainly indicative of the key causal relationship implied by the liberal literature. But they remain vulnerable to omitted variable bias and spuriousness, and because of such concerns social scientists have grown more wary in recent years about inferring causal relationships from statistical correlations in observational data alone. There have been more efforts to exploit lab, field, and natural experiments, and increased emphasis on qualitative investigation of causal mechanisms. In the latter regard, causal process observations are invaluable in determining whether the intervening events and conditions posited by a theory are actually present in relevant cases.[91] The case of Mexico in particular serves as a useful test here, given its concordance with the empirical patterns hypothesized by the liberal literature.

For studies using process tracing to investigate the political impact of ideas, Jacobs identifies a number of criteria for demonstrating the exogenous influence of an idea on some political outcome.[92] First, it must be possible to document the idea's existence not just at the moment of some key decision, but also well beforehand; this helps show the idea was not just generated by the "objective, material features of the choice situation," as Jacobs puts it.[93] Second, there must be a channel by which the idea could have plausibly been conveyed to the relevant decision-makers; it is revealing if variable channels in different contexts make a difference. For example, in Weir and Skocpol's classic study of the influence of Keynesian economics in Sweden, Britain, and the United States during the Great Depression, variable state structures either blocked or facilitated the ingress and influence of the new ideas.[94] Christensen has recently done much the same with respect to changes in tax policy[95]. Third, there should be some correspondence over time between the ideas to which key decision-makers subscribe and changes in the policies they enact or advocate.

This book is a longitudinal study of the case of North American free trade, using in-depth consideration of a single instance of a broader class of phenomena, in order to understand important features of that broader class—whose

---

[91] George and Bennett 2005; Mahoney 2010.

[92] Jacobs 2015.

[93] This criterion is similar to one articulated by Prasad (2006: 21), in her study of the rise of neoliberal tax, welfare, and industrial policies, who argues that demonstrating the exogenous impact of ideas requires showing they were not simply generated by "material and institutional incentives."

[94] Weir and Skocpol 1985.

[95] Christensen 2017.

members are each unique in some ways but alike in others.[96] While North American free trade has been unique in some ways, it has not been completely unlike other episodes of international economic integration. Viewing it this way means the case can be understood by reference to more general patterns and experiences, while also being useful for understanding them. Arguments about the globalization of individual countries sometimes focus so much on the idiosyncratic circumstances of each that they leave unclear why so many countries globalized at roughly the same time. At the other extreme, some studies have overgeneralized, ignoring differences across types of countries and suggesting that globalization has been of a kind everywhere. Some even advocate studying the world as a single unit.[97] This book shows that such an approach would be excessively abstract and would miss important cross-national differences.

A comparative-historical study is more appropriate. The important political decisions behind globalization get made by specific governments, at the national level, even when they are influenced by international circumstances and factors. North America is a useful region for studying international economic integration, as the three country cases span a diversity of contexts: democratic and nondemocratic, but also both developed and developing. This mitigates the problems of selection bias and partiality that would come from considering only certain types of countries.[98] Not considering developed and developing country cases simultaneously would come at the cost of lost perspective on the similarities and differences between them. Yet social science seldom considers developed and developing countries together, and the literature on globalization is no different. Among prior studies, some have examined single country cases, or small numbers of either of developed or developing countries. Some have considered the whole world, or large numbers of countries at once (using large-N statistical analyses), or sought to investigating globalization in more theoretical ways, or investigated central international institutions. But almost no studies have made qualitative comparisons of developed and developing country cases.[99] Studying different kinds of countries also permits thinking about cases analytically and categorically, making for better characterization, or qualitative measurement, of them. This applies to both cross-sectional and longitudinal comparisons. One challenge in explaining globalization is the minimal variation that can be exploited on the dependent variable: the countries that have most clearly eschewed globalization (North Korea, Cuba, etc.)

---

[96] Gerring 2004.

[97] E.g., Sklair 2001, 2002.

[98] Any region or country case has its particularities. Chapter 8 provides some limited comparison with cases in other world regions, showing that the North American cases are not so atypical.

[99] A paper by Fourcade-Gourinchas and Babb (2002) provide perhaps the only major exception.

are just too different to be useful comparisons for understanding others. But examining globalization more historically does yield useful variation: over time. Contrasting periods when countries embraced rather than rejected international integration makes the outcome of interest variable. The book therefore treats different time periods as separate cases, which is further consistent with Jacobs's suggestions for process tracing with respect to the impact of ideas.[100] Canada and Mexico prior to the mid-1980s and early 1990s, respectively, represent negative cases of decisions not to embrace globalization. This too is another reason North America is a methodologically useful region: the inclusion of negative cases helps reduce selection bias in qualitative comparative research.[101]

The characterization of the cases compared and analyzed in this book rests on interviews and archival research I conducted mostly in Mexico City, Ottawa, and Washington, DC. The data collection reflected the nature of each country's political system and the character of its policy process. For example, legislative debates were more important in the United States than the other countries—given the strong party discipline under the Canadian parliamentary system, and the president's control of the congress in Mexico at the time. Consequently, in considering each country case, the book does not always give the same attention to each institution or type of decision; different ones are more illuminating in different contexts. Some features of the cases, moreover, do not vary, but showing that requires attending to different kinds of processes in different countries. Other variations in the data collection across the three countries reflect that existing accounts of North American free trade have already chronicled different parts of the process for each country.[102] These existing accounts of North American free trade made some kinds of data collection unnecessary, though I still used my interviews and archival materials (described in appendices A and B respectively) to validate key claims.

I identified interviewees in two ways: first, using existing accounts naming key figures,[103] and, second, based on suggestions by earlier interviewees, or local academics (some of whom had been involved in the process). The book makes very few claims on the basis of a single interview. Far more often, I was able to verify interviewees' accounts by comparing them against each other, against

---

[100] Haydu 1998; Jacobs 2015; Lieberman 2001.

[101] Geddes 1990.

[102] Mayer (1998), for example, provides a comprehensive account of the domestic politics of NAFTA in the United States. Cameron and Tomlin (2000) describe the trilateral NAFTA negotiations; Robert (2000) discusses the negotiations in specific sectors. Doern and Tomlin (1991) and Hart et al. (1994) do the same for CUFTA, largely from a Canadian perspective. Books by Babb (2001), Flores Quiroga (1998), Shadlen (2004), and Thacker (2000) covered key events in Mexico.

[103] Cameron and Tomlin (2000), for example, provided a useful list of the main NAFTA negotiators for each country.

other accounts of the process, and against documentary evidence.[104] To allow them to be as candid as possible (particularly former civil servants) I do not quote interviewees by name in the text, though a full list of their names and relevant posts appears in appendix A. Many interviewees—particularly those who had completed graduate research degrees—were keen to step back and discuss the issues, and their experiences, from a more detached point of view. Many of those involved in the creation of CUFTA or NAFTA were proud of having played some part, and clearly enjoyed reliving the excitement of that time— even to a degree opponents who were ultimately dismayed by the outcome.[105]

The Case of North American Free Trade

I can now briefly introduce the three countries whose recent histories are the focus of this book. The United States, Canada, and Mexico reflect the two-pathway model articulated earlier, with the former two countries following more business-led and the latter technocracy-led pathways to globalization.

The US government was keen on international economic integration throughout the post–World War II period, and played the major role in building a new multilateral trading system in that time.[106] At least by the 1950s, American business was generally supportive of freer trade, and the priorities of the public and private sectors were broadly consistent. The United States was also supportive of some kinds of regional, not just multilateral, integration. This support peaked in 1979–80, when a number of American politicians called for some form of continental economic integration—maybe even a North American equivalent of the European Economic Community. The most notable instance of this was Ronald Reagan, who declared his support for the idea in November 1979, when launching his candidacy for the Republican nomination for president. The US Congress directed the president to "study the desirability of entering into trade agreements with countries in the northern portion of the western hemisphere,"[107] and even the National Governors' Association called for consideration of a North American common market.

---

[104] There was only one issue—government procurement in the NAFTA negotiations—with respect to which interviewees contradicted each other. Even in that case, however, just one interviewee was the clear outlier. And in the end, the book does not discuss the topic of government procurement, as it does not have much bearing on the major arguments.

[105] Translations of quotations from interviews and documents originally in Spanish are my own.

[106] Mastanduno 2009.

[107] Quoted in International Trade Commission 1981: 1.

But in May 1980, the Mexican and Canadian governments issued a joint state-ment rejecting such proposals and declaring their nations' interests to lie else-where. From their perspective, greater integration with the US economy would be detrimental to their national political autonomy, as well as to their prospects for economic growth and development. Mexico's was a leading voice in devel-oping countries' calls at that time for a "New International Economic Order," a direct challenge to American liberal preferences, and Mexico had already shown its skepticism about international integration in declining to join the General Agreement on Tariffs and Trade. Later in 1980, the Canadian state demonstrated its own economic nationalism in enacting a National Energy Program aimed at increasing Canadian control of the domestic energy industry—an initiative much criticized by Washington. From the perspective of the early 1980s, then, substantially enhanced integration among North America's three economies seemed a remote prospect.

In the next fourteen years, however, the governments of first Canada and then Mexico changed their mind, leading to the creation first of a bilateral Canada-US Free Trade Agreement (CUFTA) in 1989, and then a trilateral North American Free Trade Agreement (NAFTA) in 1994. Despite the events of 1980, US government officials continued to encourage their Canadian and Mexican counterparts to think about the idea. In 1984, US president Reagan raised the issue with Canada's newly elected prime minister, Brian Mulroney. Mulroney had previously rejected free trade as leader of the opposition, but in 1985 he reversed himself and decided to proceed. Similarly, at the first meeting between Mexican president-elect Carlos Salinas de Gortari and US president-elect George Bush, in late 1988, the latter reiterated US interest in negotiating a bilateral free trade arrangement. Salinas initially demurred, but then in early 1990 he too accepted Bush's standing invitation. In contrast to the United States, then, Canada and Mexico were delayed supporters of North American free trade.

In other respects, Canada had more in common with the United States, and Mexico was the outlier—especially in its authoritarianism. But, as elaborated further in Chapter 4, the state's democratic accountability was growing just as it deepened the country's economic opening and embraced world markets. Mexico therefore fits the pattern found in the democracy-centered literature. A valid theory should be capable of predictions consistent both with regressions across countries, and causal processes within them.[108] Given its simultaneously rising political and economic liberalism, the case of Mexico fits the correlations emphasized in the liberal literature, and this book provides a qualitative test of

---

[108] Lieberman 2005.

the causal processes presumed to explain the association between democracy and globalization in cases like Mexico.

During the NAFTA negotiations, Mexico's ruling party had little reason to fear that electoral politics would get in the way of NAFTA's ratification. But in Canada and in the United States North American free trade was politically vulnerable. In Canada, CUFTA became the top issue in the national election campaign of 1988, with two of three major political parties vowing not to implement it if elected. In the United States, the 1993 congressional ratification vote was not a sure thing—nor was support from the Democratic presidential candidate, Bill Clinton, in 1992. During the negotiations and the process of ratification the expected scale of free trade's impacts led to intense public debate in all three countries; civil society groups subjected the agreement to substantial criticism. The resolution of debates about North American free trade represented the moment when each country embraced modern globalization, and the intensity of the debates makes them useful for examining the politics of globalization in an unusually clear light.

Plan of the Book

The book is organized as follows.

Chapter 2 describes events and conditions up to the early 1980s, the point when an international economic recession catalyzed the Canadian and Mexican decisions to negotiate CUFTA and NAFTA. This chapter provides a baseline view of the past, allowing for contrasts with events and factors that came later, and identifying the political forces that made each country a case of nonglobalization in this period. The analysis here considers public opinion, the predominant economic ideas of the time, and the stance of the domestic business community.

Chapters 3, 4, and 5 describe the political economic pathways that led Canada, Mexico, and the United States, respectively, to North American free trade. Contrasting these three country cases validates the distinction between business- and technocrat-led pathways described earlier, while also showing that in both scenarios globalization is more an elite-driven than a democratic project. The United States was the first of the three countries to advocate North American free trade. But I discuss the US case last, because there I focus on the NAFTA negotiations of 1991–92 and the public debate in 1992–93—several years after the equivalent debate in Canada, and also after the most important decision (to negotiate) was made in Mexico.

Chapter 6 considers the role of economists in the rise of globalization. Many people have the impression that mainstream neoclassical ideas about trade have provided the intellectual foundation for globalization. But Chapter 6 explains that while academic economists are supportive of initiatives for globalization, and their endorsements make some political difference, the technical ideas behind their support are actually quite marginal. What makes much more of an impact in the political world are rather the priorities and worldviews of business, which are quite different. In other words, except if they are themselves economists, politicians are more convinced to pursue agreements like NAFTA by the ideas of businesspeople.

Chapter 7 addresses the question of how business could unite in support of North American free trade. This chapter explains how there were potential dissidents in the business community in each country, but in no case did these dissidents undermine the overall support of the private sector. Potentially unhappy industries in all three countries were gradually won over in the context of the negotiations, as the negotiators give domestic industries significant concessions, in the interest of ensuring free trade's political feasibility. These intranational consultations between the negotiators and industry representatives generated a great deal of content pleasing both to individual industries and to business as a whole. This chapter explains how the industry consultation mechanisms generated this outcome and also discusses key issues in the CUFTA and NAFTA negotiations. It speaks to the questions of how business unifies with respect to globalization generally, and why trade negotiations, including the negotiations that created NAFTA, are so mercantilist.

Chapter 8 discusses what the book means for the literatures on international political economy and on ideas in politics, and then compares the experiences of the three North American cases with those of countries elsewhere. The chapter closes with some comments about the future of globalization generally, especially in light of events since 2016, and also about the costs of mercantilist thinking. As the book will show, a world of competition among nations, like the world that mercantilist ideas suggest we inhabit, is one where high wages, strong social safety nets, egalitarian welfare states, and environmental protection are costly—and maybe unaffordable. Though advocates can make a case for free trade using mercantilist language, that language reinforces economic nationalism and perceptions of mutually hostile national interests generally. Such perceptions can engender a backlash against the international cooperation that free trade requires, and as of 2019 mercantilist thinking appears to be encouraging the rise of nationalist populism in many countries—and motivating the rollback of free trade under Trump and Brexit.

Finally, an afterword summarizes what we know about the consequences of CUFTA and NAFTA, in areas where the agreements' advocates and critics made clear a priori predictions—economic growth, employment, environmental quality, and so on. I take the measure of how the agreements have performed relative to what was said back during the intensely heated debates about them in the 1980s and 1990s.

2

Why Globalization Didn't Happen, 1948–1982

This book is about how globalization came to North America in the 1980s and 1990s. Before the rest of the book turns to the events of those decades, though, this chapter sets the context, by telling of earlier times and highlighting some key differences among the three countries of North America. It also describes how globalization very nearly came to North America, or at least part of it, much earlier: in the late 1940s. That near-miss, itself tied to one of the great what-ifs of twentieth-century global economic history, ended up influencing the shape of North American free trade decades later.

The "what-if" was the establishment of an international organization overseeing international trade in the aftermath of World War II. Toward the end of the war, as the Allies grew confident of victory, international negotiations put in place measures meant to stabilize global economic activity and to prevent the recurrence of anything like the Great Depression. These negotiations, and others like them after the war's end, established institutions that serve as important foundations for global capitalism to this day. Most famously, a 1944 United Nations conference held at Bretton Woods, New Hampshire, established the International Monetary Fund and the International Bank for Reconstruction and Development—later the World Bank. Less famously, a series of similar meetings led to the signing of a charter, in Havana in early 1948, for an International Trade Organization (ITO).

The Havana Charter was an expansive agreement, broaching not just questions of trade but also topics like fair labor standards and a commitment to full employment. Many of these broader provisions, and others granting preferential treatment for poorer countries, were included at the behest of developing countries. Their attempt to reshape the postwar international trade regime ended up backfiring, however, in the face of hostility from the United States—the world's dominant power and the leading nation in the ITO negotiations. American officials were not keen on the content added by the developing countries, and, when they got the chance to read the draft ITO character, American businesspeople were positively hostile. Some of them opposed it because they feared the threat of added foreign competition that trade liberalization would unleash. Others perceived the ITO as inadequately liberal, and biased against free market principles.[1] Rather than endorsing what they saw as a flawed agreement, then, this odd coalition stated a preference for no agreement at all, a stance then taken up by sympathizers in the US Congress.[2] As America's lawmakers refused to ratify the agreement, the Truman administration eventually gave up trying to win them over. Given America's massive weight in the global economy at that time, and the leading role of the United States in international economic affairs, other signatories of the Havana Charter also then decided not to bother ratifying it. The ITO was conceived, but never born.

For that reason, until the creation of the World Trade Organization in 1994, almost a half-century later, the central institution governing world trade was not the ITO but the General Agreement on Tariffs and Trade (GATT). The GATT was finalized by twenty-three nations in Geneva in October 1947, and was much narrower than the Havana Charter. It was originally designed just to facilitate cuts to tariffs and other trade barriers in the short run—an interim agreement that would be effective only until the more expansive ITO could replace and subsume it. The motivation to proceed so quickly was that the US president only had a limited time in which to negotiate, before the authority that Congress had granted him to do so would expire.

Later chapters in this book will more fully describe the kinds of ideas that motivate international trade negotiators, but for now suffice to say that one of the guiding principles of the GATT was nondiscrimination. That is, its authors wanted market rather than regulatory forces to shape patterns of trade and production. Trade barriers—above all tariffs, or taxes on imports—raise the price of imported goods relative to domestically produced goods, meaning that they act to protect domestic industries from foreign competition.[3] Importing countries can discriminate among imports originating in different source countries, by imposing higher or lower tariffs on them. In this way, a country can end up importing a good from a less efficient producer that just happens to be based in a country granted preferential access. The GATT therefore required that, if a member lowered barriers to imports from one country, the same benefits would have to be provided to all other countries as well; all parties were entitled to

---

[1] Johnson 2018.

[2] See Diebold 1952, which describes the coalition of "protectionists" and "perfectionists."

[3] Originally, governments levied tariffs more simply just to raise revenue, as tariffs are a relatively simple and easy tax to collect; for that reason they were a major source of public revenues in most countries until the twentieth century.

the same treatment as the "most-favored nation." The GATT did, however, allow for one exception to this general rule: discriminatory treatment under customs unions and free trade agreements. And it turns out that at the heart of the story of how a global agreement designed specifically to be nondiscriminatory nonetheless came to allow for this kind of discrimination lies a failed attempt to build a free trade zone in North America.

In the context of the massive economic readjustments and instability of the years right after World War II, Canadian reserves of US dollars were shrinking rapidly.[4] Imports surged after the relaxation in 1946 of wartime exchange controls. In the face of the imbalances threatening the country's financial system, Ottawa requested that the United States cut its tariffs on imports from Canada—which would mean Canadian exports could buy more American dollars. The Americans considered that idea politically infeasible in Washington, but came back with a different, more ambitious suggestion: to negotiate a full customs union—bilateral free trade, under which each country would eliminate tariffs on imports from the other, and harmonize its tariffs on imports from third countries. The idea of common external tariffs was in turn, though, unacceptable to the Canadians. It would amount to a major loss of autonomy, in effect handing the United States substantial control over Canada's relationship with Great Britain and the rest of the British Commonwealth. Canada therefore proposed a slightly more limited arrangement: an agreement for the lifting of trade barriers on each other's goods, but not the adoption of common external tariffs. The United States agreed, and between the fall of 1947 and the spring of 1948 officials from the two countries then negotiated the terms of a free trade agreement along these lines. The negotiators met behind closed doors, and neither government even told the public what was going on, as the level of integration that the arrangement they had in mind was expected to be highly controversial in Canada. Without giving away what they were after, and by playing off demands that other countries were making anyway, the two governments cobbled together an article in the GATT—Article XXIV—which allowed for free trade agreements applying to "substantially all the trade" between the parties to such an agreement.[5]

After the two countries' negotiators reached an agreement in principle, however, the Canadian prime minister, William Lyon Mackenzie King, decided at the last minute not to ratify it. The historical record does not reveal a great deal of what he was thinking in making this decision, but it is clear that he believed a free trade agreement would be unacceptably unpopular and politically costly in Canada. He complained in his diary about otherwise bright economic officials

---

[4] The discussion here draws heavily on Cuff and Granatstein 1977; Chase 2006.

[5] The requirement to eliminate barriers to "substantially all the trade" ruled out picking and choosing only a small number of products. Only major initiatives would meet the threshold.

"without the least knowledge of the political side of matters." His decision had the effect of putting off free trade between Canada and the United States for forty years, though decades later, when they did finally sign a free trade agreement, Article XXIV provided them with the legal basis they needed. Without that article, the 1989 CUFTA (and the 1994 NAFTA) would have been illegal under international trade law, as they derogate from the general principles of nondiscrimination otherwise required under the GATT.

Developing countries were much less central to the formation of the GATT. To some degree, they were simply marginalized by the major powers and prevented from playing a role in shaping the new multilateral trading system. The United States and United Kingdom alone did most of the work of setting up the Bretton Woods and GATT system, and they did so in ways so exclusionary that from today's perspective it is hard to believe they could ever have been considered legitimate.[6] At the same time, though, to some extent it was also developing countries' own choice not to get involved. The United States wanted all parties to adopt the norms of the multilateral trading system it was working to establish, but the developing countries were hostile to its basic character. By the 1940s, they believed they needed to pursue interventionist rather than free market policy mixes to have any chance of catching up, in economic terms, to the industrial nations. Wholeheartedly embracing this school of thought and the policy package that came with it, Mexico therefore rejected America's suggestions of closer economic integration at that time. Mexico participated in the Havana Conference but viewed the final ITO Charter as biased against developing countries, providing them with no net benefit. Like many other such countries, then, Mexico neither signed the charter nor chose to participate in the GATT.[7]

These events of the 1940s foreshadowed what was to come in subsequent decades. The United States sought to establish a liberal international economic order, Canada participated with reservations, and Mexico distanced itself entirely. The US government made clear that it was interested in regional free trade, but Canada and Mexico were reluctant, and as a consequence, if anything, the postwar period proved to be a time of deglobalization in North America. The remainder of this chapter presents the situations of the three countries in the post–World War II period, highlighting some notable differences among them, and setting out a baseline against which to compare future events. The chapter

---

[6] Gardner 1985–86.

[7] To demonstrate how many developing countries decided to stay away, the United Nations had fifty-one founding members in 1945, while GATT had only twenty-three in 1947, five of which were British colonies with limited say over their own external economic relationships. The only Latin American nations that joined the GATT as founding members were Brazil, Chile, and Cuba.

also explains why globalization did not come to North America until the major reversals of the 1980s and 1990s.

America: Liberal Hegemony

The free trade talks with Canada in the 1940s reflected the general US attitude of the time. The United States entered the twentieth century with high tariffs, like most countries, and until the 1930s that did not change. But in the course of recovering from the Great Depression the United States embraced a policy of economic openness that endured for decades afterwards.

The US Constitution grants Congress the authority to regulate foreign trade and the power to raise or lower tariffs. Historically, the northern, industrial states preferred high tariffs, to protect manufacturers from European competition; as such, the Republican Party—whose strength lay in the North—was the party of high tariffs. When in control of Congress, the Republicans tended to raise barriers to trade; Democrats, concentrated in the southern exporting states, lowered them. But in 1930, in one of the more infamous miscalculations in US public policy history, the Republicans overreached. In the depths of the Depression, two congressmen orchestrated a dramatic rise in US tariffs—the now-notorious US Smoot-Hawley tariff bill—in an attempt to deal with the severe economic contraction. Their initiative, however, proved a miserable failure, merely encouraging other countries to mimic the United States and introduce trade barriers of their own.[8] This downwards cycle of tit-for-tat protectionism led world trade to decline massively in the early 1930s. Smoot-Hawley also represented a defeat for the power of experts, as more than a thousand US economists had signed an open letter unsuccessfully urging President Herbert Hoover not to sign the Smoot-Hawley bill.[9]

After the Smoot-Hawley debacle, though, US policy swung the other way. Congressional and presidential elections in 1930 and 1932 returned the Democrats to power for the first time in over a decade, giving them a new opportunity to liberalize US trade policy.[10] They seized the opportunity by not only lowering tariffs, but also reshaping the whole structure of US trade policymaking, passing a Reciprocal Trade Agreements Act (RTAA) in 1934. The RTAA provided the legal basis for Congress to authorize the executive branch to negotiate trade agreements, under which the United States and partner nations would reciprocally agree to bind their tariffs no higher than certain fixed

[8] Irwin 1998.
[9] Fetter 1942.
[10] Irwin 1998: 337.

levels. The idea was that the presidency would take the initiative to propose and negotiate such agreements, after which Congress would vote only up or down on the resulting contents as a whole. The RTAA thereby transferred substantial authority over trade policy from the legislative to the executive branch, putting the president in the driver's seat on trade to this day.[11] The RTAA also embodied the decision to set US trade policies jointly with other countries, through international negotiations rather than unilaterally. The new framework made a big impact, with US tariffs dropping substantially after 1934.[12] Before the RTAA, as Schattschneider later observed in a classic work of political science, each member of the US Congress, acting alone, tended to favor higher tariffs as a means of protecting local industries.[13] The RTAA changed the structure of decision-making, as it aggregated decision-making to the level of the presidency—which tended to possess a different outlook.

By creating the institution of reciprocal trade agreements, the RTAA transformed tariff policy so it became as much about American exporters' access to foreign markets as about barriers against foreign imports into the United States. The man widely regarded as the inventor of this principle was Cordell Hull, US secretary of state from 1933 to 1944. A lifelong free trader, Hull believed Congress would never approve unilateral tariff reductions; but he believed reciprocity had more of a chance. Hull was proven correct, as the prospect of better access to foreign markets was what won much of the support the RTAA received. The text of the act itself identified its main purpose as "expanding foreign markets for the products of the United States."

The RTAA was not a project of American business. Some industry groups were in favor, and many of the defining ideas behind the RTAA came from internationalist business leaders and associations, like New York financiers.[14] But many others were opposed, such as the National Association of Manufacturers, which had even supported higher tariffs in the run-up to the Smoot Hawley debacle.[15] The other major US business association at that time, the Chamber of Commerce, demanded "reasonable protection for American industries subject to destructive competition from abroad."[16] While large segments of American business were hostile to tariff reductions in the 1930s, however, over the course of the 1940s and 1950s their views changed substantially.[17] Republican opposition

---

[11] Irwin 1998; Chorev 2007.

[12] Haggard 1988: 91; Schnietz 2003: 215.

[13] Schattschneider 1935.

[14] Haggard 1988: 98.

[15] James 2001: 134–35; Kaplan 1996: 49; Schnietz 2003.

[16] Quoted in Woods 2003: 412.

[17] Bauer, Pool, and Dexter 1963; Chorev 2007; Woods 2003.

to trade liberalization also weakened, and by the 1950s trade stopped being much of a partisan issue.[18] US business grew more internationalist, prioritizing opportunities for foreign exports, and the RTAA led to a gradual liberalization of trade in the post–World War II period. Under the influence and leadership of a series of US presidents, repeated rounds of negotiations at the GATT reduced tariffs among its members, and more countries joined the system.

The United States also sought to build a generally liberal international order for investment, making the world safe for American business interests. The United States was home to the vast majority of outward foreign direct investment in the immediate post–World War II period. In the mid-1950s, forty-two of the world's fifty largest firms were American, and US investment in Western Europe expanded dramatically.[19] The US government's position was that foreign investors should be able to expect the same treatment from host governments as domestic counterparts, and that public policy should be neutral with respect to investment, neither encouraging nor discouraging such flows. This was "in keeping with the basic US economic philosophy of free markets."[20]

While US officials preferred multilateral and nondiscriminatory trade arrangements, the United States did make some exceptions. In 1965, the United States and Canada agreed on an "Auto Pact" under which there would be duty-free trade on motor vehicles and auto parts between the United States and Canada. The aim was to rationalize the North American automobile industry, all the major auto manufacturers in Canada being subsidiaries of big US companies. Trade-balancing requirements nonetheless ensured that manufacturers would site substantial assembly and other operations in Canada.[21]

Similarly, the United States derogated from multilateralism in dealing with developing countries, including Mexico. In the 1970s, the United States established a Generalized System of Preferences (GSP), in principle a form of development assistance according to which imports from developing countries would be subjected to lower tariffs than those applied to imports from developed countries.[22] On the other hand, US munificence vis-à-vis the developing countries only went so far, and the United States fought developing countries' more aggressive efforts to reshape the international economic order. Developing countries were, for example, suspicious of the major post–World War II international

---

[18] Irwin and Kroszner 1999; Shoch 2000.

[19] Bergesen and Sonnett 2001; Ostry 1997.

[20] Economic Policy Group Task Force on International Investment 1977: 2.

[21] Hart et al. 1994: 202.

[22] Another notable exception to general US principles was the Caribbean Basin Initiative (see, e.g., Long 2015), in substantial part an effort to contain the spread of communism in Central America and the Caribbean.

financial institutions, as it was clear they were heavily dominated by US preferences and views.[23] Developing countries made efforts to build alternative fora and institutions; but the United States continued to insist on channeling development assistance through the IFIs. As one internal memo explained, going through the IFIs was "a means by which developed countries can take [an] assertive role in the North/South dialogue," and would allow the United States to "play a role in encouraging proper economic policies and priorities within developing countries, thus reinforcing US international monetary and development objectives."[24]

All of this was hardly bread and butter for domestic US political debate, and the public was scarcely involved in any international economic policy decisions. That was partly because the 1950s and 1960s were a famously satisfying time for American capitalism, with the US economy dominating the globe, growth consistently good, and American workers enjoying rising standards of living. As such, there is very little evidence of what public opinion vis-à-vis international economic policy even was in this period; it was not something that attracted much attention from pollsters or academic survey researchers. By some accounts, American public opinion was favorable to free trade, at least until the 1970s.[25] But such preferences were not strong. From the 1970s to the early 1990s, survey data show more Americans supported maintaining tariffs at existing levels rather than lowering them.[26] Still, the president had a fairly free hand in setting US trade policy.[27] Judging by interviews with State Department bureaucrats in the 1950s and 1960s, the preferences of the public had little impact on US foreign policy.[28]

More than public opinion, America's international economic policies reflected the views of US economists. By the end of World War II, staff members working for the lead federal agency on trade policy—the State Department—were articulating "a remarkably unadorned vision of nineteenth-century free trade."[29] Though American economists' core ideas about trade were not new (see Chapter 6), the discipline had in other ways transformed in recent years—and grown more influential. During the war, economists began participating much more in public administration and policymaking; a Council of Economic Advisers was established in 1946. Vast new amounts of

[23] E.g., Babb 2013.
[24] Council of Economic Advisers 1976: 11–12.
[25] Eckes 1992: 152–53.
[26] Holsti 1996: 87–88.
[27] Holsti 1996: 36.
[28] Cohen 1973.
[29] Ikenberry 1993: 68.

statistical data had become available over the course of the war years, while the use of mathematics had taken off in the 1930s—two trends that turned economics into a substantially more technical (and intimidating) discipline. Keynesianism and the New Deal meant that government had a new responsibility for growth and employment, and economics became a tool for meeting that responsibility. At the same time, the recently much-increased number of American economists and the unparalleled resources they at their disposal meant that US economics dominated the discipline globally.[30] American economists could disseminate their positive view of free trade not just in Washington, but internationally.

Washington was happy to offer foreign exporters access to the US market, not just on economic grounds, but also in the pursuit of foreign policy (including Cold War) aims. Such access, that is, could help win and maintain allies in the struggle against communism. Critics objected that the United States was sacrificing the interests of its firms and workers, especially as other countries began catching up to and soon matching American leadership in technology and industry. By the 1970s, industrial competition from Japanese firms in particular began eroding the security and confidence of US manufacturers—most notably in the auto sector. By the early 1980s, for the first time in decades, many US manufacturing firms found themselves seriously struggling with foreign competition. This led some American business leaders to demand protection that few had previously thought necessary.

But while some US industries adopted defensive postures, others made aggressive calls for new international institutions that would give them increased access to foreign markets and favorable treatment for their international operations.[31] This led to growing American interest in the liberalization of trade in services, and stronger protections for foreign investment and intellectual property rights. While starting to campaign for the inclusion of investment in the Uruguay Round of GATT negotiations (after 1986), the United States also began seeking better protections for its firms' overseas investments, launching a bilateral investment treaty (BIT) program in 1983. In this, the United States was only doing what Europeans had been doing for some time, giving investors the opportunity to sue host governments directly in case of conflicts.[32] The US BIT program differed from its European predecessors, however, in also seeking to *liberalize* host countries' investment rules—such as by prohibiting

---

[30] Backhouse 2010.

[31] Ostry 1997.

[32] Host countries have signed BITs in hopes of increasing investors' confidence in the security of their assets, thereby leading them to invest more.

performance requirements and opening up new sectors to investment.[33] The United States also began making more assertive demands for other countries to protect intellectual property, US firms being major players in the invention of new products and technologies. The United States pushed developing countries hard for changes in their intellectual property laws starting in the 1980s, using both threats and rewards for compliance. For example, the United States started making benefits under the GSP conditional on the effective protection of intellectual property.[34] This development came despite objections from some influential trade economists that intellectual property rights were not even a trade issue.[35]

It was in the 1970s that US leaders began expressing renewed interest in some form of deep North American integration. The US Trade Act of 1974 included a statement that "it is the sense of the Congress that the United States should enter into a trade agreement with Canada." The US secretary of state raised the prospect of a trilateral common market while on a visit to Mexico with President Jimmy Carter in 1979.[36] And in 1979–80, early contenders for both the Democratic and Republican nominations for US president seized on the idea. Both California governor Jerry Brown (a Democrat) and former US Treasury secretary and Texas governor John Connally (a Republican) proposed some kind of trilateral North American common market. Later that year, Ronald Reagan, Connally's Republican rival, also endorsed the idea in prominent fashion, in a November 13 speech formally announcing his intention to seek the nomination. Reagan discussed the idea of a "North American accord" at some length, albeit not in very specific terms. Around the same time, in 1979, in the same bill by which it ratified the Tokyo Round of multilateral trade negotiations (1973–79), Congress instructed the president to "study the desirability of entering into trade agreements with countries in the northern portion of the western hemisphere to promote the economic growth of the United States and such countries and the mutual expansion of market opportunities."[37] Even the National Governors Association expressed enthusiasm at that time, passing a resolution at its February 1980 conference calling for an international forum to explore the idea.[38]

---

[33] American efforts to open up other countries to US capital were not new. Even in the immediate postwar years, US officials tried to use promises of development aid to persuade Latin American governments to liberalize (Rabe 1978).

[34] Sell 1995: 323.

[35] E.g., Bhagwati 2008: 73.

[36] According to Serrano 1993: 337.

[37] International Trade Commission 1981: 1.

[38] *Globe and Mail* 1980.

Events later in 1980, though, led Americans to moderate their advocacy for North American free trade. In May of that year, on the occasion of a rare bilateral summit, Canadian prime minister Pierre Trudeau and Mexican president José López Portillo issued a joint statement firmly rejecting the idea of regional economic integration. Given this chilly response, US politicians and officials subsequently backed off. They knew it would not help politically in Canada and Mexico for regional integration to look like a project the US government had bullied its neighbors into accepting.

Canada: Manufacturing Nationalism

Like the United States, Canada entered the twentieth century with high tariffs. These were the legacy of a "National Policy," adopted in 1879, which established an enduring pattern of trade protectionism. The smallness of Canada's economy relative to that of the United States meant it would always do a lot of business with the much larger market to the south, but would also worry about its national economic autonomy and the risks of excessive dependence.[39]

Despite its tradition of economic nationalism, however, Canada's politicians occasionally tried something different. In 1911, for example, the Liberal government of prime minister Sir Wilfred Laurier proposed to sign a free trade arrangement with the United States. The US president at that time, William Taft, had indicated his administration was amenable. The Liberals gambled and lost on the issue, however, as it proved deeply unpopular with Canadian voters; the Liberals lost badly in a federal election in 1911 fought largely over the question of free trade. That chastening experience would live long in the memories of Canadian politicians, as would the catchy slogan of free trade's opponents: "No truck nor trade with the Yankees!"

Behind a "tariff wall" maintained well into the twentieth century, Canada turned into an industrial nation; on a per capita basis, by the end of World War II Canada was one of the wealthiest countries of the world. The war had shattered the economies of Japan and most European nations, whereas manufacturing capacity in Canada and the few other industrial nations outside of Europe had expanded well beyond prewar levels. As described earlier in this chapter, the 1940s were again a time when Canadian politicians thought seriously about signing a free trade agreement with the United States. But as in 1911, the initiative came to a fast end, and for political reasons, with Liberal prime minister Mackenzie King's skittishness likely reflecting his party's bitter experience under Laurier

[39] Hart 2002.

decades earlier. Mackenzie King was persuaded by the economic case for free trade, stating "from the economic point of view, there was everything to be said for the proposal and little against it." But politically he believed the proposal would never be viable: "The Conservatives would seize on this issue, if it were placed before them, in order to force an early election. They would distort and misrepresent the proposal as an effort on the part of the Liberals to sell Canada to the United States."[40] At least from his point of view, free trade was not a potential vote-winner.

Because of nationalist sensitivities of the kind that led Mackenzie King to drop the idea in the 1940s, Canada eschewed free trade with the United States for forty more years. Still, the Canadian government endorsed trade liberalism on a multilateral basis, and actively contributed to the establishment of the postwar international trade regime.[41] For Canada, multilateralism served the purpose of balancing its twin allegiances to Britain and the Commonwealth, on the one hand, and the United States on the other. The liberalism of the Canadian state in the mid-twentieth century also reflected the influence of the internationalist and economically trained career bureaucrats who dominated international economic policymaking at that time.[42] Many of these officials held advanced degrees in economics, and by the mid-twentieth century Canadian economics was squarely neoclassical, barely if at all distinguishable from economics in the United States, with Canadians making notable contributions to the otherwise US-dominated literature on trade.[43] The mandarins were so scholarly that the atmosphere in the upper echelons of the civil service itself became remarkably academic; in the early postwar period "the economists ruled in Ottawa."[44] To underscore the links to their counterparts in American government and academia: the de facto head of the Canadian delegation at Bretton Woods held a PhD in economics from Harvard, was one of two people called on to second Keynes's motion to adopt the conference's Final Act, and would go on to head the economics department at Queen's University. In academia, probably the most influential Canadian economist ever, Harry Johnson, also held a PhD from Harvard (plus MA degrees from Toronto and Cambridge), and he spent most of his career as a professor at the University of Chicago.

Despite their influence, though, Canada was a lukewarm liberalizer even on a multilateral basis. In the 1960s Kennedy Round of GATT negotiations, for instance, Canada demanded and won an exemption from the tariff-cutting formula

[40] These quotes appear in Weihs (1974: 79–80).
[41] Granatstein 1985; Muirhead 1992: 59.
[42] Weihs 1974; Porter 1958.
[43] See Wonnacott 1993.
[44] Granatstein 2015: 158.

applied to all other developed countries.[45] Due to efforts such as that, Figure 1.1 shows, Canada's trade integration barely increased in the 1950s and early 1960s; Canadian trade policy still included a heavy dose of protection, particularly for manufacturing.[46] Though that policy to a degree reflected Canadians' hesitation about getting too close and therefore vulnerable to the much larger United States, it did not reflect public opinion about bilateral free trade specifically. If we judge by polls in the 1950s and 1960s and the early 1980s, there was actually majority support in Canada for free trade with the United States.[47] In 1963, fully half of Canadians were in favor, versus 32 percent opposed; in 1968, the percentages were 56 and 27, with the rest expressing no opinion.[48]

The enthusiasm for trade among Canada's foreign policy elite, and in a more diffuse way among the public at large, was not reflected in the views of business. Manufacturers in particular—an influential part of Canada's business community—demanded protections from threatening international markets, seeing themselves as relative minnows in the world economy. Industry demands for tariff protection were not new; the main voice of industry, the Canadian Manufacturers' Association (CMA), had been campaigning for protection since the 1800s. Originally founded in 1871 (as the Ontario Manufacturers' Association), the CMA was by the twentieth century one of the two most powerful business associations in Canada.[49] Even after World War II had decimated industries in many other countries, the CMA repeatedly emphasized its opposition to further opening of the Canadian economy, saying, for example, in 1948:

> The Canadian tariff is already reduced to a level lower than the tariffs of most other industrial countries in the world and further reductions would endanger our industrial economy.... Tariff concessions beyond those made at [the GATT] last year should not be entertained.[50]

The CMA complained the GATT wasn't working, as other countries (most importantly the United States) were in the CMA's view not living up to their

---

[45] Reuber 1978: S131.

[46] Hart 2002: 75.

[47] Lyon and Leyton-Brown 1977; Robinson 2015.

[48] Sigler and Goresky 1974: 655; see also Bothwell, Drummond, and English 1981: 262.

[49] As an executive assistant to the federal minister of trade and commerce put it in 1963 in response to a naive query about the importance of the prime minister's speaking to the CMA: "The annual dinner of the Canadian Manufacturers' Association . . . along with the annual meeting of the Canadian Chamber of Commerce, is probably the most important gathering of businessmen in Canada. If it is the Prime Minister's wish to make a major address . . . to Canadian business, he could not pick a better audience" (McCabe 1963).

[50] Canadian Manufacturers' Association 1948: 2–3.

commitments. Arguing for a restrictive rather than increasingly liberal trade policy, the president of the association wrote to the federal cabinet in 1950:

> Since Canada's positive leadership towards lowering of trade barriers has failed to promote comparable action among other countries then it must be admitted that the experiment has been a failure and we should direct our energy towards building up Canada as a market for Canadians.[51]

The liberal mandarins in Ottawa ran up against this industry resistance on a regular basis in the postwar years. To some degree, they pushed back. C. D. Howe, the minister of trade and commerce, responded angrily to the CMA that "it is not the intention of the Government to withdraw or in any way to weaken its support of the international programme for the reconstruction of world trade along lines that seek to regain for Canada greater freedom of access to markets throughout the world."[52]

Manufacturers argued that protecting Canadian jobs demanded that Canada change the status quo, under which the country was (so they claimed) exporting largely labor-light raw materials and agricultural goods, and importing labor-intensive manufactures:

> In 1954 we imported more foreign fully manufactured goods than any other country in the world, not just on a per capita basis, but in actual volume. . . . Conversely, the great bulk of our exports are foodstuffs, raw materials, semi-processed materials and articles requiring only a few manufacturing steps. . . . This situation poses the question whether Canada has gone too far in tariff reduction.[53]

Manufacturers portrayed Canada as a relatively underdeveloped country, and therefore in need of strong protection for industry, with businesspeople complaining about competition from "low-wage countries":

> In some fields the most difficult competition comes from low wage countries such as the United Kingdom, Western Europe and Japan. Nor must it be forgotten that while wages in these countries are much lower than Canadian wages, their factories are equipped with the most modern of machinery and their technical skills are high.[54]

---

[51] Holding 1950.

[52] Canadian Manufacturers' Association 1948: 2–3.

[53] Canadian Manufacturers' Association 1955a. See also Holding 1952.

[54] McLagan 1961.

When asked specifically about free trade with the United States, the president of the CMA stated it "would completely destroy great segments of the Canadian manufacturing industry, and . . . we would lose a great deal of our identity and autonomy as a country."[55]

This attitude changed little over time. During the Tokyo Round of GATT negotiations, in the 1970s, manufacturers demanded that the new round not result in foreign manufacturers controlling any more of the domestic Canadian market:

> Whatever concessions Canada is alleged to have obtained in previous negotiations for improved access to foreign markets have been more than offset in aggregate terms both by the access that foreign suppliers have gained to the Canadian market and by the non-tariff barriers protecting their own markets.[56]

Canada's tariff wall effectively moderated outside competition, but it also provided a major incentive for foreign—mostly American—investment in Canada. After World War II, capital poured into the country, as parent companies abroad opened branch plants to serve the Canadian market; high tariffs meant they could not do so using imports instead. Much of the Canadian manufacturing sector soon comprised the assets of large American firms, and FDI grew to represent an unusually large share of the whole Canadian economy.[57] As one 1968 report summarized, "The extent of foreign control of Canadian industry is unique among the industrialized nations of the world."[58] At that time, Canada was so much more of an FDI destination than a source that it decided not to sign the OECD's Code of Liberalization of Capital Movements, and was the only OECD country that did not partake of the International Centre for Settlement of Investment Disputes.[59] American participation in the Canadian economy was sufficiently widespread that some claimed Canada was at risk of a de facto "silent surrender" to the United States.[60] In response to concerns about this increasing foreign control of Canadian industry, politicians began taking steps to limit it.[61]

---

[55] Sheils 1953.

[56] Canadian Manufacturers' Association 1974. As late as 1977, the CMA was expressing largely negative views of international economic opening, complaining that "at this stage in Canada's development as an industrial nation, our industry is in general not as capable of benefiting from trade concessions gained as it is vulnerable to trade concessions granted" (Stevens 1977).

[57] Litvak and Maule 1981; Laux and Molot 1988.

[58] Task Force on the Structure of Canadian Industry 1968. Wonnacott and Wonnacott (1982) put it differently: "The United States is big, wealthy, and owns much of Canadian industry."

[59] Litvak and Maule 1975–76.

[60] Levitt 1970.

[61] Bothwell, Drummond, and English 1981: 262.

Most notably, in 1973, Canada introduced a Foreign Investment Review Act. This new law, in the interest of "the ability of Canadians to maintain effective control over their economic environment" (as its Section 2 explained) allowed the federal government to begin screening all foreign investments, and to block those not—in regulators' eyes—of "significant benefit to Canada."[62]

Aside from the CMA, the other important voice of business in Canada in the postwar period was the Canadian Chamber of Commerce.[63] In contrast to the CMA, the more broad-based Chamber, which encompassed not just manufacturers but also more export-oriented primary sector industries, was more liberal in its trade policy recommendations. The chairman of its Trade Committee argued to the federal cabinet in 1966,

> We shall continue to support your efforts towards a successful outcome of the [current round of GATT negotiations]. It is obvious that Canada will have to make those tariff concessions necessary to obtain the balance of advantages required to increase our export trade. . . . Canadian manufacturers must be prepared, in [the] future, to meet greater exposure to foreign competition, not only abroad, but at home.[64]

But overall the Chamber devoted little attention to the issue of trade. Its policy activity was more focused on domestic concerns, like labor market and tax issues. The Chamber also tended to embrace free markets as a matter of principle—setting it at odds with policies of trade interventionism. But even the Chamber argued, in 1974, that "adequate safeguards must be retained to protect essential Canadian manufacturing industries."[65] And much the same held for other business groups at the time. Some business-allied think tanks in the postwar period—particularly those not linked to manufacturing—were interested in free trade with the United States.[66] But they had little motivation to campaign on the issue.

Businesspeople who took an active interest in trade tended to be those motivated to campaign against rather than for liberalization. They expressed their hostility toward public officials perceived to be too smitten with free market ideas.

---

[62] Intriguingly, the CMA was not so concerned about the ingress of foreign investment, and did not support the 1973 legislation.

[63] The Chamber is still "the largest business association in Canada, and the country's most influential," at least according to its website. The Chamber certainly has more members than any other business association in Canada: currently about two hundred thousand (again according to its website).

[64] Valle 1966: 2.

[65] King 1974: 12.

[66] Ernst 1992.

The CMA complained that Canada's international trade "negotiators and the back-up team of public servants, while highly competent, are relying too heavily on theoretical free-trade principles."[67] The Canadian Textiles Institute, similarly, decried "the elegant mathematics of officials more familiar with economic theory than international reality."[68] And because businesspeople distrusted Canada's trade negotiators, they made frequent requests for opportunities to participate more directly in trade negotiations and the policy process.

The free market officials about which business was complaining were well versed in the neoclassical trade theory that led leading academic economists in Canada to support free trade both generally and with the United States specifically. Canadian professors of economics contributed influential studies to the neoclassical literature on trade economics, and when they weighed in on questions of policy, their recommendations were consistently liberal.[69] A widely cited 1967 study by Wonnacott and Wonnacott recommended the negotiation of an FTA with United States, as did a report by the Economic Council of Canada, a policy research institute funded by the federal government.[70] Studying the economics of a possible free trade arrangement, the council released a report on its findings in 1975, concluding that bilateral free trade with the United States would be of significant benefit to Canada—a conclusion "remarkably close to that advocated by most Canadian academic economists over the years and quite at odds with the popular and 'business' views on the subject."[71] Given the power of the bureaucracy, its close connections to academic economics, and the liberalism of the discipline in Canada by that time, it is no surprise that protectionist businesspeople were hostile to it. At the same time, Canadian business had reason to be satisfied that their opposition to free trade was successfully keeping Canadian trade policy distinctly restrictive.

Mexico: Development and Deglobalization

The post–World War II period looked rather different from the perspective of the developing world. In the mid-twentieth century, it is important to remember that the manufacturing sector was very small in all but a dozen or so countries—and some of those had come under heavy fire during the war. The conflict had fostered a measure of industrialization in some nations, by forcing combatant

---

[67] Canadian Manufacturers' Association 1977: 2
[68] Canadian Textiles Institute 1983.
[69] E.g., Johnson 1968; Wonnacott 1993.
[70] Abelson 2002.
[71] Rea and MacLeod 1976: 82.

countries' manufacturers to redirect production away from consumer goods and toward the war effort. The sudden scarcity of imports available from those nations both enabled and effectively forced the developing countries of the time to build up their own manufacturing sectors. Moreover, the prices of many primary commodities had declined substantially in the 1930s, reducing the buying power of the developing countries that were exporting them. Developing states sought to make a virtue out of necessity, and introduced policies they hoped would replace imported manufactures with home-grown products.

In doing so, they were also taking on board new ideas and advice about the merits of protecting infant industries from international competition. At that time, the mainstream of the international economics profession mostly accepted, and in some respects even welcomed, developing countries adopting interventionist trade policies for the sake of industrialization.[72] John Maynard Keynes, the most influential and celebrated economist anywhere, was saying that free trade might sometimes need to be subordinated to the higher purposes of macroeconomic growth and stability.[73] And according to an emerging subdiscipline of development economics, the challenges and needs of developing countries were in crucial respects quite different from those of wealthier, already industrialized nations. Specifically, development required more interventionist policies, with the state playing a bigger role in the economy. State-centered development was consistent with previous European history, insofar as more backward countries had typically used state intervention to catch up to earlier developers, and they had also often sought to protect new industries from foreign competition.[74] It was thought that developing countries would do well to shift employment from agriculture to manufacturing, not least because international trade was unfavorable to primary sector producers.[75]

The field of economics and the substance of economic thought in Mexico tracked these "structuralist" perspectives.[76] When Mexico's national university opened the country's first economics program, in 1929, largely with the aim of training new bureaucrats and politicians, these were the kinds of ideas that future policymakers absorbed.[77] As a consequence, like many other developing countries, Mexico introduced a policy of state-guided import substitution industrialization (ISI)—building on the high tariffs Mexico had always had.[78]

[72] Bruton 1998; Waterbury 1999.

[73] Eichengreen 1984; Sachs and Warner 1995.

[74] Chang 2002; Gerschenkron 1962; Helleiner 2003.

[75] Lewis 1954; Prebisch 1959; Economic Commission for Latin America 1950.

[76] Whitehead 2006.

[77] Babb 2001.

[78] Coatsworth and Williamson 2004.

That Mexico's ISI program was not radical for the time is shown for example by the fact that international institutions were largely unbothered by it.[79] And even though the interventionism entailed by ISI bore some similarity to the state socialism of the Soviet Union (whose economic record at that time looked quite good), planning and ISI were by no means inevitably left-wing projects; in Mexico, much of the import substitution program was introduced under the relatively conservative president Miguel Alemán, between 1946 and 1952.[80] ISI policies were also easily understood in nationalist terms, dovetailing comfortably with Mexican sensitivities about sovereignty and in particular the loss of half the country's land area to the United States in the nineteenth century.

Mexico's development strategy entailed remaining outside of GATT and using a complex system of tariffs, quotas, regulations, and import licenses to restrain its international economic integration via both trade and investment.[81] Mexico made increasing use of quantitative import restrictions, which granted considerable power to the state, giving bureaucrats control of many markets.[82] Starting in 1962, Mexico also employed a series of "Auto Decrees" in building up the domestic auto sector, requiring substantial local content and restricting the use of foreign inputs.[83] As a consequence of all these measures, until the 1980s Mexico was if anything deglobalizing (see Figure 1.1). The system yielded impressive economic growth, with standards of living more than doubling within a quarter of a century after 1950.

During all that time, Mexico was governed by a single party, the Partido Revolucionario Institucional (Institutional Revolutionary Party, or PRI). The PRI, which had consolidated its control of the country in the 1920s, embodied a rather unique form of authoritarian, dominant party rule. The PRI ruled Mexico using a mix of state corporatism, frequent recourse to vacuous revolutionary rhetoric, patronage, corruption, populist economic policies, occasional repression, and crooked elections.[84] Under the PRI, incumbent presidents handpicked their own successors (each president ruled for a single six-year term) and controlled not only the executive branch, but also the legislative and judicial branches, subnational governments, and to a large extent the PRI itself. Elections were held, but they were a mere formality. The press was free to present some criticism, but for practical reasons could not go too far. The state, for

---

[79] Urzúa 1997: 54.

[80] Gauss 2010.

[81] Lustig 1998.

[82] Balassa 1983; García Rocha and Kehoe 1991.

[83] This was not unlike what Canada demanded the right to do under its own 1965 Auto Pact with the United States.

[84] See e.g., Knight 2001; Middlebrook 1995; Riding 1984; Teichman 2001.

example, controlled the supply of newsprint and was itself a major purchaser of advertising; any newspaper that objected too strenuously to government policies could find itself suddenly deprived of a major revenue stream.

The PRI's authoritarianism operated more through inclusion than exclusion; its basic logic was to incorporate its opponents rather than repress them. The party organization had formal branches for workers and peasants, which gave these groups opportunities to participate in political life. That was partly a reflection of the fact that Mexico's postrevolutionary 1917 constitution was very sympathetic to labor, and in some ways the PRI could lay claim to being a party of the labor movement. But the incorporation of workers and peasants within the PRI also constrained their influence, as for example the party tended to buy off their leaders and make them very poor representatives of the rank and file.[85]

By contrast, businesspeople were never afforded any formal place or role in the party. The public and private sectors maintained a kind of balance of power, with business leaders not interfering in politics or questioning the PRI's revolutionary rhetoric, while the PRI ensured an agreeable business climate. A "Law of Chambers" (Ley de Cámaras) enacted in 1941 required firms to join officially recognized associations, which allowed for some representation of private sector concerns to the state—but also constrained business lobbying and thereby limited its influence. Businesspeople could deal with the government only via their chamber, or individually through personal contacts.[86] All this meant that postwar state-business relations in Mexico had a very different character than in the United States and Canada. On the basis of extensive biographical research, Camp provides evidence that economic and political elites in Mexico were very distinct groups—unlike in C. Wright Mills's famous study of the "power elite" in the United States, and Clement's slightly later study of Canada.[87] The Mexican state was more insulated from private sector influence than in countries with more familial and social ties spanning the worlds of business and government, and/or where elites move easily from one sector to the other over the course of their careers. There was little such rotation in Mexico, and public officials were often sons of public officials.[88] Compared to the United States and Canada, but as was more typical in Latin American countries, Mexican businesspeople made few efforts to start or take over any political parties, or to seek positions inside the state to pursue their interests.[89]

---

[85] Middlebrook 1995.

[86] Mizrahi 1992.

[87] Camp 1989; Clement 1977.

[88] Cleaves and Stephens 1991; Smith 1979.

[89] Story 1986: 6; Schneider 2002.

The Mexican state also ensured its own strength vis-à-vis the business class, and its independence from it, by accumulating economic resources, such as by nationalizing much of heavy industry. Nationalization was economically appealing, as in recent years the Soviet Union had achieved impressively high growth rates under central planning, and developing countries saw state-owned enterprise as a promising industrialization strategy.[90] Politically, the nationalizations and interventionist policies were facilitated by the fact that industry was internally divided, not able to take much coordinated political action, and regularly unable to reject unwanted government proposals.[91] As a consequence, by the 1970s, the strength of the state relative to the domestic private sector clearly distinguished Mexico from the other two countries of North America. The eleven largest firms in the country, including in sectors such as railroads, electricity, oil, and finance, were all state-owned.[92]

In contrast to its domestic strength vis-à-vis Mexican society, however, the state's position was more tenuous internationally. Where possible, it sought to protect its independence by shaping its external relationships, such as by limiting the influence of international economic institutions and the United States. A 1969 briefing paper to World Bank president Robert S. McNamara explained: "There is little more that we can expect to achieve in the way of institution-building or influence over policy. . . . They can reasonably claim to have made a pretty good job of economic development. . . . Mexico is the last country in the world in which the overt exercise of leverage can be expected to pay off."[93] In the 1970s, Mexico became a strong and active advocate of a New International Economic Order, a developing country-led initiative to, as the name implies, substantially reshape the organization of the global economy—such as by stabilizing and setting commodity prices at levels favorable to the developing countries.[94] The campaign for a NIEO reflected stark inconsistencies between the visions and preferences of developed and developing countries, with the latter seeking a much reduced role for markets in international economic affairs.[95] Disagreements with the developed countries had already led the developing countries to develop new international institutions more to their liking, such as the United Nations Conference on Trade and Development.

At the same time, the Mexican state could not go it alone entirely. In a modest and very regulated way, the state did make some use of foreign investment.

[90] Bruton 1998.
[91] Cleaves and Stephens 1991; Story 1986.
[92] Story 1986: 43–44.
[93] Quoted in Urzúa 1997: 63.
[94] See Bockman 2015.
[95] Krasner 1985.

Before the Mexican Revolution, in the late nineteenth century, foreign capital had poured in to railroads and mining, but after the mid-twentieth century
manufacturing became the favored destination sector. Mexico's experience with
policies on (and actual receipt of) foreign investment was not atypical for a developing country. Such policies were, however, sometimes contentious. The
postrevolutionary constitution of 1917 forcefully claimed all land, water, mines,
and oil for Mexico, and in 1938 Mexico expropriated the largely foreign-owned
oil sector, engendering substantial conflict over the issue, particularly with the
United States. Contrary to US preferences, Mexico subscribed to the Calvo
Doctrine, according to which foreign investors should have no recourse to any
dispute resolution other than that available to domestic investors.

And Mexico had an ambivalent attitude toward foreign investment.[96] Just like
Canada, Mexico passed a law in 1973 aimed at regulating foreign investment—
a Ley para Promover la Inversión Mexicana y Regular la Inversión Extranjera,
or Law to Promote Mexican Investment and Regulate Foreign Investment. As
the name implied, the law banned foreign investment in some sectors, and limited foreign investment in any given firm to 49 percent. Foreigners could also
not acquire more than 25 percent of the shares of a Mexican company without
prior authorization from the National Commission on Foreign Investment,
a semiautonomous agency whose decisions were slow and whose decision-
making criteria were uncertain and discretionary. Mexican policymakers would
have liked not to have so much foreign investment, and therefore influence,
in the country, but at the same time they viewed foreign investment as useful
for achieving a faster rate of economic growth.[97] The law was not aimed at
preventing foreign investment entirely, but to establish constraints on foreign
investment and to encourage investments deemed beneficial by the host state.
Some exemptions from the general principles were possible, such as for facilities
established under Mexico's export-oriented, maquiladora program, which pur-
posefully sought out foreign investment with the aim encouraging the development of light manufacturing in Mexico.[98]

State intervention in the economy expanded further in the 1970s. Under
President Luis Echeverría, between 1970 and 1976, the number of state-owned
enterprises increased from 84 to 845.[99] As a consequence, between 1978 and

---

[96] Hellman 1983.

[97] Hellman 1983.

[98] In 1976, Mexico also enacted a new law on patents/inventions and trademarks. This modified
an existing law, shortening patents to ten years and making it easier for the government to assign a
patent to a different holder, if the previous owner did not bring a product to market. By comparison,
US patents at the time were for seventeen years, giving holders a longer period of high returns on
their inventions.

[99] Hellman 1983: 200.

1991, investment by state-owned enterprises (SOEs) as a share of gross domestic investment was 21.5 percent for Mexico, in contrast to just 3.7 percent for the United States.[100] This difference between the relative scales of the public and private sectors reflected a general divide between developing and developed countries: the share of SOE investment for the former group was 21.1 percent of gross domestic investment (or 24.1 percent if weighted by each country's GDP), and 13.2 percent for the latter (7.7 percent if weighted).

The previously cooperative relationship and tacit agreement between the state and business broke down, however, as the private sector resented Echeverría's interventionist policies. Businesspeople established new associations to better represent themselves, including most notably a Consejo Coordinador Empresarial (CCE, or Business Coordinating Council), an "organization of organizations," encompassing among others the Consejo Mexicano de Hombres de Negocios (Mexican Council of Businessmen) and traditional associations of industry, commerce, and agriculture. The organization and decision-making procedures of the CCE favored large firms and liquid asset holders, who grew increasingly vocal in their objections to the statist character of Mexico's economic policies.[101] Growing business hostility to the overly interventionist state was not directed against the country's import substitution and trade protection policies, however; those were reasonably popular among businesspeople, even if there were certainly some who were would have preferred opening. In fact, Mexican business had long supported the policy of autarky, with criticism by industrialists and major business associations having been a major reason for Mexico's rejection of the Havana Charter in 1948.[102] Industries welcomed the subsidies and other forms of state support they received under ISI, and broadly embraced structuralist economic ideas.[103]

We can therefore understand some important events in 1980 in light of this traditional position of business. Mexico decided to participate in the Tokyo Round of multilateral trade negotiations in the 1970s and negotiated an accession protocol. In early 1980, however, at a ceremony honoring the nationalization of the Mexican oil industry in 1938, President López Portillo suddenly announced that Mexico would not join the GATT after all. This decision divided the business community, as it did the state.[104] There were firms, and government

---

[100] World Bank 1995: 276–81. This source provided no equivalent data for Canada, but according to the OECD (1985), public enterprises represented 4.7 percent of gross capital formation in the United States in 1975–79, compared to 15.7 percent for Canada.

[101] Schamis 1999: 40.

[102] Gauss 2010; Story 1986.

[103] Love 1996.

[104] Story 1982.

agencies, that had supported joining the multilateral trading system. But on the whole the decision aroused little antipathy, as most groups were comfortable with the country's closed economy. Among others, the national association of economists (Colegio Nacional de Economistas) argued against joining GATT.[105]

Conclusion

Until the 1980s and 1990s, Canada and Mexico restrained the depth of their integration with the neighboring, much larger United States economy. They both passed nationalist, restrictive foreign investment laws in 1973, and in 1980 they jointly rejected US-based proposals for continental economic integration. So when CUFTA went into effect in 1989 and NAFTA in 1994, it was a major reversal of past policy.

Compared to Canada and Mexico, the United States started supporting continental economic integration much earlier in the twentieth century. As the capitalist world hegemon, starting in the 1930s the United States sought to build a liberal international economic order for trade and investment. Initially US business leaders were divided and on the whole unenthusiastic about trade liberalization. But over time they grew to support this agenda, which also enjoyed the strong endorsement of American economists, and to some degree reflected their influence. So even if free trade with Canada and Mexico did not come to the United States until late in the twentieth century, that was not for lack of earlier interest on the part of the US government, or interested parties in US society.

Canada devoted itself to multilateralism after World War II, balancing an old allegiance to Britain and the Commonwealth with a newer pragmatic one to the United States. Canada became an active participant in multilateral negotiations at the GATT, but the hostility of domestic manufacturers meant initiatives for trade liberalization could only go so far. Professorial Canadian officials weighed their liberal instincts—which resembled those of their counterparts in Washington—against the political costs of displeasing the domestic private sector. From the perspective of today's globalized world, the objections of Canada's manufacturers back in that earlier time are striking. In 1920, the CMA called for policies that would "diminish, as far as possible, the importation of goods from foreign countries which can be produced at home," and would "make Canada self-contained by developing and encouraging within her boundaries all legitimate activities that will give occupation to Canadian citizens."[106] It is now

---

[105] Gutiérrez-Haces 2015: 219–20.
[106] Canadian Manufacturers' Association 1920: 3.

almost unthinkable that a major business association would argue in this way against liberal trade policies.

For Mexico, like Canada, economic nationalism was not unrelated to political sensitivities about sovereignty and the risk of American domination, and Mexican leaders were ambivalent about US investment in their country. In other respects, though, Mexico's political economy was distinct from the other two countries. The state exercised more control vis-à-vis the business community and asserted itself abroad in advocating a New International Economic Order. Consistent with the preferences of Mexico's business and economics communities, and reflecting mainstream international thinking about economic development at the time, Mexico adopted a strategy of heavily regulated import substitution industrialization. As a consequence, Mexico not only maintained restrictive trade policies, but remained outside of the GATT system entirely until the 1980s. Though politically the state's authoritarianism was a black mark, the track record of ISI in Mexico was impressive, as consistent economic growth from the 1950s to the start of the 1980s substantially raised the living standards of ordinary Mexicans.

Any assessment of the role of public preferences in shaping all of these events is limited by the fact there were very few surveys of people's attitudes in any of the three countries with respect to international economic policy. Public opinion polling in Mexico, in particular, was very limited before the late 1980s. In none of the countries is there much evidence that the public's thinking about international economic policy generally is very sophisticated, much less about North American trade and investment specifically. And in no country is there evidence of public opinion shaping the state's embrace or rejection of free trade. In Canada especially, in the period covered here, there was a clear contradiction between public opinion and public policy: surveys show people supported free trade with the United States, but successive governments chose not to act on that preference. Their decision not to pursue free trade was consistent, however, with the preference of the Canadian private sector.

This baseline helps explain what happened later. When the openings came in the 1980s and 1990s, changes in actors' views compared to before are signs of whose preferences made a difference; the rise of globalization cannot have been due to the priorities of actors whose views did not change. The liberal literature points to a factor—democratization—that clearly changed over time and could in theory explain the onset of globalization. The critical literature is comparatively vague about an event or secular trend that triggered the rise of globalization. If anything, the critics imply that businesspeople always stood to gain from international economic integration and should therefore have favored it. From this perspective, elites could have used globalization whenever they wanted, to beat back social democracy, to reassert their class power, and to redistribute wealth upward to the rich. If so, however, this chapter has shown the theory is at odds with reality. In all three countries, there used to be lots of businesspeople critical if not dead set against globalization. Future chapters will show how that changed.

3

Canada

To Secure and Enhance

At the start of the 1980s, North American free trade seemed like a fairly remote prospect. American politicians were talking about more regional economic integration, but the governments of Canada and Mexico were having none of it. In May 1980, after meeting in Ottawa, Canadian prime minister Pierre Trudeau and Mexican president José López Portillo let it be known they were opposed to "current informal proposals for trilateral economic cooperation among Canada, Mexico and the United States." Later that year, the Canadian government also announced plans to introduce an interventionist National Energy Program aimed at expanding domestic control of the Canadian energy sector. This policy was anathema to American preferences for secure access to Canadian energy: a further sign that the Trudeau government was little concerned about US opinion, and not much interested in cooperating with Washington.

By 1985, though, a new Canadian government, led by Progressive Conservative ("Tory") prime minister Brian Mulroney, invited the United States to negotiate an expansive bilateral free trade agreement. This decision reversed in dramatic fashion Canada's long-standing policy of restraining rather than deepening integration with the American economy (see Chapter 2). Mulroney announced Canada's interest in 1985, negotiations followed from 1986 to 1987, and CUFTA went into effect on the first day of 1989—after the Tories won an election in 1988 that was effectively a referendum on free trade. This chapter shows how events and changing circumstances over the course of the early 1980s led to this major transformation in Canadian economic and foreign policy. Before the 1980s, most Canadian economists had already endorsed free trade with the United States; key business groups however—particularly manufacturers—had been hostile. The views of business reversed themselves in the early 1980s, though, and the priorities of policymakers soon followed. This sequence of events is telling, and given its importance this chapter makes detailed use of primary sources in documenting it.

Mulroney made the decision to negotiate in the context of a major public enquiry on Canadian economic policy. Partly as a consequence of a steep recession in 1982, late that year Trudeau's Liberal government established a Royal Commission on the Economic Union and Development Prospects for Canada. The Macdonald Commission (so named for its chairman) was tasked with holding public and private hearings across the country, drawing on the analyses and ideas of numerous experts, and bringing them together in a major final report. When it released that report in September 1985, its most notable recommendation was to negotiate a free trade agreement with the United States; three weeks later Mulroney announced that he would proceed. By that point, his decision came as no great surprise, as the Tories had already dropped many hints that they were enthusiastic about the idea. When campaigning in 1984, they promised to improve relations with the United States generally, and once in power they quickly reversed the previous Liberal governments' nationalist energy and foreign investment policies. Giving a speech in New York a couple months after being elected, the new Tory prime minister signaled his government's priorities in proclaiming Canada "open for business."

Even so, the new Tory government made no mention of free trade specifically until well after November 1984, when the chairman of the Royal Commission, a former Liberal politician, suddenly announced his support for a "leap of faith" into free trade with the United States. This endorsement—made almost a year before the commission completed its final official report—gave the idea of free trade substantial legitimacy, including of a bipartisan character. This chapter therefore considers that call for a leap of faith, and the forces and circumstances that led to it. Above all, it shows that the preferences of the Canadian private sector changed substantially just before the Tories accepted Washington's long-standing offer to make a deal. On the other hand, there was no discernible change in the positions of the general public or of Canadian economists.

A Business Victory

Among the country's business groups, the Canadian Manufacturers' Association (CMA) had the most striking change of heart. As explained in Chapter 2, the CMA had historically resisted trade liberalization, and at the start of the 1980s it was still doing so. An internal survey of its membership in 1980 found that roughly equal parts believed that free trade with the United States would lead them to increase employment, decrease employment, or would have no effect. Given that distribution, the organization's spokespeople conveyed at best a lukewarm view about trade liberalization. A 1981 report by the New York–based Conference Board found that, among 167 business executives surveyed in the

three countries of North America, "any increase in economic and political dependence on the United States is viewed as a disadvantage by most respondents
from both Canada and Mexico."[1] Overall, as one business association leader put
it, Canadian manufacturers were "always sort of dragging their feet" with respect
to trade liberalization, "and that was true very much until the recession of the
early 1980s."

In 1982, the growth rate turned negative in Canada for the first time in decades;
Canadian businesspeople were alarmed. The more than 3 percent contraction
was not just worrying in itself, it also led to a burst of US trade protectionism, in
the form of the application of several countervailing and antidumping actions.
These measures meant that under US trade law, and according to assessments
by the US International Trade Commission and Department of Commerce,
subsidized imports from Canada were harming US industries, such that protective measures for those industries were warranted. As is typical in such cases the
Canadians did not agree. Firms reliant on exports to the United States found
the rulings especially worrying (above all those firms whose products were hit
by the American duties). But even the manufacturing sector as a whole, with its
history of opposing free trade, began to re-evaluate the importance of some sort
of institutionalized, legal assurance of export access to the US market. Though
support for free trade among some parts of the Canadian business community
was not new, the breadth of interest had become unprecedented.

As a consequence, within a short time, a striking transformation took place. In
the early to mid-1980s, the CMA reversed itself and suddenly began calling for
a free trade agreement. In September 1984, for example, the association stated:

> Industry needs further multilateral trade liberalization. . . . Moreover,
> it needs to explore *all* means of securing dependable and preferential
> access to the U.S. market [including] giving consideration to entering
> into a trade agreement with the U.S. under Article XXIV of the GATT.[2]

By 1985, the CMA started "actively supporting government attempts at
trade liberalization. CMA views have been presented to the government on a
number of occasions and the organization is encouraging its members to make
their support public in speeches and public statements."[3] As one interviewee
reflected later, "The manufacturing sector adopted a position fully and aggressively supporting the free trade negotiations, which was diametrically opposed
to the historical position of the association." The CMA president reported that

[1] Cook 1981: B1.
[2] Canadian Manufacturers' Association 1984.
[3] Montgomery 1986: 23.

the launching of free trade negotiations with the United States was entirely consistent with what the CMA had advocated:

> The CMA's views and concerns about Canada-U.S. trade were adopted largely intact by the Macdonald Royal Commission and then by the Mulroney government. And today, the trade negotiating process with the U.S. (as well as with the GATT) is unfolding along the lines advocated by the CMA.
>
> Ottawa's decision during the past year to initiate negotiations for a bilateral trade agreement with the United States represents a major victory for the CMA's lobbying efforts.[4]

The importance of the CMA's change of perspective notwithstanding, it was another voice of business that ultimately led the private sector push for free trade: the Business Council on National Issues (BCNI), an association of 150 corporate CEOs, partly modeled on the US Business Roundtable. Within a few years of its establishment in 1976, the BCNI had become a key conduit by which the heads of the largest and most multinationalized firms in Canada had expanded their influence over public policies in a wide range of areas.[5] A club for the country's corporate elite, the BCNI was the first business association openly to advocate for free trade, discussing it 1983 with US vice president George Bush for example while he was on a visit to Ottawa.[6]

Still, it was not just big business that had changed its views; the owners and managers of smaller firms had too. Distancing itself from its own previous input into trade policy, the Canadian Federation of Independent Business stated in 1984 that "positions on industrial policy are in a state of constant evolution; much of what we believed in 1978 is *not* what we believe [today]. Our position would be much more free trade, free market oriented now."[7] The membership of the CFIB was, judging by internal polls, strongly supportive of free trade.[8] In the end, not only the BCNI and CMA, but also the Canadian Chamber of Commerce, Quebec Chamber of Commerce, Canadian Federation

---

[4] Thibault 1985–86: 1.

[5] Cameron 1986; Langille 1987; Carroll and Shaw 2001; Richardson 1992. The CMA and the much smaller Canadian Exporters' Association later merged and became the Canadian Manufacturers and Exporters. The BCNI changed its name to the Canadian Council of Chief Executives, and then in 2016 to the Business Council of Canada.

[6] Gordon 1983; King 1983.

[7] Lightman 1983.

[8] Doern and Tomlin 1991: 310. An influential Canadian economist, similarly, observed that over the course of the 1970s there had been, with respect to free trade, "a number of quite important changes.... I believe that the most important change is a shift in business attitude" (Wonnacott 1981).

of Independent Business, and the Canadian Exporters' Association all called for a comprehensive bilateral agreement.[9]

Why did the views of Canadian business shift so much in the early 1980s? It is telling that support was led and coordinated above all by the executives of large and international firms. Canada was a substantially larger recipient than source of foreign direct investment (FDI) for a long time after World War II, so much so that (as discussed in Chapter 2) it stoked fears of a total takeover of the Canadian economy. By the late 1960s foreign (and overwhelmingly American) control had grown to 57 percent of manufacturing, 65 percent of mining and smelting, and 74 percent of petroleum and natural gas.[10] But the inflow of foreign capital largely dried up after the mid-1970s. The percentage of nonfinancial corporations' assets under foreign control declined from a high of 35 percent in 1971 to a low of 21 percent in 1985—seemingly because of the new regulations the Canadian government introduced in 1973.[11] At the same time, outward FDI started to grow, as Canadian firms began to internationalize, as shown by Figure 3.1.[12]

Consequently, domestic control of Canada's largest corporations increased substantially, and Canadian firms grew bigger.[13] These changes transformed the outlook of the Canadian business community, which suddenly became outwardly oriented, even aggressively so, and began perceiving international markets as opportunities rather than threats. The nationalist, antiliberal ideas that were previously so characteristic of many Canadian business leaders were quickly displaced by more globalizing ones, and many more firms grew confident in their ability to compete with counterparts elsewhere. Capturing that spirit, in its submission to the Macdonald Commission in the 1984, the Canadian Chamber of Commerce stated: "Canada is no longer merely a passive recipient of foreign investment. Canadian companies are increasingly becoming active overseas investors in their own right." In times past, smaller firms had been less enthusiastic about free trade. A CMA representative had reflected in 1980 that "many Canadian companies are obviously not of a size sufficient that they can feel very confident in jumping into a very large market, as would be implied if the trade

---

[9] Doern and Tomlin 1991: 310; Langille 1987: 68; Litvak 1986; Graefe 2004.

[10] According to Laux and Molot (1988: 53–54).

[11] Baldwin and Gellatly 2005. Data on FDI before the 1980s are hard to come by. As of 1980, Canada's inward stock of FDI was 20.4 percent the size of its GDP. To set that figure in context, for the world as a whole FDI was 5.3 percent of GDP; for the United States it was 3 percent. Among the developed countries, only Ireland was host to more inward FDI relative to GDP (UNCTAD n.d.).

[12] E.g., Niosi 1981; Litvak and Maule 1981.

[13] Carroll 2004; Chow 1993.

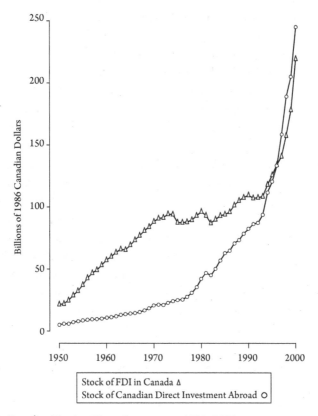

Figure 3.1 Canadian Foreign Direct Investment, 1950–2000. Source: Statistics Canada 2013a, 2013b.

were entirely free."[14] But over time large firms worked to reshape the conversation within the business community, and to build business solidarity in support of free trade. As one business representative put it, building unanimity within the sector "required a lot of leadership from senior executives . . . who tended to be with larger companies."

In a Pliant State

The Mulroney government's policy change did not come from within the government itself. The prime minister was not originally a fan of the idea of free trade, and he had previously avoided the issue. He did not mention it in the 1984 election campaign that brought him to power, and is even reported to have said he was

[14] Thibault 1980.

opposed before that, at the June 1983 convention that had made him Tory party leader.[15] In July 1983, Mulroney told an interviewer that he was more interested in domestic policy changes, not any major new trade initiatives with the United States.[16] Doern and Tomlin also provide another reason to think that Mulroney did not originally want free trade, but was converted to the idea over time: he made policy changes unilaterally (liberalizing regulations in the areas of investment, energy, and banking) that he could otherwise have used as bargaining chips in the CUFTA negotiations—had he seen the negotiations coming.[17]

Nor is there reason to believe that many other Tory politicians were life-long free traders who waited to reveal and pursue their liberal trade policy preferences once in office. Mulroney's economic cabinet and the top bureaucrats advising them were certainly not technocrats. Among the prime minister; the ministers of trade, industry, finance, and external affairs; the ambassador to the United States; and the deputy ministers of trade and industry, four had their highest degrees in law, two in business, one in political science, and just one in economics.[18] In the mid-1980s, if anything, and as in the United States, the upper echelons of the state in Canada were dominated by lawyers, and Watson describes the Mulroney government's ideology as "more business-oriented than market-oriented."[19] The Tory government had numerous ties to the private sector, shared many of its views, and generally sought to pursue business priorities as a matter of course. Mulroney only took the decision to negotiate free trade once the government had consulted extensively with Canada's major business associations, ascertaining that they were strongly supportive.[20] As one business association leader observed, Mulroney "took what was generally seen as a political risk for the country as a whole, but . . . not a political risk in terms of being in tune with the business community. In fact, quite the opposite."

The two most comprehensive accounts of CUFTA's creation, by Doern and Tomlin and Hart et al., present Canada's decision to negotiate as a largely technocratic one.[21] That is, it was the consequence of deliberations among bureaucrats

[15] Hunter 1985.

[16] Business Week 1983.

[17] Doern and Tomlin 1991.

[18] Lumley 2005. I am referring here to Mulroney, James Kelleher, Sinclair Stevens, Michael Wilson, Joe Clark, Allan Gotlieb, Sylvia Ostry, and William Teschke. Ostry was the only one of the eight with a PhD (from Cambridge). Five of the eight had their highest degrees from Canadian universities, one the UK, and two the United States (Gotlieb's LLB from Harvard and Teschke's MBA from Michigan State). Future chapters will compare these people's backgrounds to those of their counterparts in Mexico and the United States.

[19] Watson 1987: 345; Dye, Schubert, and Zeigler 2011: 184–85.

[20] Doern and Tomlin 1991: 26; Simeon 1987.

[21] Doern and Tomlin 1991; Hart et al. 1994.

and neutral, disinterested experts in universities and think tanks. This view is especially unsurprising in the case of Hart et al., given that the authors were former bureaucrats who participated in the process. Another official involved (and a future Canadian ambassador to Washington) provides a similar, largely autobiographical, account.[22] Outsider academic research has also sometimes presented bureaucrats and economists as the key advocates of free trade in Canada.[23] Studies of the Macdonald Commission argue that economists exercised considerable influence over its deliberations, and that the commission provided a crucial impetus to the free trade project.[24] Clarkson goes so far as to argue that "neoclassical economics took over the Macdonald Commission."[25] Some economists agree that their work influenced the commission, and therefore the Tories' decision to negotiate CUFTA.[26] In embracing free trade, the Tory government certainly did what trade officials in the state bureaucracy, and many outside policy experts in think tanks and universities, were advising them to do. But how influential, really, was that advice? The influence of the economists needs to be compared with the influence of business.

Aside from the Macdonald Commission, around 1983 a routine internal review of trade policy by the federal bureaucracy suggested a variety of new initiatives for the cabinet to consider taking. One possibility, departing from the 1965 Auto Pact, was negotiating some sector-specific free trade agreements with the United States.[27] The Canadian trade minister of the time, Gerald Regan, met with US trade representative Bill Brock in Washington in February 1984 to talk about this idea, and they identified steel, urban transit equipment, agricultural machinery, and computer services as four potential candidate industries. But the American industries expressed little interest, and in any event the more the two countries' officials thought about it, the more free trade for only specific sectors looked impermissible under the GATT. By June 1984, then, they decided not to explore the idea any further.[28]

But by then, and well before any clear decision on the part of the state to seek a comprehensive free trade agreement, the BCNI had internally "concluded that an overall free trade deal is probably more likely than a sectoral arrangement."[29]

---

[22] Burney 2005.

[23] Golob 2003.

[24] Bradford 1998; Inwood 2005; Simeon 1987.

[25] Clarkson 1993: 64. See also Bradford 1998: 116.

[26] Wonnacott 1993.

[27] Hart et al. 1994.

[28] Doern and Tomlin 1991. As explained in Chapter 2, GATT's Article XXIV allowed for discriminatory trade agreements only if they applied to "substantially all the trade" among the parties to such agreements. Otherwise the "most-favored nation" rule had to apply.

[29] Clarke 1984.

This, remarkably, was in February 1984, several months *before* the Canadian state had decided to pursue a free trade agreement, and even before the 1984 election won by Mulroney and the Tories. The conclusion was in effect a self-fulfilling prophecy: such was the confidence of the BCNI in its own political influence that it could tell the future through its own preferences. And the BCNI's statement shows that the organization's members, leading CEOs of large firms, were enthusiastic about free trade several months before the Canadian political elite showed signs of seriously considering the idea.

The BCNI promoted the idea of free trade in a variety of ways. In September 1984, it proposed a Canada-US "trade enhancement agreement"—a mechanism to explore ways of reducing trade barriers, an idea that the federal trade minister agreed to explore.[30] Meanwhile, the heads of the BCNI, CMA, Chamber, and CFIB organized a forty-five-person task force to address Canada-US trade relations. And all this time the Macdonald Commission was holding hearings at which the Canadian private sector expounded its vision of how Canada should engage internationally.[31] It was in that context, in the fall of 1984, that Donald Macdonald suddenly said Canada should take a leap of faith and ask the United States to negotiate an agreement.

The Macdonald Commission had a team of internal researchers at its disposal—a mix of academics and bureaucrats seconded from their home departments. Many of the staff were economists who believed strongly in the benefits of free trade. They made their case directly to the members of the commission, and prepared background reports and documents to shape the debate. A study by Harris and Cox claimed that integration with the United States would produce major productivity gains in Canada, and thereby raise GDP per capita on the order of several percentage points.[32] Another, sponsored by the C.D. Howe Institute (a center-right think tank) pointed to similarly substantial benefits.[33] The head of the institute and the study's lead author used their connections to ensure that government ministers, their aides, and senior officials knew of its conclusions.[34]

But it is important to recognize that Canadian economists' support for free trade was not at all new; these sorts of studies were not really saying anything different from what the economics community in Canada had been saying for decades. Most notably, Wonnacott and Wonnacott and the Economic Council of Canada had long before argued that free trade with the United States would

[30] Langille 1987: 68.
[31] Inwood 2005.
[32] Harris and Cox 1984. See also Whalley and Hill 1985.
[33] Lipsey and Smith 1985.
[34] Doern and Tomlin 1991: 27; Hart et al. 1994: 78.

substantially improve the productivity of the Canadian economy.[35] Little changed over time in the outlook or policy advice of Canadian economists, and their influence cannot have been a major reason why policymakers' view of free trade changed so much in the 1980s. Some accounts place government bureaucrats at the heart of the story, and suggest that the work and views of economists inside the state were decisive.[36] It is certainly true that Canadian bureaucrats play a major role in advising elected politicians about trade policy, and staff trained as economists make up a significant share of the federal bureaucracy. But many of the people at the center of bureaucracy-based accounts of the rise of free trade in Canada were not actually economists; instead, they were trained in law, political science, or even history. Compared to before (see Chapter 2), the 1980s were not a time when economists dominated the Canadian state. Nor did the upper echelons of the civil service turn over any more than usual, after Mulroney's election in 1984;[37] so there is little reason to think new people brought in any substantially new economic ideas. The decision in Canada was therefore neither as technocratic as it might appear nor the product of new thinking coming to the state from professional economists.

The bureaucrats who eventually endorsed free trade were reluctant to do so until it was politically safe—because business had endorsed it first. Only by about 1985, as the government organized a long series of hearings, consultations, and public policy reviews, did it became clear that the private sector was now strongly in favor. A meeting in Florida in May between representatives of the US and Canadian Chambers of Commerce led them to write a joint letter to the president and prime minister announcing their support for comprehensive negotiations.[38] During the late spring or summer of 1985, Mulroney read a draft version of the almost two-thousand-page final report soon to be released by the Macdonald Commission. With one dissenter—the sole labor representative[39]— the bipartisan commission recommended that Canada negotiate a free trade agreement with the United States. Not long after the release of the official final report, in September 1985, Mulroney announced that his government had decided to proceed. He may have thought initially that free trade was too risky an undertaking, as had Mackenzie King back in the 1940s, when his fears of a political backlash outweighed enthusiasm for the potential economic benefits of free trade. But by the time Mulroney announced the decision he knew where

[35] Wonnacott and Wonnacott 1967; Economic Council of Canada 1975. See also Chapter 2.

[36] E.g., Golob 2003.

[37] Bourgault and Dion 1990.

[38] Hart et al. 1994: 77.

[39] Drache and Cameron 1985.

just about every possible constituency sat on the issue, and he decided the risks were worth it.

Electing Free Trade: Public Opinion and the 1988 Election

At almost the same time that Mulroney made the announcement, a public relations strategy memo written by the Prime Minister's Office was leaked to the *Toronto Star*. Saying the public had little understanding of the issue, the document called for a "selling job":

> The strategy should rely less on educating the general public than on getting across the message that the trade initiative is a good idea. In other words, a selling job. The public support generated should be recognized as extremely soft and likely to evaporate rapidly if the debate is allowed to get out of control. . . . Benign neglect from a majority of Canadians may be the realistic outcome of a well executed communications program.[40]

Even free trade advocates had to concede this was a bit cynical.[41] And this strategy document suggests that the Tories were not motivated by electoral considerations, as even advocates of free trade appear to have believed there was little public support for it. A report on public opinion for the Macdonald Commission reported surveys showing that Canadians were strongly opposed, while the Tory trade minister warned that "to the man in the street free trade conjures up an image of the United States as a blood-sucking Dracula."[42] That said, other surveys found higher support; this was seemingly because different question wordings could elicit quite different responses.[43] By some indications, support for free trade with the United States had previously been quite high in Canada (see Chapter 2), but it went into decline just around the time the Tories decided to go for it.[44] Either way, the research literature on Canadians' trade

---

[40] Reprinted as Cameron 1986: 8.

[41] Hart et al. 1994: 103.

[42] Quoted in Laver 1985: 25. See Johnston 1986; see also Petry and Mendelsohn 2004.

[43] Johnston 1986: 145.

[44] See Bélanger and Pétry 2005; Dasko 1986; Robinson 2015. Robinson (2015) suggests that in the mid-1980s, as free trade turned into a more concrete possibility, public support for it (which was already more than 50 percent) increased. But after that it dropped substantially, in the later 1980s and into the early 1990s.

policy preferences does not suggest their views were very firm or rested on a very deep understanding of the issue.[45]

Given that CUFTA's advocates understood that public views of trade are rather malleable, and they knew the agreement would face strong opposition, they prepared from the beginning to campaign publicly in support of it. Different flavors of nationalism, economic and otherwise, would play big roles in the debate. Canadians have long worried about the real or perceived encroachment of US influence. In the 1970s, particularly under the leadership of prominent cultural figures such as writers and book publishers, campaigning of this kind led to the introduction of many of the nationalist economic policies, like foreign investment screening, that Mulroney undid a decade later.[46] In the mid-1980s, when it became clear that Canada might negotiate a free trade agreement with the United States, there were associations and communities who did not wait to begin organizing against the idea. A clear warning sign, from their perspective, was a March 1985 visit by Ronald Reagan to Ottawa. Clearly enjoying excellent personal rapport, the US president and Canadian prime minister instructed their ministers to spend six months looking into ways of reducing barriers to bilateral trade.

Seeing the writing on the wall, a mix of artists, writers, publishers, intellectuals, academics, labor leaders, environmentalists, and some leaders from the opposition political parties soon formed what they called a Council of Canadians. This, they announced, would campaign for national sovereignty—economic, political, and cultural—in the face of the threat embodied by CUFTA. Later in 1985, a similar but somewhat less cultural/elite and more activist/grass-roots network of organizations—largely led by Canada's largest feminist organization along with ecumenical social justice groups—formed another campaign organization, which they called the Coalition Against Free Trade.[47] Eventually, despite historically being broadly accepting of trade liberalization, the labor movement also got heavily involved.[48] For the unions, free trade with the United States specifically threatened to force Canadian workers into downward competition with American counterparts suffering under less favorable labor laws.

When the CUFTA negotiations began, in 1986, these groups succeeded in turning free trade into a major public controversy. In April 1987, during another Mulroney-Reagan summit, the Council of Canadians and variety of other organizations held a parallel "Maple Leaf Summit" in Ottawa and pasted

---

[45] Mendelsohn and Wolfe 2001.

[46] Sigler and Goresky 1974.

[47] Ayres 1998.

[48] Historically, Canadian unions supported free trade, and even at the time of the CUFTA debate they were welcoming multilateral liberalization at the GATT (Bleyer 1997: 140).

a "Declaration of Canadian Independence" onto the doors of parliament. The Council of Canadians and the Coalition Against Free Trade gradually joined forces, fusing the concerns of nationalists with those of the unions, feminist organizations, and other social movements. The combined coalition expanded yet further and incorporated yet more groups, such as antipoverty advocates and the main confederation of aboriginal peoples in Canada.[49] In 1987, the whole alliance decided to call themselves the "Pro-Canada Network," a coalition of coalitions that would seek to share information and coordinate joint action.[50]

This opposition coalition was united around two main convictions. First, as one interviewee put it, CUFTA "was an agreement which was being negotiated and organized on American terms, and Canada was losing out on largely everything." In opponents' eyes, Canada had already lost a lot of control over its own destiny and laws, and free trade would only make the subjugation worse. They pointed out that it was signing an FTA in 1875 that led Hawaii to join the United States. Second, as one interviewee stressed, they "were thinking about jobs," and about the status of workers more broadly. Free trade, its critics believed, would empower firms by making them mobile, and disempower workers by pitting them against each other, forcing them to accept lower wages and poorer working conditions. And the rules and market forces of the global economy would discourage governments from pursuing the public good through taxes on business, environmental regulations, and many policies effective for encouraging economic development. One interviewee explained:

> You have arguments from corporations in Canada, for example, that they can't compete with the Americans—either because of the strength of the Canadian dollar, or because of our tax system, or because of the severity of our regulatory laws over either labor or environment. So what you have, then, is extraordinary pressure to change this, extraordinary pressure put on governments.

The Tories had been elected in 1984, and by 1987 the opponents could see another national election on the horizon. They decided to try to make that election into, in effect, a referendum on free trade.[51] In May 1988, the leader of the

[49] See Ayres 1998; Barlow 1998.

[50] Massicotte 2001. Founding organizations included the Canadian Labour Congress, Council of Canadians, Assembly of First Nations, Canadian Teachers' Federation, Coalition Against Free Trade, the Coalition québécoise d'opposition au libre-échange, GATT-Fly, the National Action Committee on the Status of Women, the National Anti-Poverty Organization, and the National Farmers Union. It was arguably the civil society mobilization against CUFTA in Canada that gave rise to the entire global justice (or, to some, antiglobalization) movement.

[51] Barlow 1998: 109.

Pro-Canada Network met with the leaders of Canada's two major opposition parties—both of which had stated their opposition to CUFTA—and presented them with a petition asking for an election before the agreement's implementation. The two opposition leaders agreed to try to force an election, and in July the Liberal Party leader asked his party's majority in the senate to hold up passage of CUFTA.[52] Mulroney accepted, and on October 1 he dissolved parliament and called an election for November 21. As the agreement's opponents had hoped, the election came to be dominated by the issue of CUFTA. The Liberals—the party that had governed Canada for most of its history—made their opposition to CUFTA a focus of their campaign, and public opinion grew more critical.[53]

Given the opposition of the opposition Liberal and New Democratic Parties, CUFTA's depended on the re-election of the Tory government. In the end, the result of the November election was that the Tories took 43 percent of the popular vote, the Liberals 32 percent, and the NDP 20 percent. But while the Tories were defeated in terms of the total popular vote, the Liberals and NDP split many constituencies, and the incumbent party won 169 out of the parliament's 295 seats—a clear majority. This therefore allowed the Tories to enact CUFTA on schedule at the start of 1989. Nevertheless, there is good reason to think that these vote shares show more voters were opposed to free trade than supported it. A poll taken in the same month as the election found 39 percent support and 51 percent opposition to the FTA.[54] Public support would likely have been even lower, and the Tories might have lost the election, but for substantial campaigning by business between 1986 and 1988. To contribute to the victory of the pro-CUFTA Tories, the Canadian business community established the Canadian Alliance for Trade and Job Opportunities (CATJO), with the aim of influencing public opinion.[55] CATJO represented the BCNI, Chamber of Commerce, Canadian Exporters' Association, Canadian Federation of Independent Business, and the Canadian Manufacturers' Association. Donald Macdonald, the chair of the commission that had recommended free trade, became one of CATJO's two co-chairs, while the BCNI's chairman headed its executive committee.[56] Through CATJO, the largest interest group by spending in the 1988 election, business campaigned in support of both free trade and the Tories; large firms spent liberally.[57] For example, they paid for a four-page insert, entitled

---

[52] This was highly unusual for the upper house of Canada's parliament. Senators are appointed rather than elected, and typically do not play a very visible role in lawmaking.

[53] Bélanger and Pétry 2005.

[54] LeDuc 1989.

[55] Ayres 1998: 71; Doern and Tomlin 1991: 216.

[56] Langille 1987: 69.

[57] Ayres 1998: 104–5.

"Straight Talk on Free Trade," in more than forty daily newspapers, two weeklies, and one national magazine. To avoid falling foul of electoral laws, CATJO's advertising carefully avoided naming the Tories (or any other party), but the implications were clear. As the prime minister's then-chief of staff explains in his memoirs, in the 1988 election "the business community rallied in unprecedented fashion to demonstrate support for the agreement."[58] Or, as a business association leader put it, "The manufacturing community fought on [Mulroney's] side." The support helped, as supporters of free trade spent seventy-seven cents for every dollar the Tories spent on advertising.[59]

Two years later, when word got out in early 1990 that Mexico had approached the United States about negotiating a free trade agreement, the Canadian government faced a dilemma. By that time, free trade was extremely unpopular in Canada. The economy had gone into recession soon after CUFTA's implementation, and rightly or wrongly the two things were connected in the mind of the public.[60] But, as a US embassy cable put it in 1990, while "polls show that free trade as a concept does not play all that favorably with the Canadian 'man on the street,' trade and business organizations actively support an agreement with Mexico."[61] The trilateral NAFTA never grew as important to Canada as CUFTA; economic modeling predicted it would have little impact on the Canadian economy beyond what the bilateral CUFTA had already had.[62] But think tank economists still favored converting CUFTA into a trilateral agreement with Mexico, rather than leaving the United States and Mexico to negotiate a separate bilateral agreement on their own. They warned that a "hub and spoke" arrangement, with the United States at the center, would make Canada less competitive in attracting investors.[63] Mulroney therefore requested that Canada be allowed to join the talks, and after some deliberation the US and Mexican governments accepted.

During the subsequent negotiation and ratification of NAFTA in the early 1990s, public opinion in Canada turned even more negative about free trade. In 1993, 33 percent of respondents to one survey reported supporting free trade, while 60 percent were opposed; regarding the still-to-be-enacted NAFTA, 23 percent were in favor and 69 percent were opposed.[64] That year, five years

---

[58] Burney 2005: 131.

[59] Hiebert 1991: 23. By comparison, groups opposed to CUFTA spent only thirteen cents for every dollar spent on advertising by the two political parties against the agreement. In absolute terms, the Pro-Canada Network spent about $752,000 on advertising, while CATJO (the biggest purchaser of advertising other than the parties) spent $2.3 million (Hiebert 1991: 20).

[60] Mendelsohn, Wolfe, and Parkin 2002.

[61] National Security Council 1990.

[62] See International Trade Commission 1992.

[63] Lipsey 1990.

[64] Mendelsohn and Wolfe 2001.

since the free trade election of 1988, Canadians again went to the polls. The election occurred in the fall, after the negotiation of the side-agreements, and just months before NAFTA was due to go into effect. The Tories, in power for almost a decade, had by this time become deeply unpopular, and the election was the Liberals' to lose. But the issue of free trade presented them with a dilemma. By this time the party elite had quietly dropped their opposition to CUFTA, and they accepted advisers' arguments for why they should ratify NAFTA.[65] But free trade was not going to be popular with the voters.

The Liberals therefore finessed the issue, promising to renegotiate NAFTA before implementing it. The strategy worked, insofar as the Liberals were elected in a landslide. Then, after the election, the Liberals' "renegotiation" took all of a couple days—and resulted in only trivial changes, before the new government implemented NAFTA on schedule at the start of 1994. One business association leader summarized the strategy: "The Liberals campaigned on renegotiating it, but I think everyone realized, including my organization at the time, that by 're-negotiate' they meant doing a bit of tweaking around the edges." Another said: "I don't recall any concern that we had when the Liberals actually won the election that we wouldn't be going ahead with the NAFTA." When it came to NAFTA, as for CUFTA, elites in Canada did not make the decision to embrace free trade because the decision was popular with the electorate.

Conclusion

> History has shown that no country has been able to create a well-balanced and prosperous economy . . . without a policy of adequate tariff protection.
>
> —Canadian Manufacturers' Association, 1955

> History shows that no country can aspire to become or to remain a great nation by looking inward.
>
> —Canadian Manufacturers' Association, 1989[66]

CUFTA phased out tariffs on Canada-US trade within ten years, restricted the imposition of many performance requirements for foreign investors, and— most importantly from the Canadian side—established a binational dispute settlement process. The Canadian negotiators hoped this would help constrain

---

[65] The Liberal leader had signaled the party's change of perspective in 1991, when he called globalization just a "fact of life."

[66] These two quotes come from Canadian Manufacturers' Association (1955b) and Vice (1989).

the Americans' use of countervailing and antidumping duties. From the point of view of Canadian businesspeople, this was critical. For them, the most important purpose of the free trade agreement was "to secure and enhance Canadian access to export markets," as one trade ministry discussion paper put it.[67] Such was the contentiousness of the issue of dispute settlement with respect to trade remedies that the entire negotiation almost collapsed entirely because of it. The Canadian negotiators proposed a number of different strategies for exempting Canada completely from US trade remedies, but their American counterparts considered those ideas completely unacceptable. In the end—this was the very last provision of the agreement to be decided—they settled on a mechanism for bilateral review of the application of trade remedies laws.[68] This system would rely on binational panels that would constrain each government, issuing binding rulings on whether importing countries' administrative agencies were applying their own trade laws in correct and unbiased ways. Still, even that was only a glass half-full for Canadian business. One interviewee explained: "The biggest disappointment that the business community had in the context of the Canada-US agreement was the failure to make much headway on trade remedies."

Though this process was not quite as robust as the Canadian private sector might have liked, businesspeople were still very motivated to see CUFTA ratified. Previous accounts have suggested that the rise of free trade in Canada, like globalization in many other countries, was a function of corporate preferences. But few studies draw much attention to the fact that the preferences of Canadian business changed substantially over time; if anything, in dwelling on reasons why business should enjoy massive benefits from globalization, critical accounts imply that business always had reason to want economic opening and integration. That business preferences changed dramatically in a short period of time actually strengthens the claim that CUFTA was a project of economic elites.

Prior to the 1980s, Canadian economists but not businesspeople strongly endorsed trade liberalization—including free trade with the United States—and the Canadian state embraced only modest international economic integration. As Figure 1.1 shows, trade as a share of GDP actually declined in Canada in the 1950s and early 1960s, and in the next two decades it grew only modestly. But that changed after the private sector changed its views in the early 1980s, and the preferences of Canada's leaders soon followed. Businesspeople and politicians sympathetic to business eventually became so committed, moreover, that they campaigned for free trade in 1988 and thereby averted the Tory government's electoral defeat. Public opinion, both that year and in 1993, weighed against the

---

[67] Kelleher 1985; see also Finlayson and Thomas 1986.

[68] Gagné 2000.

embrace of continental free trade, but policymakers pushed forward regardless. Canadian business played a crucial role in winning public support—against opposition by organized labor and a variety of civil society groups, as well as two of Canada's three major political parties. There was no correspondence between shifts in public opinion and government policies with respect to free trade.

Some studies have said that free trade was a consequence of trade policy experts' changing input and recommendations—at the extreme that governments' pursuit of free trade was social learning, with economists finally able to make politicians see sense. Rather than self-interested actions by economic elites, it would clearly suit advocates of agreements like CUFTA for them to be seen as products of sober, unbiased reflections by wise and experienced specialists. Expertise and disinterested deliberation possess more legitimacy than the self-interested preferences of industry. But economists' ideas about trade policy did not really change much in Canada in the 1980s, and they mattered a lot less than what the private sector wanted. Bureaucrats inside the state endorsed free trade, but only once it was safe for them to do so—because business had done so first.

4

Mexico

Rise of the Technocrats

Mexico decided to negotiate and ratify North American free trade five years after Canada. Relative to Canada, Mexico had previously been even more opposed to the idea. Mexico remained outside the GATT well into the 1980s and was centrally involved in an international alliance of developing countries that was critical of the US-dominated multilateral trading system. After the mid-1980s, though, Mexico reversed course dramatically and embraced international trade and investment. Mexico joined the GATT in 1986, substantially liberalized its regulations on inward foreign investment in 1989, and began talks with the United States and then Canada about a free trade agreement in 1990.

Before the 1980s, free trade with the United States was hard to imagine in Mexico. In a period when inward-oriented policies were working well to grow the economy and raise standards of living, proposals for significantly increased integration were anathema to the autonomy that most Mexican policymakers believed the country needed. Over the course of the 1980s, however, the worldviews of Mexico's political and bureaucratic elite changed dramatically. A new generation of policymakers, notable for holding economics PhDs from top American universities, gained control. Bolstered by the support of allies outside of Mexico, these adherents to more market-oriented economic ideas gradually displaced the older, statist-nationalist competitors who had previously decided Mexico's policies.[1] It was this new team of technocrats that brought Mexico into the multilateral trading system, opened up the economy, and negotiated NAFTA. Just as Chapter 3 focused on documenting the evolution of business views in Canada, then, this chapter focuses on changes in the backgrounds, circumstances, ideas, and priorities of Mexico's public officials. It also details, like Chapter 3, that there is little evidence that Mexico's change of

[1] See, e.g., Babb 2001; Centeno 1997; Thacker 2000.

stance on free trade had anything to do with shifts in public opinion, or changes over time in politicians' accountability to it.

Aligning the Stars

At the start of the 1980s, Mexico was enjoying the fruits of a twenty-year period of fast, uninterrupted economic growth, the country's leaders even daring to speak of a convergence in living standards with the world's industrial nations. Historically a fairly modest oil producer, Mexico had discovered large new deposits in its territory over the course of the 1970s. Exports of oil rose sixteen-fold between 1978 and 1981, and, flush with the revenues, the government borrowed liberally on international credit markets, expecting further sales to cover the cost of repayments.[2] Substantial financial independence in hand, Mexican leaders voiced blunt criticisms of the liberal and US-dominated character of the global capitalist economy, arguing for changes in its institutions and guiding principles. At that time, Mexico could afford to thumb its nose at its hegemonic neighbor to the north.

An economic crisis unleashed in 1982, however, put an end to all this optimism and the assertiveness that went with it. Global economic activity began to decline in 1981, and oil prices fell. At the same time, the US Federal Reserve began adopting anti-inflationary policies that had the knock-on effect of increasing the interest rates on sovereign debt. At first, public officials and commercial banks expected these shocks to be short-lived; but eventually it became clear that oil prices and interest rates were not about to return to their previous levels. Mexico began losing its ability to service its debts, and by the summer of 1982 announced it was not in a position to continue repaying them. On September 1, the state nationalized the banking system and imposed exchange controls in an effort to prevent capital from leaving the country. With no good options, Mexican representatives approached the International Monetary Fund (IMF)—the world's lender of last resort—for assistance. The result of their negotiations was a financial rescue package requiring Mexico to implement a program of "shock treatment": devaluing the currency, cutting government spending, and capping wage increases.[3] Thus began a long period of negotiations with the international financial community over Mexico's debts and what it would do about them, as Mexico negotiated a series of IMF rescue packages, none of which worked to revive the economy.[4] Annual GDP growth, already

[2] Balassa 1983.
[3] Urzúa 1997: 72.
[4] Ortiz Mena 2004: 217.

slightly negative in 1982, dropped several percentage points further in 1983. The 1980s—during which time oil revenues continued to decline, adding to the state's fiscal misery—turned into a "lost decade" for Mexico, as for many other developing countries.

Asking for help from external creditors put Mexican officials under considerable pressure—as staff from the IMF, and the US government, were well aware. The Mexicans had little choice but to undertake at least some of the policy changes its creditors wanted. The IMF's managing director, for example, met with Mexican representatives in 1983 specifically to impress upon them the merits of liberalizing the country's trade barriers, in return for Mexican access to developed country markets.[5] Not long after that, Mexico joined the GATT (see below). What put the Fund in an especially strong position was that private creditors were reluctant to roll over repayments on Mexico's debt without a reassuring stamp of approval—such as a standby arrangement with the IMF. That in turn required that the Mexicans identify a plan for reducing the public sector deficit, and in a way that was convincing to the IMF. At the same time, Fund staff knew that debt repayments would hinder economic growth. A confidential cable from the US embassy in Mexico reflected this tension in the mid-1980s:

> Continued infighting among key cabinet members and the reluctance of [the Mexican government] to take strong actions cast serious doubt on the government's desire and ability to implement a serious multi-year economic adjustment program.... The IMF will take a fairly tough position vis a vis Mexico regarding the public sector deficit but perhaps not as strong as it has historically because of [a new emphasis on] economic growth.[6]

In contrast to the 1970s, when Mexico's leaders could afford to be assertive with their foreign counterparts, the 1980s gave them more reason to compromise, as they felt the effects of the policy "conditionality" imposed on them by the IMF and other lenders. In this respect Mexico was not unlike many other developing countries, and recent statistical research has shown that officials in countries receiving IMF assistance have tended to last longer in office if they share the policy preferences of the international financial institutions (IFIs)—the IMF and the World Bank.[7] Conversely, IMF lending favors countries whose

---

[5] Boughton 2001: 361.

[6] Busby 1986.

[7] The World Bank had previously been somewhat sympathetic to restrictive trade policies enacted with import-substitution industrialization in mind; but over the course of the 1970s and 1980s the Bank grew more critical of them (Broad 2006).

key economic policymakers subscribe to the same beliefs as IMF officials—as proxied by their holding degrees from elite American economic departments or having worked previously for either of the IFIs.[8] Officials subscribing to the same kinds of policy ideas as the staff of the IFIs are more likely to survive, while their countries get programs with fewer, less stringent conditions—and more time to implement them. So the nature of the policymakers in a government makes a difference to the policies governments enact, with countries at risk of macroeconomic crisis more willing to give officials with recognized credentials control over policy.[9]

Mexico's international creditors began taking an interest in the competition among Mexico's officials for promotions up the bureaucratic hierarchy. It was obvious to anyone familiar with Mexican politics that such movements were important, as the occupants of key posts could substantially change the direction of economic policy. In subtle and not-so-subtle ways, external constituencies supported and encouraged the competitors for these posts in whom they had the most confidence. In this way, over the course of a few years in the mid-1980s, an older generation of more nationalist bureaucrats were forced out, and a younger cohort with much less statist and nationalist outlooks took their place.[10] A dramatic shift took place in the intellectual foundations of the people running the Mexican government, reflecting that back in the 1970s Mexico had substantially increased the funding available for Mexicans to study abroad.[11] Academic exchanges and scholarship programs helped "good economics" come to Mexico, like the rest of Latin America, by allowing top economics students to do their graduate study in elite US departments.[12]

One of the features of Mexico's political economy that changed the most in the context of the country's indebtedness, and the influence of foreign creditors, was its trade policy. In the mid-1980s, the Mexican government dismantled many impediments to economic opening.[13] By the early 1980s, importing almost anything required a license, but in July 1985, the Mexican government reversed that policy and announced large cuts in the percentage of imports requiring licenses.[14] The share of imports, by value, that were subject to permits fell from 100 percent in 1983 to 35 percent in 1985.[15] Mexico then acceded to GATT in 1986—a process that was considerably simplified by the fact that Mexico's prior

---

[8] Nelson 2014, 2017.

[9] Chwieroth 2007; Dargent 2014.

[10] Babb 2001; Teichman 2001; Whitehead 2006.

[11] Camp 2002: 155.

[12] Harberger 1996.

[13] Urzúa 1997.

[14] Lustig 1998; Page 1992.

[15] García Rocha and Kehoe 1991.

policy changes meant it had little to do to meet the expectations of its new partners in the GATT—and unilaterally reduced barriers to imports still further in
1987.[16] The maximum tariff dropped from 100 percent in 1982 to 20 percent in
1988.[17] Erstwhile private sector critics of trade liberalization were by that point
devoting themselves less to resisting the opening generally than to campaigns for
retaining policies protecting their own specific firm or industry.[18]

Carlos Salinas de Gortari, secretary of planning and budget between 1982
and 1988, was one of the new cohort of bureaucrats making free market policy
changes such as these. Salinas held a PhD from Harvard, though unlike many
of the other ambitious officials climbing the state hierarchy in that period,
Salinas's doctorate was in political economy (from Harvard's Kennedy School
of Government) rather than economics. By mid-1986, he was the clear front-
runner in the race to succeed the incumbent president, Miguel de la Madrid,[19]
and the following year he was officially named the candidate for president for the
Partido Revolucionario Institucional (PRI). From an American point of view,
Salinas was highly appealing as Mexico's prospective leader. A State Department
memorandum said of him:

> We expect him to continue his predecessor's profound economic
> reforms, to pursue changes aimed at bringing new pluralism to Mexico's
> political system, and to follow a more pragmatic foreign policy. In all of
> this he faces . . . strong opposition . . . committed to moving Mexico in
> directions deeply inimical to U.S. interests.[20]

His attractiveness to the Americans notwithstanding, Salinas's administration
did not start well. The presidential election in the summer of 1988 proved surprisingly dramatic. Historically the PRI exercised such control that the results
of presidential elections were never in any doubt, but Salinas faced an unexpect-
edly serious competitor: Cuauhtémoc Cárdenas, an erstwhile *priísta* who had
split from the party a year prior. Cárdenas, the son of a former Mexican president, was from the party's left wing, and that branch was unhappy about the
PRI's turn toward free market policies.[21] Cárdenas's campaign was surprisingly
effective, and early results on the day of the election indicated he might even

---

[16] Page 1992.

[17] Kose et al. 2005: 45.

[18] Cronin 2003: 88.

[19] Salinas had been de la Madrid's deputy during the previous administration, when de la Madrid
was budget minister.

[20] Levitsky 1988.

[21] Cárdenas was also unhappy not to be selected as the party's presidential nominee.

win. But then the computer system used to count the votes suddenly crashed, and in highly suspicious fashion. When the system was restored, the PRI quickly claimed victory and announced that Salinas had received 50.7 percent of the votes. Whether Salinas really won a majority of the votes cast in that election remains unknown. He certainly benefited from the PRI's usual dirty tricks, though whether he completely stole the election is less certain.

Despite the less than ideal process by which he assumed the presidency, the US government did what it could to support Salinas in the months after his election. In the fall of 1988, Mexico was again suffering from a fall in foreign reserves and declining oil prices, but the United States arranged a $3.5 billion bridge loan, which was (unofficially) intended to support the president-elect. The loan was, in the words of a Reagan administration official, "designed to encourage President Carlos Salinas de Gortari to continue with the current reform program. A second and equally important motive, [officials] admit privately, is to demonstrate to the left-wing political opposition inside Mexico that the Salinas regime will have the full political and financial backing of the United States."[22] During the presidential transition, an analyst in the US Department of State's Bureau of Inter-American Affairs summarized:

> De la Madrid is the inheritor of the economic disaster visited upon Mexico by the policies of his two immediate predecessors. . . . The profound reforms he and Salinas have been carrying out are precisely what Mexico needs. . . . Salinas, a brilliant political economist, knows [an economic] turnaround will come about only through structural change and modernization . . . though he will have to fight strong opposition within his own party and a widely perceived political need to compromise with the Cárdenas forces. . . . We believe it is strongly in the United States interest that Mexico achieve visible growth within the new two years. . . . We should be prepared to go out of our way to help make this happen.[23]

Similarly, another analyst wrote: "Though regarded as a statist, Salinas' record as Secretary of Programming and Budget suggests that he may now be committed to fiscal restraint, privatization, and reduced government intervention."[24]

---

[22] Bailey 1988.

[23] Abrams 1988.

[24] Sorzano 1987. Less auspiciously, this analyst also observed of Salinas: "Short, bald, with an unimpressive speaking style, he is devoid of the charisma that PRI politicos had hoped could breathe new life into the Party."

The American officials got what they wanted: Salinas zealously pursued an ambitious program of market-oriented policy changes, making Mexico into a poster
child for neoliberalism. The economic team under Salinas that undertook all this
was remarkable. All of his economic cabinet ministers, and many high-level staff
in the state bureaucracy, held PhDs from prestigious American universities like
MIT, Yale, and Chicago. During the years of the Salinas presidency (1988 to
1994), Mexico's was an exceptionally technocratic state—governed by a like-
minded team of highly educated policymakers who had pursued generally similar kinds of careers, and whose shared *forma mentis* reflected their training in
elite American economics departments. In contrast to Canada, among eight key
economic policymakers in Mexico at the time of its decision to negotiate free
trade (the head of state; secretaries of trade, budget, finance, and foreign affairs;
ambassador to the United States; and undersecretaries of trade and industry),
six had PhDs. All six PhDs were from the United States (Harvard, MIT, two
from Yale, and two from Chicago), and all were in economics, with the exception
of Salinas's in political economy. One of the other two had an MA in economics
from Yale.[25]

Salinas's first priority was renegotiating his country's external debt, and in
1989 Mexico became the first country to restructure under the Brady Plan,
named for US Treasury secretary Nicholas F. Brady. The Brady Plan acknowledged the need to relieve some of the debt weighing on many developing
countries and allowed debtor governments to make payments on more man-
ageable terms. This allowance reflected that by the end of the 1980s, many nations were no closer to clearing their debts than they had been years earlier,
and creditors were recognizing that some debt would simply never be repaid; a
measure of forgiveness was therefore inevitable. The Mexicans negotiated with
hundreds of private banks, who exhibited some flexibility because of their confidence in the technocrats and the credibility of Salinas's plans for reducing the
public deficit—plus the stamp of approval given to those plans by the IMF and
World Bank.

Having renegotiated the debt, the Salinas team turned their focus to the transformation of the Mexican economy. Building on similar efforts by the previous
administration, one important step was the continued privatization of many of
Mexico's numerous state-owned enterprises, including the banks that had been

---

[25] I have taken biographical information from Camp (1995) and Presidencia (1992). The
eight here are Salinas, Jaime Serra Puche, Ernesto Zedillo, Pedro Aspe, Fernando Solana, Gustavo
Petricioli, Herminio Blanco, and Fernando Sánchez. Unlike Canada, Mexico had a single minister for
both trade and industry, but unlike Canada a separate minister for the budget. Mexican *subsecretarios*
rank immediately below the secretary, roughly like Canadian deputy ministers.

nationalized in 1982.[26] The Salinas administration pursued the privatization of firms in sectors like telecommunications, airlines, and banking.

In May 1989, the Salinas administration also dramatically liberalized Mexico's regulations on foreign direct investment (FDI). Mexico had passed a restrictive law on inward FDI in 1973, and though the Salinas administration did not change the law, it decided to begin implementing it in only the most liberal possible way. The law had been aimed at restricting foreign investment, but far from seeing foreign investment as a threat, the technocrats now wanted more of it. A presidential decree repealed a 49 percent limit on foreign ownership for most sectors, and the decree simplified the procedures for getting approval. Joint ventures with up to 49 percent foreign participation no longer required authorization. New sectors were opened up to FDI, while foreign participation in the stock market was made much easier and bureaucratically simpler; a large influx of portfolio investment followed.[27] Previously, up to 49 percent ownership was allowed automatically, in sectors not reserved for the state or Mexicans; now, more than 80 percent of sectors would be open to 100 percent foreign investment automatically.[28] A National Foreign Investment Commission would continue to screen investments, but only those over US$100 million.

The most dramatic policy change was yet to come, however. It was in early 1990 that Salinas made the decision to accept the long-standing US offer to negotiate a free trade agreement. Being surrounded by PhD economists, Salinas had already been asked to think about the idea. But initially, as one interviewee explained: "President Salinas did not want a free trade agreement. We proposed it to him, at the end of 1988." At that time, before his inauguration, "He opposed it and shut us off." That was also despite George Bush raising the idea with Salinas when the two met in 1988 as presidents-elect.[29]

It was ultimately a chastening trip to the World Economic Forum, in Davos, that changed Salinas's mind. Salinas had hoped that his debt renegotiations, privatizations, investment liberalization, and other market-oriented policy changes would get the attention of many foreign investors and lead to a surge of capital inflows. In Davos, however, Salinas found that all this had failed to make much impact on the international investor community. The Berlin Wall had come down only a couple months prior, the end of communism in Eastern Europe was in sight, and regional integration initiatives in Asia and Western Europe were attracting more attention than anything happening in

---

[26] Mayer 1998: 38. Mexico had 1,155 state-owned enterprises in 1982, and only 433 by 1988 (Aspe 1990: 125).

[27] Ros 1992.

[28] Amigo 1991.

[29] Salinas de Gortari 2000: 52.

Mexico. Mexico therefore needed to do something dramatic, Salinas decided, to regain investors' attention. He was impressed by a meeting with German chancellor Helmut Kohl, who reinforced what Salinas's own officials had told him and suggested that Mexico could really get investors' attention by signing a major integration agreement with the United States.[30] Before even leaving Davos, Salinas informed the officials traveling with him that he had decided to pursue this idea; not long after, his chief of staff approached American officials in Washington. Salinas's decision to accept America's offer to negotiate a free trade agreement was therefore motivated as much the pursuit of foreign investment as by the goal of liberalizing trade and increasing economic integration with the United States per se.[31] For Salinas, export access to the US and Canadian markets was attractive predominantly as a means of encouraging more capital flows to Mexico: a clear instance of what Appel and Orenstein call "competitive signaling."[32]

The technocrats around Salinas (with their highest degrees in economics rather than political economy like him) saw NAFTA somewhat differently: more a means of deepening and institutionalizing the structural transformation of the Mexican economy. They hoped to reap the gains of market efficiencies while guarding against the caprices of corruptible and fallible bureaucrats. As one interviewee explained, the technocrats' goal was to use NAFTA to do something dramatic, "more fundamental. . . . Really go into the core, and redo the foundations, and retrofit this economy, really, and not just paint the outside."[33] These were true-believers, and they subscribed (as Chapter 6 will explain) to a view of trade wherein reducing barriers to imports was in itself a good thing, irrespective of what any other country might do. As one bureaucrat (with a US economics PhD) stated: "We would have opened everything, unilaterally!"[34] Another Mexican official explained: "The negotiating team—all of us, from [the president] down to people like me— were free traders. All of us." In the Salinas years, as another interviewee put it, "The stars aligned."

---

[30] Salinas de Gortari 2000: 48.

[31] Ros 1992; Mayer 1998; Cameron and Tomlin 2000; Thacker 2000; Espinosa Velasco and Serra Puche 2004.

[32] Appel and Orenstein 2018.

[33] Gruber (2000) claims that the Mexicans decided to negotiate free trade because they regarded the Canada-US bilateral agreement as a threat. But archival evidence provides no support for this thesis, and it is also inconsistent with what I was told by interviewees from both the public and private sectors. Ortiz Mena (2004) also reports knowing of no evidence to support Gruber's interpretation.

[34] This shows the difference between the ideological currents dominant inside the Mexican and Canadian governments. Remember that, of eight key Canadian officials, only one held a PhD (in economics, though not from the United States).

Not Naturally Popular

The dubious circumstances in which Salinas took over as president in 1988 could be taken as evidence that he was above the law and beyond the constraints of electoral democracy. But in actual fact he was acutely concerned about public opinion and public preferences, including with respect to the country's economic opening. Salinas knew, and political science data sets confirm, that democracy was growing in Mexico. According to the binary criteria of Przeworski et al., Mexico became a democracy in 2000, when the ruling PRI lost the presidency for the first time in decades.[35] But even before that year, opposition parties had been growing in popularity and influence. The PRI's seat share in the lower house of the congress declined from 1961 to 2000.[36] The percentage of the vote that went to the PRI candidate in presidential elections dropped monotonically from 1976 to 2000.[37] Opposition parties won increasing numbers of subnational elections over the course of the 1990s.[38] The first non-PRI state governor was elected in 1989 (in Baja California). Secular sociodemographic and economic changes in Mexico fostered the emergence of an increasingly autonomous and assertive mass media, important elements of which were clearly critical of the ruling regime.[39] Internal decision-making within the PRI itself also grew more horizontal in the 1990s, with the power of the president increasingly constrained.[40] One final sign that Mexico was getting more democratic and that Salinas cared what the voters thought is that his was the first administration in Mexico to hire an in-house pollster. According to Pemstein et al.'s Unified Democracy Scores, which treat democracy as gradational, there was therefore a gradual increase in the country's level of democracy starting in the early 1970s—see Figure 4.1.[41]

Still, on NAFTA, there is little if any evidence that the decision to negotiate had anything to do with public opinion. One interviewee familiar with Salinas's thinking stated that "the decision to initiate the process to sign a free trade agreement with the United States and Canada . . . was taken without taking any surveys beforehand. . . . The decision did not depend on whether people wanted it or didn't want it." On the contrary: "There was *never* a direct, immediate rationale

[35] Przeworski et al. 2000.

[36] Greene 2007.

[37] Cameron and Wise 2004.

[38] Lucardi 2016.

[39] Lawson 2002.

[40] Langston 2001.

[41] Pemstein et al.'s (2010) scores are a weighted average of those from a number of other credible data sets. So we can think of them as the assessment of a typical political scientist.

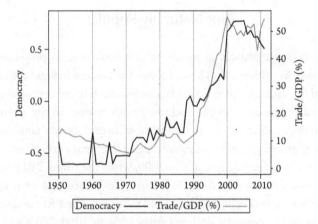

Figure 4.1 Mexico's Trade Openness and Democracy over Time. Sources: Penn World Table 8.0; Pemstein et al. 2010.

for the structural reforms in terms of the effects they could have on voting. To the contrary. There were two very large concerns. Losing the support of the PRI ... and losing voters." Similarly, when Salinas instructed his staff to broach the subject of an FTA with their American counterparts in early 1990, interviewees say they expected much more public backlash than enthusiasm. They made no announcement about the talks until the *Wall Street Journal* broke the story, specifically because they did not expect the news to be well received.[42] They had hoped to manage the news much more deliberately than they ended up doing.

When the question was eventually put to the public, the available polling data—from 1990 onward—suggest that Mexicans generally accepted the idea of free trade with the United States.[43] Surveys commissioned by the office of the presidency found more enthusiasm for NAFTA than hostility, with support ranging from 49 to 69 percent and opposition from 9 to 19 percent. Polling being somewhat rudimentary in Mexico at that time, however, these results were based on samples that were far from perfectly representative, and they must be taken with a grain of salt. Moreover, other data suggest different conclusions. One survey in 1991 found only 17 percent of Mexicans thought they would actually derive any benefit from NAFTA.[44] Mexicans seemed to assess free trade according to what they expected the impacts to be on the country as a whole, not just their own situation, and also depending on their views of Salinas and the PRI generally.[45] Based on qualitative interviews, Hellman argues that Mexicans

---

[42] Truell 1990.
[43] E.g., Dyck and Greenfield 1994.
[44] Basáñez 1995.
[45] Wilson 2001; Pastor and Wise 1994; Kaufman and Zuckermann 1998.

simply could not make very informed assessments of NAFTA, as they were not getting enough information to do so.[46] In her view, people in the United States and Canada were somewhat more informed, because of the greater political openness in those countries, and the freedom of their media. On the other hand, at least by the late 1980s, sample surveys suggest that Mexicans were about as politically engaged, pro-democracy, and understanding of economic issues as voters in wealthy democratic countries.[47] Given that survey research suggests voters in the latter category of countries do not hold particularly well-informed or clear preferences with respect to international economic policy, though, that does not suggest Mexicans' attitudes toward NAFTA were very sophisticated either.[48]

Free trade became subject to substantial civil society criticism in Mexico, much like in Canada. Critics organized a broad-based alliance in opposition to the agreement. The opposition to NAFTA in Mexico built on mobilization by leftists within the PRI, who had grown angry about its turn to free markets and the loss of labor and campesino influence in Mexico in the 1980s. In October 1990, the opposition conservative Partido de Acción Nacional asked a professor at Mexico's Universidad Nacional Autónoma de México, known to have contacts in Canada, to organize a conference on Canada's experience under CUFTA. The professor, María Teresa Gutiérrez Haces, invited twenty Canadians (ten supporters and ten critics of CUFTA) to Mexico City to discuss CUFTA and hear their views on a wider North American FTA. The event turned into a spirited microcosm of the heated debate on CUFTA in Canada and was widely publicized in Mexico.

The ten Canadian critics stayed on in Mexico, were joined by representatives of other Canadian organizations opposed to CUFTA, and met with Mexican counterparts—representatives of independent labor unions, women's groups, environmentalists, indigenous rights advocates, academics, and farmers' organizations.[49] The independent labor confederation Frente Auténtico del Trabajo (FAT) hosted an *encuentro*, as it was called, which eventually led to the formation of the Red Mexicana de Acción Frente al Libre Comercio (RMALC, or Mexican Action Network on Free Trade)—modeled on the Pro-Canada Network.[50] Most

---

[46] Hellman 1993.

[47] Domínguez and McCann 1996.

[48] Some later surveys do not suggest Mexicans are very supportive of free trade at all. Three-quarters of Mexican respondents to the 1996 World Values Survey favored "stricter limits on selling foreign goods here, to protect the jobs of people in this country," versus only 16 percent who said they favored allowing "goods made in other countries [to] be imported and sold here if people want to buy them."

[49] Calderón and Arroyo 1993; Massicotte 2001; Robinson 1994; Thorup 1991.

[50] By this time the Pro-Canada Network had renamed itself the Action Canada Network (Ayres 1998).

of organized labor in Mexico was closely tied to the PRI, but the FAT played a key role in RMALC, providing funding and office space. RMALC developed strong ties to NAFTA opponents in the United States and Canada, even though most Mexican critics sought a different kind of North American integration— more social democratic, regulated, and European in style—while opponents in the other two countries were more critical of integration per se.[51] Many of NAFTA's opponents in NAFTA expressed concerns about the possibility that Mexico would try to compete internationally on the basis of lower labor costs, workplace safety, and unions' bargaining power.[52]

In the face of the criticism directed at NAFTA, the state used a variety of tools to build public support. Because of the political resources and means at the PRI's disposal, opponents of North American free trade were not able to generate public debate about it on the same scale as in the United States and Canada. While the authoritarian Mexican state could not make use of repression (partly because to do so would reduce the chances of NAFTA's ratification in the United States, as Chapter 5 will explain), it still possessed powerful tools for stifling criticism.[53] The PRI still had control of Mexico's official union confederation, for example (the Confederación de Trabajadores de México, or CTM). While the CTM had opposed the economic opening in the 1980s and criticized NAFTA behind closed doors, in public the CTM and National Peasant's Confederation endorsed NAFTA and made only moderate calls for adjustment assistance and other favorable terms.[54]

Salinas was also able to make use of a Consejo Asesor (Advisory Council), comprising representatives from a diversity of social sectors.[55] The secretary of trade and industry, Jaime Serra Puche, served as president of the Consejo Asesor and presided over all its meetings, with Blanco Mendoza (chief of the NAFTA negotiations) its technical secretary. The council's membership was dominated by the private sector. Nine of its twenty-four members, more than any other sector, were drawn from the Coordinadora de Organismos Empresariales de Comercio Exterior, Consejo Coordinador Empresarial, Confederación de Cámaras Industriales, Confederación de Cámaras Nacionales de Comercio. Four came from the elite Consejo Mexicano de Hombres de Negocios.[56] The Consejo Asesor worked to involve friendly opinion leaders, who could then

---

[51] Ayres 1998; Kay 2005.

[52] Aguilar Zínser 1992.

[53] Poitras and Robinson 1994; Centeno and Maxfield 1992.

[54] Flores Quiroga 1998; Grayson 1993: 15; Poitras and Robinson 1994.

[55] See e.g., Bustamante 1994.

[56] The Consejo Mexicano de Hombres de Negocios was an association of chief executives, roughly comparable to the US Business Roundtable or Canadian Business Council on National Issues.

disseminate pro-NAFTA messages among their own colleagues and networks. Using a typically inclusive approach for the PRI, the Consejo Asesor provided an opportunity for expressing input and even criticism, but then dismissed critics as having been heard.[57] One Mexican bureaucrat, summing up the overall process by which Salinas and his team worked to promote free trade, said: "We manipulated things so as to make NAFTA popular. It was not naturally popular. There was a great salesmanship. Salinas was a salesman."

Salinas also made use of a new rural development program called PRONASOL (Programa Nacional de Solidaridad), which proved an effective tool for winning consent to many of the policy changes the technocrats made.[58] Rural opposition was heavily muted by the introduction of this ingenious new antipoverty and community development program, which distributed modest financial and infrastructure benefits in return for effective loyalty to the PRI. It was a traditional PRI tactic to co-opt critics with patronage.[59] Salinas had personal control of the program, and it reflected the thesis of his PhD at Harvard, which had argued that involving people in the design and management of projects would win their political support much better than just giving them money. PRONASOL did exactly that, and on a very modest budget, paid for in part by the privatization of previously state-owned enterprises. PRONASOL channeled funding into infrastructure for poor areas (roads, schools, clinics), but specifically via local groups loyal to the PRI and not critical of the government.[60] Linking privatization to these benefits also helped to legitimate the former.

The PRI regime could, in an important sense, simply impose the economic policies it wanted, and then use its extraordinary resources and traditional nondemocratic means to deal with any criticism. The slow erosion of authoritarianism notwithstanding, in the 1990s the PRI was still in a position to buy people's loyalties and repress dissent.[61] Though the PRI did not have the same control as before, Salinas still had the means to shape the debate in a way that leaders in Canada had not, using both its authoritarian political control and its social control via the party's corporatist arms. In that sense, in the eyes of many, many of Mexico's free market policy changes would have been impossible without the PRI's authoritarianism.[62] The PRI's traditional expertise in the use of clientelism and corporatism served the technocrats well in pursuing their goals.

---

[57] There were also extensive congressional hearings. Given the lack of congressional independence from the presidency, however, these had little critical perspective.

[58] Centeno 1997; Poitras and Robinson 1994: 11–12.

[59] Centeno 1997.

[60] Dresser 1991.

[61] Centeno 1997: 232.

[62] Long 2015.

Business: On the Other Side

When news of the preliminary talks about free trade leaked out in early 1990, it was not initially clear how Mexican businesspeople would react. The state had not consulted the private sector about the idea beforehand, and the announcement came as a surprise. NAFTA was going to build on the opening that had unfolded over the previous several years, and large parts of Mexican business had been opposed to those prior liberalization initiatives.

There is some evidence that the preferences of Mexican firms changed in the early 1980s, similarly to how they did in Canada around the same time; but overall the number of businesspeople advocating free trade was limited. Unlike in Canada, proactive business advocacy was the exception in Mexico, not the rule. In 1984, executives from some large Mexican companies reached out to the heads of major American firms operating in Mexico and organized a series of meetings to discuss the two countries' economic relationship.[63] This group of businessmen was interested in the idea of some kind of trilateral North American economic union—and this was even before Canada had agreed to negotiate CUFTA. According to one interviewee, they "weren't thinking about an FTA. We were thinking about a European model, about a common market." Still, these talks led to little concrete action, and it would be several years until an important voice of business made the first *public* call for free trade. In February 1989, the outgoing head of Mexican Business Council for International Affairs (Consejo Empresarial Mexicano para Asuntos Internacionales) called for a North American common market.[64] This was, however, the very same man, Enrique Madero, who had coordinated the Mexicans in the meetings with the Americans back in 1984. And in the face of Madero's speech, as explained earlier, Salinas was initially unmoved. One interviewee described the president's initial reaction as "virulent. . . . He told us Mexico would never belong to any kind of North American bloc."

While some large, internationally integrated firms—whose weight was growing in Mexico's economy—were enthusiastic about liberalization, other parts of the business community were hostile, or at least skeptical, as previous studies have emphasized.[65] As explained in Chapter 2, Mexico had many small- and medium-sized, domestically oriented manufacturing enterprises that depended on government contracts, subsidies, and continued protection from foreign competition. These firms were mostly critical of trade liberalization, as

---

[63] Interviewees, and Grayson (2007), reported that Rodman Rockefeller and Enrique Madero, joint heads of the Mexico-US Business Committee (MEXUS), coordinated these talks.

[64] Pizarro 1990.

[65] Flores Quiroga 1998; Shadlen 2000; Thacker 2000.

were state-owned enterprises, such as the national energy company PEMEX.[66] In the words of one Mexican technocrat: "The private sector in Mexico ... had learned how to work with the inefficiencies and the corruption and the semi-openness." Another interviewee explained even more bluntly:

> Mexican business didn't have the foggiest idea. . . . Remember that we had just begun opening up the Mexican economy. Mexican business depended basically on government giveaways, government contracts, government permissions to import, government permissions to export. So Mexican business and businessmen didn't exist! . . . If anything, businessmen were very much opposed to trade opening. Because they saw that—correctly—as a direct threat to them, because they were not particularly competent at competing at a worldwide scale. They had had protection for many years. So Mexican businessmen were not at all a part of [the decision to negotiate].

Smaller manufacturers were represented by an association named Canacintra, one of the vehicles by which the PRI had both incorporated and constrained the political voice of business (see Chapter 2).[67] For many years, this had helped the PRI to marginalize the private sector politically. But in the 1970s, business grew more active, and established means of representation and consultation came to an end, as new associations emerged. One such body was the Consejo Coordinador Empresarial (Business Coordinating Council), a new umbrella organization established with the explicit goal of uniting the previously disparate factions of Mexican business. Though business-government tensions eased in the late 1970s, the economic crisis in 1982 exacerbated them once again, particularly when the state nationalized the banks.[68] In the 1980s, then, some businesspeople grew motivated to participate in the unprecedented private sector activism—stimulated by resentment about state intervention in the economy—while others did so out of opposition to the increasingly free market orientation of the technocrats. Some of the old business allies of the PRI felt betrayed by the newly liberal policies the party enacted over the course of the 1980s.

[66] Johnson Ceva 1998; Shadlen 2000; Thacker 2000. This is hardly surprising given their subordination to the PRI.

[67] The Ley de Cámaras (1941) required businesses to affiliate with either of two main confederations—CONCAMIN or CONCANACO. But that same year, the government also created Canacintra, which was affiliated with CONCAMIN but became relatively independent—particularly because of its large membership (Mizrahi 1992).

[68] Alba Vega 1997.

Canacintra continued working with the government, but some of its members grew disenchanted with the organization's leadership and its commitment to the PRI. After 1986, dissidents within the organization therefore established a rival National Association of Manufacturers (Asociación Nacional de Industriales de la Transformación, or ANIT). Giving up the institutional advantages associated with Canacintra, ANIT opted for a more autonomously critical posture vis-à-vis the state and its increasingly free market policies.[69] Confronting this challenge, the state acted to strengthen Canacintra, such as by rejecting ANIT's application for a separate official chamber, meaning that joining the voluntary ANIT would not absolve members of the responsibility to pay dues to the official Canacintra.

Even if the dissidents felt Canacintra was insufficiently critical, from the outside it seemed to Mexican officials that Canacintra and the small manufacturers it represented were quite a tough group to please. As a consequence, according to one NAFTA negotiator, "The internal negotiations [within Mexico] were more intense than the external negotiations [with the US and Canadian representatives]." Another interviewee described Canacintra as "always very on the other side." Nevertheless, despite the abundant criticism from small manufacturers, in the end the Mexican state succeeded in mitigating business opposition to NAFTA in Mexico. All the country's major business associations ultimately endorsed the agreement, even if some of them did not do so until the bitter end, after the formal negotiations had concluded. Canacintra, as reported in its monthly periodical, endorsed NAFTA in 1993.[70] Chapter 7 will elaborate on how Mexico's technocrats managed to dodge the threat of a business backlash. Compared to in Canada, broad-based private sector support for North American free trade was much more the end outcome of a process, and resulted from organization and influence on the part of the state.

Conclusion

Economic policy debates in the 1980s fractured the Mexican business community, as different sectors and firms settled on different strategies. Some opted to support economic opening, others to fight it, and still others to compromise with it. With respect to NAFTA, though larger and more international firms were generally supportive, overall it is not the case that in Mexico free trade was a project of economic elites. There is much less evidence of the kind of proactive, broad-based support on the part of businesspeople that there had been in Canada. But

[69] Shadlen 2000.
[70] *Transformación* 1993.

nor did NAFTA have much to do with democracy and the preferences of the mass public. Even though Mexico was certainly democratizing, NAFTA was a project of technocratic politicians who pursued free trade for reasons of their own, reflecting their educational backgrounds.

The US government did not compel Mexico to negotiate free trade, and international agencies like the World Bank and IMF had no direct influence either.[71] Mexico's own policymakers grew strongly committed anyway, seeing in NAFTA a means of making wide-ranging changes to domestic economic policies that they favored irrespective of any action by the United States or Canada. In some ways, Mexico went *beyond* what international actors were asking for—showing that free trade and other neoliberal policies they embraced were not just in some sense an international imposition.[72]

But while Mexico's economic opening was not a foreign imposition, the rise of the technocrats and the decisions they made reflected the country's weak position vis-à-vis external influences. Challenging economic circumstances made Mexico dependent on external financial constituencies with whom the technocrats were well placed to negotiate, and which in turn endorsed and encouraged them and their agendas. While the preferences of business did not change as much over time as they had in Canada, and were not the impetus behind free trade in Mexico, it is also true that business was not nearly as hostile as the liberal literature would suggest. Democratization certainly did not undermine the power of a domestic economic elite strongly committed to autarky: Mexico's top businesspeople were advocates of opening, as were—at least by the end—all the country's major business associations.

The technocrats were not unconcerned about public opinion; for the first time in decades the PRI felt accountable to the public. Polls suggest that public opinion was supportive, but also—as in Canada—that free trade's advocates were able to shape public opinion to a significant degree how they wished. Mexico's opening was therefore not a consequence of the state's growing accountability to a mass public autonomously desirous of economic opening. But nor was it, as in the case of Canada, a function of changing private sector worldviews and policy demands. In Canada, by the time the Mulroney government decided to negotiate bilateral free trade, the announcement came as no surprise. In Mexico, in contrast, the announcement came as a shock; there had been no prior public discussion, even despite a well-known, standing US invitation to negotiate.

---

[71] Ortiz Mena 2004: 221; Urzúa 1997: 95.
[72] Thacker 2000.

5

The United States

Divided Hegemon

CUFTA did not generate great public interest in the United States, but NAFTA was another story.[1] A range of critics assailed the agreement, and advocates responded with more than corresponding intensity. The debate reached a peak when NAFTA came up for a vote in Congress in the fall of 1993, legislative approval being a much greater challenge in the United States than in either Canada or Mexico. The parliamentary system and its tradition of party discipline meant that a majority government in Canada could count on support in the legislature, while at the time of NAFTA's creation Mexico was a nondemocracy governed by a ruling party with clear control of the congress. So in both Ottawa and Mexico City, a majority of legislators were sure to vote with the executive branch. In Washington, by contrast, low party discipline and the greater autonomy of the legislative branch meant that the president could not count on the support even of legislators from his own party.

Many members of Congress were concerned about the potential consequences of siding against public opinion on NAFTA; this in turn led both opponents and proponents to campaign aggressively to shape the public's views. A few months before the vote, public opinion leaned against NAFTA. But the Clinton administration and a business campaign group called USA*NAFTA succeeded in shifting public views, such that by the fall of 1993 public opinion was roughly balanced between pro and con. NAFTA was made safe, in other words, because economic and political elites promoted it.[2] Businesspeople were keen to see the

---

[1] The main reason for this was probably the greater wage differential between the United States and Mexico compared to between the United States and Canada. Lechner (2016) shows that workers tend to be more concerned about trade integration with countries poorer than their own.

[2] Ayres 1998; Center for Public Integrity 1993; Dreiling and Darves 2011, 2016; Kay and Evans 2018; Kay 2005; MacArthur 2000; Rupert 2000; Shoch 2000.

agreement ratified, given that the US negotiators had succeeded in including much of the content they had wanted.[3]

The administration that steered NAFTA through the ratification process was not the same as the one that negotiated it. The administration of President George H. W. Bush negotiated NAFTA in 1991 and 1992, and Bush signed the agreement in December 1992, though by then he had been voted out of office. Bush had hoped to conclude the NAFTA negotiations early enough so that congressional approval could be conferred before the presidential election of November 1992, but the negotiations ran on too late in the summer. Securing the agreement's congressional approval therefore fell to Bill Clinton, whose different, more compromising stance on NAFTA maybe made it possible.

Only Something Good for Us

When the Canadian government approached the United States about a free trade agreement in 1985, the Reagan administration was receptive right away. And when Mexican officials broached the topic in early 1990, their US counterparts were also immediately enthusiastic.[4] When asked soon afterward for her views, the US trade representative, Carla Hills, reported to President Bush that "there is broad support among your economic and foreign policy advisers."[5] So there was little debate within either the Reagan or Bush administration about pursuing North American free trade.[6] As previous chapters explained, US officials worked for a long time to promote free trade to America's neighbors, citing reasons Canada and Mexico should like it. Behind closed doors, US officials discussed how to achieve it. The US ambassador to Mexico had said confidentially in 1988 that "free trade between the two countries is a long term goal."[7] Having finally won over the Canadian and Mexican governments, though, Washington's focus turned quickly to a new challenge: securing the content the United States wanted in the agreements.

---

[3] Chapter 7 discusses the market access parts of the negotiations in greater detail.

[4] The 1984 Trade and Tariff Act had authorized the president to negotiate bilateral free trade agreements, and named Israel and Canada as two prospective parties to such agreements. Shortly thereafter, the United States signed its first bilateral FTA, with Israel. Similarly, the Congress included authority for the administration to continue negotiations on trade and investment with Mexico generally in a bill in 1988 (PL 100-418).

[5] Hills 1990: 1.

[6] Some American trade officials were hesitant about negotiating a free trade agreement with Mexico, simply because they did not want to lose focus on the Uruguay Round of GATT negotiations. But this concern fell away fairly quickly.

[7] Pilliod 1988.

Among the top US priorities were commitments from Canada and Mexico in the areas of intellectual property and investor rights, demands that the Americans knew Ottawa and Mexico City would resist. The United States had been seeking commitments from Canada and Mexico in these areas for years; in the mid-1980s the United States had started proposing negotiations on these topics at the GATT as well. Though the goal of fostering economic development, democratization, and improved governance in Mexico was an important motivating factor in America's pursuit of an agreement, that goal declined in importance once it was time to negotiate over NAFTA's content. Similarly, CUFTA represented an opportunity for the United States to address a mix of what trade negotiators call "irritants" (miscellaneous sector-specific trade conflicts) and also to establish precedents for including new content in international trade negotiations.[8] Given the relative sizes of the countries' markets, economists did not expect that free trade with either Canada or Mexico would have a big impact on the United States. But from the moment officials began talking about the substance of CUFTA and NAFTA, there was a lot of motivation on the US side to win content that would please American business.

Intellectual property rights (IPRs) comprise patents, copyrights, and trademarks, and especially since the early twentieth century a large share of all the world's inventions and content that could be covered by these instruments have been generated by US firms. In the domestic market, American law ensured that US firms could profit from sales of their creations; but in other countries consumers could often acquire copies without paying equivalent compensation. As a consequence, especially in the 1980s, US firms began pressing their government to lean on others to pass stricter intellectual property laws of their own, and to work harder to enforce such laws.

Within North America, American officials working on the issue of intellectual property were focused above all on the issue of patents for pharmaceuticals. Both Canada and Mexico were making abundant use of "compulsory licensing": giving domestic manufacturers legal permission to produce generic drugs, copying patented drugs developed by foreign firms and paying the latter only modest compensation for the right to do so. US opposition to this practice was not new. Almost a decade before the start of the CUFTA negotiations, the US Department of Commerce had argued that "Canada's compulsory licensing system is a matter of no small concern to U.S. industry. . . .If the system itself cannot be eliminated, the U.S. industry has suggested that increasing the royalty payment from 4% to 12% would mitigate the adverse effects."[9] Similarly, a

---

[8] Hart et al. 1994: 297–98.
[9] Department of Commerce 1977: 1.

memo to Vice President Bush, briefing him ahead of a trip to Canada in 1986, suggested as a talking point: "I cannot overemphasize our continued unhappiness over your reluctance to introduce legislation modifying the compulsory licensing system affecting pharmaceutical patents."[10] In much the same vein, US officials threatened in 1986 that "unsatisfactory action on [the issue of patent protection could] cost Mexico hundreds of millions of dollars" in discretionary access to the US market, under its Generalized System of Preferences (GSP).[11] Mexico did indeed fall foul of US pressure, and subsequently lost some discretionary benefits under the GSP in 1987.[12]

In the CUFTA negotiations, the United States sought to include a chapter on intellectual property, but Canada objected (wanting to maintain its compulsory licensing system), and in the end no such chapter was included. Nevertheless, the issue was highly contentious, and in 1987, under pressure from the United States, the Canadian government made substantial modifications to its patent laws—most notably adding three more years of patent protection before pharmaceuticals could be subject to compulsory licensing.[13] Much the same happened four years later, in the run-up to the NAFTA negotiations. Like Canada, Mexico wanted to maintain its compulsory licensing regime, while the United States wanted the system eliminated. In the spring of 1991, the US Congress was debating whether to give the Bush administration authority to negotiate a free trade agreement with Mexico.[14] As explained in Chapter 2, legally the US Congress has final authority over foreign economic relations, and so it must formally ratify any international trade agreement for it to be implemented. But under a process established in 1934, Congress began delegating authority to the executive branch to conduct the negotiations.[15] In 1991, industry associations took the opportunity to pressure the US negotiators in turn to demand that Mexico make changes to its intellectual property law. Some threatened not to support the negotiations at all, unless they got what they considered an initial commitment from Mexico. Leading members of Congress also made it clear to both the American and Mexican negotiators that this was a minimum condition for them to support the start of negotiations. The Mexicans recognized that they would have to agree, and subsequently enacted substantial changes to their

[10] Khedouri 1986.

[11] Bennett 1986.

[12] Sell 1995: 330.

[13] Burns 1987.

[14] Under the delegation process invented long ago as part of the 1934 Reciprocal Trade Agreements Act.

[15] This was known as "Fast Track" authority for many years, and is now called Trade Promotion Authority.

intellectual property law in June 1991.[16] The new law substantially increased the scope and stringency of patent protection.

The United States made use not only of threats, but also positive encouragements—offering additional access to Mexican imports under its GSP program in return for the change in Mexico's intellectual property law. One US negotiator explained: "We were trying to determine interest, willingness, and ability to negotiate a free trade agreement, and make the type of structural reforms that are of interest to the United States—patents and copyrights being a prime example. And we used our GSP program to provide an incentive or a reward for doing that." This was not controversial in Washington; within the United States, there were no voices raised against pressuring Mexico in this way. Stronger protection for intellectual property rights was, as this official put it, "only something good for us."

Mexico later agreed also to include intellectual property in the text of NAFTA itself. As a consequence, the US private sector Advisory Committee for Trade Policy and Negotiations stated that NAFTA's "provisions on intellectual property as they pertain to Mexico substantially meet most of the ambitious negotiating objectives."[17] The intellectual property provisions in NAFTA were much broader than anything the United States had previously managed to include in any international agreement, and subsequently served as a model for America's approach to IPRs in the Uruguay Round of GATT negotiations.[18] Among other things, NAFTA introduced stringent restrictions on the use of compulsory licensing.[19]

Another top priority for American business and the American negotiators was liberalization of Canadian and Mexican rules on foreign investment. By

---

[16] For example, eight large US business associations, drawn principally from the film, publishing, music, and software industries, wrote to US negotiators to tell them that the government of Mexico "must not fail to implement . . . its promise of much needed reform extending copyright protection to sound recordings and computer software. Such failure would inevitably threaten congressional support" for the launching of negotiations over NAFTA (International Intellectual Property Alliance 1991). Inside the US government, one analyst recommended as a message to the Mexican foreign secretary: "I understand that your Congress expects to adopt new intellectual property rights legislation early in the session beginning next month. This issue has aroused considerable interest on Capitol Hill since it is important to a number of US industries. This legislation is particularly important to fast-track re-authorization and FTA negotiations" (Cowal 1991: 2).

[17] Advisory Committee for Trade Policy and Negotiations 1992.

[18] International Trade Commission 2016: 76.

[19] Sell (1995) argues that, in general, developing countries have not been persuaded that stricter protection of intellectual property is really in their interest, but that pressure from the United States has forced many of them to change their intellectual property laws. Sell names Mexico as an exception to this pattern, though, saying the Mexican technocrats believed stricter IPRs would yield benefits to Mexico.

the start of the CUFTA negotiations, the Mulroney government had already substantially liberalized Canada's regulations on inward FDI (substantially modifying the 1973 Foreign Investment Review Act by replacing it via new legislation in 1985), and investment never became an especially contentious issue in the negotiations. The 1985 Investment Canada Act reduced the range of investments that would require screening and eliminated the requirement that any new investment would have to be a "significant benefit" to Canada: a "net benefit" was now sufficient. In CUFTA, the United States wanted a commitment to "national treatment" for American investors in Canada, meaning they would be treated the same as domestic investors, and Canada agreed to this.[20] On the other hand, Canada insisted on the right to continue screening company acquisitions by foreign investors above C$150 million.[21]

In the case of NAFTA, given that a major motivation was a US desire to protect its investors in Mexico, and the Mexicans hoped NAFTA would draw more FDI to their country, the investment provisions were much more central for the whole negotiation. And in the area of investment, like intellectual property, the Americans took the opportunity to negotiate provisions well beyond what they had managed in any prior agreement. The NAFTA investment chapter (Chapter 11) brought together commitments that had never been combined before. First, Chapter 11 stipulated the elimination of many regulations that Mexico had previously used to shape the behaviors of foreign investors, such as local content rules and foreign exchange balancing requirements. The definition of investment for the purposes of Chapter 11 would be very broad, and parties could never introduce any new performance requirements.[22] The Americans wanted to eliminate any sectoral restrictions on foreign investment in Mexico, and also to encourage the privatization of state-owned enterprises; the Mexicans insisted on excluding the energy sector, for the most part, but otherwise they excluded very few sectors.[23] Given their enthusiasm for free markets (see Chapter 4), as one of them said, "It's hard to think of any sector in which foreign investment had no reason to be." Though Canada and Mexico did maintain the right to review

---

[20] Khedouri 1986.

[21] Raby 1990.

[22] Haggard 1995; Maxfield and Shapiro 1998. The concurrent GATT negotiations about investment did not affect NAFTA much, since the investment provisions negotiated at a multilateral level were much narrower—largely just about performance requirements. NAFTA's investment chapter was much broader.

[23] It should be said that every country had its constitutionally sensitive areas. The US excluded maritime transport services—the 1920 US Jones Act requiring that domestic goods shipping be conducted by American-owned ships—and Canada its cultural industries. Mexico nationalized its oil industry in 1938, expropriating the assets of US and British companies, in an action enshrined in the constitutions and taken as a defining assertion of sovereignty in the face of foreign domination.

certain foreign takeovers (as Canada had done in CUFTA), overall, NAFTA liberalized investment flows in many ways—to an unprecedented extent in an agreement spanning the developing and developed worlds.

Second, aside from limiting the measures that governments could take to regulate foreign investment, Chapter 11 gave foreign investors from NAFTA countries controversially expansive legal options in settling disputes with host governments.[24] The United States (as well as many other developed countries home to multinational enterprises) had for many years offered to sign bilateral investment treaties (BITs) with developing countries, under which the signatory governments committed not to expropriate foreign investors—and if they did, quickly to provide full compensation. The appeal of BITs for the United States was that many developing countries' judicial systems (including Mexico's) were, the Americans believed, too slow and open to political interference to offer for- eign investors credible protection against expropriation. On the other hand, de- veloping countries appreciated BITs insofar as the added assurance they provide to investors should, at least in principle, lead to more inflows of foreign capital. In other words, BITs would help attract foreign investment by making a country appear safer to investors, and they did that using dispute settlement procedures by which investors could bring complaints about host governments to binding international arbitration.[25]

The starting point for the United States in negotiating the investment provisions in NAFTA, then, was that Chapter 11 would merge their standard ("model") BIT with the commitments of a free trade agreement. This had not been done before, and the trade agreement, moreover, would include a broad investment chapter—proscribing performance requirements, ensuring na- tional treatment, and prohibiting any new restrictions on the right of investors to establish themselves in a partner country. By comparison, CUFTA had not provided for investor-state dispute settlement (ISDS) and defined investment much more narrowly. Confronted with the Americans' demands, the other countries' negotiators were taken aback.[26] Attracting investment was not a major Canadian goal, and the Canadian investment negotiators were opposed to ISDS. Canada had previously signed some BITs, but in the role of a source rather than host nation. The Mexican negotiators were initially ambivalent, but grew more accepting of the US demands, thinking that the more assurance they

[24] See Barenberg and Evans 2004; Shadlen 2005.

[25] BITs were not new, but there were few of them until the 1980s—at which time the number expanded dramatically.

[26] The offense-defense quality of the investment negotiations was not unlike what unfolded in the negotiations over investment in the Uruguay Round at the GATT, as countries split on the issue depending on whether they were capital-exporting or capital-importing (Dattu 2000: 290).

could provide to foreign investors, the better. In the end, Mexico sided with US preferences, Canada lost out on the issue, and NAFTA contained sweeping investor rights. Unlike the trade provisions in NAFTA, the investment chapter as written allowed private firms to initiate disputes *directly* with governments.[27] The United States subsequently used these principles as precedents, and after NAFTA further trade agreements signed by the United States consistently included similarly extensive investment chapters.[28]

A Bare-Knuckle Fistfight

Given NAFTA's contents, US business groups were delighted. The Investment Policy Advisory Committee, a private sector-based body with official responsibility for advising US trade negotiators on investment policy issues, stated that it strongly supported NAFTA's investment-related provisions.[29] The agreement would, as American business leaders had wanted, open up new opportunities for them in Mexico, and it would lock in the market-oriented policy changes that had been made there in recent years. A US business association official explained US private sector interest in NAFTA as follows:

> People had a lot invested in Mexico and were making a lot of money on their exports from Mexico. . . . And they didn't want Mexico to backslide on any of the openness and liberalization efforts that they had adopted under Salinas, mostly on investment, but also in terms of trade openness. And they wanted to get better protection for intellectual property, and better protection on investment. . . . You have low labor rates so that you can invest there and compete globally. . . . People were looking at Europe and East Asia at the time. . . . Europe was becoming a really large, integrated market with very few barriers. And it was making their companies more competitive globally. It was appealing to be able to draw on the larger range of wages and that sort of thing that you found in Europe at that point.

The National Association of Manufacturers (NAM), the US Chamber of Commerce, and the Business Roundtable—the country's three major national business associations—all offered the agreement their strong endorsement.

---

[27] Simmons 2014.

[28] International Trade Commission 2016: 81. At the time of writing (early 2019), the newly renegotiated NAFTA eliminates NAFTA's investor-state dispute settlement mechanism.

[29] MacMillan 1992.

And an internal memo within the office of the president reported in late 1992 that, out of six trade policy advisory committees, only one was opposed to NAFTA: the Labor Committee. All but one of seventeen Industry Sector Advisory Committees supported NAFTA, as did all three Industry Functional Advisory Committees. Agriculture was slightly more divided; out of ten Agriculture Technical Advisory Committees, five were supportive, and the other five were internally divided.[30]

But though businesspeople were very happy about NAFTA, other constituencies were not. As soon as it became known that the US government was negotiating a free trade agreement with Mexico, critics of the idea began campaigning against it. The debate grew increasingly intense between the fall of 1990 and the fall of 1993, to a degree that was remarkable given that trade had never previously attracted so much public attention in the United States. And NAFTA's opponents almost won.

The first clear sign of the scale of the civil society hostility to NAFTA was when opponents of NAFTA brought their grievances to Capitol Hill in January 1991. Congress was starting to look ahead to the "fast track" vote later in the spring, by which it would grant or deny the Bush administration the authority to negotiate a free trade agreement with Mexico. Dozens of organizations contributed to a meeting and then press conference blasting the proposal—labor unions, environmental organizations, church groups, development NGOs, family farm advocates, and others.

Labor unions and the AFL-CIO, the US labor confederation, were strongly opposed to free trade with Mexico, as were a number of prominent environmental organizations, and from early 1991 through late 1993 these groups campaigned vigorously against ratification.[31] NAFTA was one of their core issues in that time, unions being very worried about the threat of potential job losses, especially given the possibility of US firms moving to Mexico to take advantage of the lower wages there. The labor members of the official US trade policy advisory body were highly critical of NAFTA, saying it was "impossible to support."[32] By the time of the NAFTA negotiations, American trade unions were familiar with many instances of firms moving operations to Mexico, or at least threatening to do so, in the face of workers' demands for better pay or conditions in the United States. Organized labor warned that NAFTA would give firms an incentive to further drive down wages, and that the government in Mexico might want to lower standards in order to compete and attract investment. Critics of NAFTA who warned the agreement would lead to a southward

---

[30] Hrinak 1992.
[31] See Kay 2005; Evans and Kay 2008.
[32] MacMillan 1992: 14.

outflow of investment were derided by its proponents, but given the nature of the investment negotiations (as described earlier) the agreement was written to allow for exactly that. Some mainstream economic modeling also suggested that NAFTA could mean costs rather than benefits for low-skilled workers.[33]

There was similar criticism from the environmental movement. NGOs from all three countries urged the inclusion of environmental safeguard clauses and improved protection and enforcement.[34] By the time of the NAFTA negotiations, it was well known that air and water quality in the US-Mexico border region were very poor, due to rapid unplanned growth, including as part of the maquiladora program. This did not augur well for a future with even more trade and economic activity in that area. Much like labor, environmentalists also worried that NAFTA would foster pernicious international competition, with governments discouraged from protecting the environment if they wanted their country to remain "competitive." And environmentalists' concerns about NAFTA only deepened in 1991, when in August of that year, a GATT dispute settlement panel ruled in favor of a Mexican challenge to the US Marine Mammal Protection Act. The dispute revolved around a US law restricting imports of tuna caught in ways dangerous to dolphins, and the law was struck down by an international organization on the grounds that it was an illegitimate constraint on trade. Critics pointed to the decision as evidence of trade agreements' nefarious impacts. The case quickly turned into a public relations disaster for the Mexican government, which quickly backtracked and promised both to ignore the ruling and to pass a new law to protect dolphins.

The labor and environmental critics of NAFTA generally sought to build and sustain alliances with foreign counterparts, claiming they did not want to achieve their goal of killing the agreement at the expense of Mexican workers.[35] Strategically, nor did they want to be seen taking a racist or chauvinist stance—as some NAFTA advocates said they were.[36] Seeking an internationalist image, and to avoid scapegoating Mexican workers, US union activists' main argument was that firms were playing off the two countries' workforces against each other—to the benefit of workers in neither country.

There were, however, other critics of NAFTA in the United States who were unabashedly nationalist in their views. Another of the agreement's prominent opponents was the conservative Pat Buchanan—an adviser to several former presidents and a right-wing populist candidate for the Republican Party's presidential nomination in 1992 and 1996. In a similar vein, Ross Perot, a

---

[33] International Trade Commission 1992.
[34] Hogenboom 1998.
[35] Thorup 1991.
[36] E.g., Von Bertrab 1997.

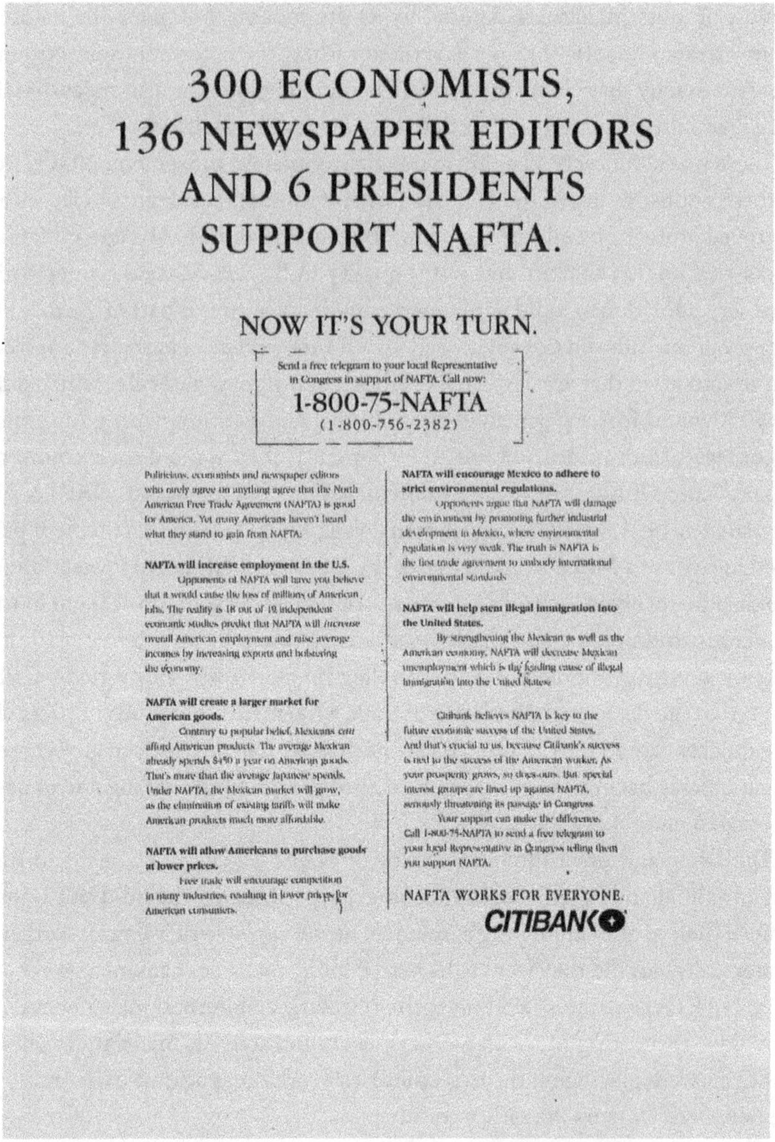

Figure 5.1 Advertisement appearing in the *Boca Raton News*, November 8, 1993

wealthy Texan entrepreneur and an independent presidential candidate in 1992 and 1996, used his ample wealth to publicize his objections to NAFTA. Perot mainly appealed to nationalist Republican voters; he released a book criticizing NAFTA, entitled *Save Your Job, Save Our Country*. This became so successful that he eventually debated the issue with Vice President Al Gore on national television in the fall of 1993, and he also appeared before Congress. Perot became famous for predicting that NAFTA would lead to a "giant sucking sound" of jobs moving from the United States to Mexico—probably the most memorable soundbite from the whole debate about NAFTA in the United States, even though many other opponents of free trade would not otherwise have sympathized with Perot or his perspective. The opposition to NAFTA therefore comprised a wide range of nationalist and internationalist criticisms; taken together, the number of people who subscribed to one or other of these views was substantial.

In the face of all this opposition, the American business community was highly motivated to see the agreement become a reality—so keen, in fact, that businesspeople funded and coordinated a large-scale public campaign in the lead-up to the congressional ratification vote in November 1993. In October 1992, the Business Roundtable established a campaign group called USA*NAFTA to promote the agreement both to the public and to legislators.[37] Individual firms also paid for advertisements in local newspapers, such as that shown in Figure 5.1. As one US business association staff person put it, "The people who were running the NAFTA coalition were absolutely rabid about it." NAFTA's business advocates promoted the agreement above all as a jobs machine, saying free trade would expand US exports to Mexico and thereby contribute to American employment.

The Business Roundtable was an association of chief executives of large US firms, describing itself in the 1980s as "founded in the belief that business executives should take an increased role in the continuing debates about public policy. The Roundtable believes that the basic interests of business closely parallel the interests of the American people."[38] The Roundtable always worked not just to influence public policy directly, but also to shape executives' thinking about national issues relevant for American business generally.[39] In the context of the public debate about NAFTA in the early 1990s, the Roundtable both campaigned publicly for NAFTA and encouraged more commitment to NAFTA among American business leaders. One of the two co-chairs of the Business Roundtable at that time, the CEO of American Express, was even the chair of the official private sector trade advisory body.[40] He was therefore in a position to convey the Roundtable's priorities and positions directly to the US negotiators. He was also one of the founders of the USA*NAFTA campaign group.

One business association staff person summed up the NAFTA debate in the United States as "a bare-knuckle fistfight between labor, environment, and business." The financial resources each of these groups could bring to bear did

---

[37] Rupert 2000.
[38] Business Roundtable 1981.
[39] Vogel 1983: 34.
[40] Dreiling and Darves 2011.

not make that fight a very fair one, however. Assessing the spending on the issue of NAFTA (including by the Mexican government), the Center for Public Integrity (an investigative NGO) summarized that "the anti-NAFTA forces have been financially 'out-gunned' by the Mexicans and the US business community in this lobbying effort."[41]

Clinton and the Side-Agreements

Despite all the campaigning by American business, NAFTA would probably have fallen at the last hurdle if not for Bill Clinton. He and his team committed to winning the agreement's ratification and worked hard to that end. That was despite the fact that NAFTA was probably not something Clinton initially wanted to deal with, since it was a project of the incumbent Republican president against whom he was campaigning in 1992. Moreover, Clinton faced the serious dilemma that his own Democratic Party was internally divided on the issue, with many grass-roots members being opposed, while the party establishment and centrist leaders were in favor. Reflecting this division, some of the Democratic candidates in the primaries in early 1992 had come out against NAFTA. Sooner or later Clinton would have to take a position on the agreement, and it was not a given that he would support it. In the summer, addressing a labor audience in San Francisco, Clinton had said that "from everything we read, the treaty has a whole lot of things in it for people who want to invest money and nothing for labor practices (nor) for the environment. . . . It looks like they're going to take a dive and just go for the money and it's wrong."[42]

It was in the fall of 1992, after he was selected as the Democrats' candidate, that Clinton finally settled on his message about North American free trade. In a speech at North Carolina State University on October 4, Clinton announced his support for NAFTA—but only on condition that it be accompanied by supplementary agreements on labor and environmental issues. Clinton said that free trade could be a force for either good or ill, depending on how the agreement was implemented. He talked about how Mexico had already done some positive things from an American point of view, helping to shrink the trade deficit and contributing to employment for US workers. Clinton's position reflected that some of his associates and advisers recommended he drop the agreement, while others were trying to persuade him to support it. The latter group included,

---

[41] Center for Public Integrity 1993: 2. This report concludes that the lobbying by the Mexican government and business communities was "the most expensive, elaborate campaign ever conducted in the United States by a foreign government."

[42] Quoted in the *Los Angeles Times*, August 1, 1992.

according to interviewees, Gene Sperling, George Stephanopoulos, Eli Segal, Barry Carter, and Hillary Clinton. Notably, none of these people studied economics at the graduate level; they were predominantly lawyers instead. Clinton appears to have pursued NAFTA because these kinds of generalist advisers convinced him it could do a lot of good, if "our jobs, our businesses, our farmers and our environment" could be protected from "unfair practices," as he put it in his speech in North Carolina.[43] In Clinton's worldview, NAFTA could help America compete in an increasingly challenging global economy, but the fairness of that competition—and its consequences for the US trade balance, jobs, and workers' well-being—would depend on foreign nations' labor and environmental standards. It made sense, then, to introduce a mechanism to prevent nations from competing unfairly in the global marketplace. That mechanism was the supplementary agreements he proposed.

On the other hand, there is little reason to think that he gained an electoral advantage from pursuing NAFTA. One adviser explained later that Clinton's decision to support the agreement was "agenda driven and not poll driven. . . . You didn't have to take more than a week of Democratic Politics 101 to know what a free trade agenda was going to do to the party . . . [Clinton] paid a huge political price."[44] That was likely an exaggeration, but there was certainly no strong electoral reason for Clinton to spend scarce political capital getting NAFTA ratified. In 1992, Gallup polling found more Americans perceived international trade as a threat than an opportunity, and at various points in 1993 surveys found more public opposition than support for NAFTA.[45]

Comparing Clinton's team at the start of his presidency to those of Mulroney and Salinas, the Americans were much like the Canadians and nothing like the Mexicans. In 1993, out of the president and vice president; secretaries of commerce, treasury, and state; USTR; White House chief of staff; chair of the Council of Economic Advisers; ambassadors to Canada and Mexico, and head of the Office of Management and Budget, only one person had a PhD in economics. Fully seven of the rest of these people were lawyers.[46] The Americans, like the Canadians, were far from being technocrats.

---

[43] Clinton may also have been convinced by longtime friends then working for the US Council of the Mexico-US Business Committee (one of whom had previously served on the US International Trade Commission), who produced a study predicting two hundred thousand new US jobs because of NAFTA (Center for Public Integrity 1993).

[44] Galston, quoted in Riley 2016: 133.

[45] Mayer 1998; Newport 2016.

[46] The one holder of a PhD was Laura D'Andrea Tyson. The equivalent people in the Bush administration in 1990 also counted among them only one person with a PhD in economics: Michael Boskin. Tyson and Boskin were both economics professors taking a break from academia while heading the Council of Economic Advisors. Clinton's team was Al Gore, Ron Brown, Lloyd Bentsen, Warren Christopher, Mickey Kantor, Mack McLarty, Laura D'Andrea Tyson, Peter Teeley, James

Given Clinton's stated position on NAFTA, after he was elected in November 1992, his new administration informed Mexico and Canada that the three countries would need to return to the bargaining table in 1993 to decide the substance of the labor and environmental "side-agreements." The Canadian and Mexican governments were not at all enthusiastic about this. Nevertheless, the U.S. Environmental Protection Agency (EPA) and State Department kicked off the negotiations. Staff from the EPA viewed the negotiations positively, as an opportunity to encourage Mexico to strengthen its environmental laws, and their enforcement. According to one interviewee: "Environmental people within the government did believe that NAFTA [and] trade liberalization generally can do a lot of good. But if a country doesn't have a strong environmental regime in place, it can also do harm." The EPA staff were less worried about the United States lowering its own environmental standards to attract investment (an argument made against NAFTA by its critics).

Initially the negotiators had no clear sense of what the side-agreements would look like. But given Clinton's position, they would need to establish monitoring mechanisms, and provide some kind of means by which each national government would be held to account for its performance in implementing and enforcing its own laws. There was a great deal of debate about whether the side-agreements would provide for any kind of enforcement capabilities, such as trade sanctions. USTR Mickey Kantor, for example, was initially in favor of sanctions, while staff members at the USTR's office were opposed, as were— even more vehemently—the governments of both Canada and Mexico. In the end, the negotiations on the side-agreements came to an end in August 1993, twelve months after the end of the main NAFTA negotiations. The result was two agreements: the North American Agreements on Labor Cooperation (NAALC) and Environmental Cooperation (NAAEC). These specified labor and environmental standards that each party would be expected to meet, with failures to comply being punishable, after a long bureaucratic process, by trade sanctions or fines. This outcome reflected an elaborate balancing act, a compromise among the agendas of the Clinton administration, various US federal agencies, members of Congress, the Canadian and Mexican governments, US business, and the US environmental and labor movements. Canadian officials were especially opposed to trade sanctions, and there were officials from both Canada and Mexico who strongly disliked the idea of broaching labor and environmental issues in a trade agreement. Nevertheless, the governments of both these countries accepted that the US political situation meant the side-agreements were inevitable.

Robert Jones, and Leon Panetta. For Bush, the equivalents were Dan Quayle, Robert Mosbacher, Nicholas Brady, James Baker III, Carla Hills, John Sununu, Michael Boskin, Edward Ney, John Negroponte, and Richard G. Darman.

And they did help facilitate NAFTA's ratification, by increasing the number of votes for it in Congress. The side-agreements helped in particular by providing "cover" to Democratic members of Congress who wanted to support NAFTA but had concerns about its labor and environmental consequences—or at least electoral concerns about appearing indifferent to these concerns.[47] Republicans in Congress, who knew full well that their votes were critical to NAFTA's passage, were on the other hand staunchly opposed to the side-agreements, as were American business groups. The latter, as one representative put it, fought the Clinton administration over the issue "tooth and nail until the end." Some business leaders, however, recognized the political usefulness of the side-agreements and accepted them because they really wanted to see NAFTA ratified.

The labor side-agreement did little to reduce the opposition of US unions. One Clinton administration interviewee said labor was so hostile to NAFTA that really there was no way the NAALC could ever win it over. Labor simply did not care about the substance of the side-agreement, even if NAFTA was a given. In the eyes of union leaders, the side-agreement's enforcement mechanisms were so complex, and involved so many steps, that there was little chance of trade sanctions or fines ever being imposed.[48] The NAAEC, in contrast, succeeded in winning endorsements from some environmentalists. In the spring of 1993, several large environmental organizations presented Mickey Kantor with their recommendations for the content of the environmental side-agreement and stated they would support NAFTA if their demands were met.[49] In the NAAEC, these groups got more or less what they wanted, and so they endorsed NAFTA—an action that other, more grass-roots environmental organizations deeply resented.[50]

Having finalized the substance of the side-agreements, in the fall of 1993 the Clinton administration made passing NAFTA its top priority. Final congressional approval required heavy lobbying by the executive branch. The Clinton administration provided wavering members who finally voted in favor with a range of benefits, from product-specific import restraints to minor tax code changes.[51] In September, Clinton kicked off his fall campaign for NAFTA by

[47] Mayer 1998.

[48] The NAALC stipulated that countries should enforce their own labor laws—laws with respect to occupational safety and health, child labor, wage standards, equal pay for men and women, and protection of migrant workers. As discussed in this book's afterword, despite unions' criticisms, the NAALC ended up helping to build a measure of labor transnationalism in North America (Kay 2005).

[49] Hogenboom 1998: 208–9.

[50] The six were the National Wildlife Federation, World Wildlife Fund, Audubon Society, Environmental Defense Fund, National Resources Defense Council, and Conservation International.

[51] Eisenstadt 1997.

inviting former presidents Bush, Carter, and Ford to join him at the White House and demonstrate their bipartisan commitment to the agreement. On November 9, as mentioned earlier, Vice President Al Gore debated populist conservative NAFTA critic Ross Perot on live television. At the same time, Clinton pushed business leaders to campaign harder on his side. He spoke to the US Chamber of Commerce on November 1, asking its leaders to work harder on NAFTA's behalf. Business groups subsequently dominated the congressional hearings about the agreement.[52]

There was one last constituency worth mentioning that supported the campaign for NAFTA: economists. The American economics community was overwhelmingly supportive, US economists being strong believers in liberal trade and investment policies. On September 1, 1993, 283 economists (including twelve Nobel Prize winners) sent Clinton an open letter declaring their support for the agreement. They did so even despite the fact that, from the perspective of neoclassical economics, both the greatest benefits and the greatest adjustment costs would be borne by the smallest member of the new free trade zone— Mexico. From a US perspective, therefore, many economists viewed NAFTA much more as a foreign policy than economic policy issue—a means of fostering Mexico's economic development, and thereby its political stability, but not a big potential influence on the US economy.[53] Stiglitz recalled later that "when President Bill Clinton first asked the Council of Economic Advisers about the economic importance of NAFTA, early in his administration, our response was that potential geopolitical benefits were far more important than the economic benefits."[54] That was because, as summarized, for example, in an investigation by the US International Trade Commission, almost all economic models predicted NAFTA would expand US GDP by about 0.5 percent at most.[55]

The tenor of the public debate did not reflect that view, though. Instead, both critics and advocates of NAFTA presented it as a potentially major influence on the US trade balance and employment (for reasons to be discussed in Chapter 6). Nor were members of Congress thinking of NAFTA predominantly in terms of its potential benefits for Mexico. When asked about this many years later, the US ambassador to Mexico at the time of the NAFTA negotiations said: "I don't think that the top leadership of our country thought of it primarily in terms of

---

[52] Velasco (1997) found that witnesses at US congressional hearings on NAFTA included businesspeople 39 percent, public officials 20 percent, members of Congress 11 percent, union representatives 10 percent, NGOs 8 percent, academics 4 percent, politicians 4 percent, think tank staff 3 percent.

[53] Krugman 1996.

[54] Stiglitz 2004.

[55] International Trade Commission 1992; see also Krugman 1993.

its beneficial political impacts. They cared about economics."[56] And that was not just true of the executive branch, but also Congress, whose members voted largely according to what they expected the impacts of NAFTA would be on jobs and wages in their districts.[57]

Conclusion

Just a few weeks before the congressional vote in the fall of 1993, NAFTA's ratification was far from certain; polls were finding that slightly more Americans opposed than supported the agreement.[58] Many members of Congress were wavering. In the end, though, on November 17, the House voted 234 to 200 in favor of NAFTA, and three days later the Senate voted 61 to 38. There were 132 Republicans and 102 Democrats in favor in the House, and 156 Democrats, 43 Republicans, and 1 independent opposed. Most representatives from Clinton's party opposed his position on NAFTA. Judging by donations from political action committees, not just export-oriented industries but even import-competing industries spent money in efforts to ensure the agreement's passage.[59] Donations from labor encouraged representatives to vote against NAFTA, and corporate contributions the opposite.[60]

The battle over NAFTA in the United States was almost as intense as that over CUFTA in Canada five years prior. Public opinion never grew exactly enthusiastic, but pro and con were roughly balanced by the time Congress voted on the agreement. The American private sector strongly supported NAFTA, and for the sake of ratification major business groups promoted it to an ambivalent electorate. Views vary as to whose efforts—those of the Clinton administration or American business—made more of a difference. One interviewee argued that the role of the Clinton administration had been exaggerated: "It wasn't the Clinton administration who got it done; it was the American business community that got it done."

Still, without Clinton, NAFTA might never have been ratified. Members of Congress tend to support trade liberalization more reliably if the president is a member of their own party.[61] But most congressional Republicans voted for NAFTA anyway, such that it was Clinton's presence that convinced just enough

---

[56] Quoted in Estévez 2012: 70.
[57] Baldwin and Magee 2000.
[58] Mayer 1998; Holsti 1996.
[59] Beaulieu and Magee 2004.
[60] Baldwin and Magee 2000.
[61] Magee 2010.

Democrats to get it through. Far fewer Democrats had voted to approve the start of negotiations back in 1991, when the president had been a Republican. Clinton also met with many more House Democrats than Republicans, and statistical analyses suggest that these meetings raised the probability of Democrats voting for NAFTA.[62] Had Bush been re-elected in 1992, fewer Democrats would probably have supported the agreement—maybe too few to ensure the agreement's survival. Clinton's strategy of imposing side-agreements—against the opposition of Republicans, US business, and the Canadian and Mexican governments—may also have been vital. He was an excellent compromiser, and his support for NAFTA in combination with the supplementary labor and environmental accords was possibly the only kind of position that could have allowed NAFTA to become a reality.

[62] Uslaner 1998.

6

Did Economists Cause Globalization?

The central tenet of international economics is that free trade is welfare improving. We express our conviction about free trade in our textbooks and we sell it to our politicians. Yet the fact of the matter is that we have one heck of a time explaining these benefits to the larger public.[1]

Much of the literature presents economists as central players in the rise of globalization. Chapter 4 examined one role that economists can play, for example, in the case of Mexico, as technocrats: economist-policymakers occupying key posts inside the state. This chapter now turns to economists in another guise: as the source of ideas adopted by, and motivating, other agents of globalization. According to some accounts, economists' neoclassical trade theory has been the core motivating vision of the policymakers who have made globalization happen.[2] Based on the history of free trade in North America, this chapter shows, on the contrary, that contemporary globalization does not rest on neoclassical foundations. While it is true that economists have been strongly supportive of initiatives for globalization, and their endorsements have made a difference to its legitimacy, the technical ideas behind their support are politically marginal. Instead, the priorities and worldviews of business, which are in some respects very different, influence policy outcomes to a much greater extent. In economists' formalized theory of trade, market liberalism yields substantial benefits for consumers, and trade is not a zero-sum competition among nations. In contrast, businesspeople and politicians see trade in a more informal and practical way, as a win-lose international contest, and they support free trade largely because of its benefits to producers. It is hardly surprising that economists and

---

[1] Trefler 2004.

[2] I define an "economist" as a holder of an advanced degree—a master's degree or PhD—in economics (or economics-heavy public policy).

businesspeople think about trade differently; they are after all paid to do very different things, and academic research requires different skills and dispositions than making profits. But how then have two groups of people, with substantively inconsistent sets of ideas, each supported the common project of globalization? This chapter shows how the ideas of the one, in the real worlds of both domestic politics and international trade negotiations, push aside the ideas of the other.[3]

Some critics of globalization, and neoliberalism more broadly, take neoclassical economics as little more than an intellectual derivative—a useful fiction helping to legitimate the preferences and agendas of business elites.[4] Other studies present economists, and experts more generally, as much more autonomous and intellectually influential in their own right.[5] From this perspective, policy changes can be the consequence of evolutions or revolutions in "knowledge regimes."[6] Many critics of neoliberalism see economists as highly unified around a free market agenda rooted in neoclassical ideas. It would seems then that the rise of globalization, reflecting the political success of neoliberal policies of various kinds, must be proof that, in terms of ideas, economists rule.[7]

In a more implicit way, the liberal literature also takes neoclassical economics as the ideational basis for policymakers' understanding of trade and their motivation to liberalize it. This literature predicts that policymakers will act on the basis of objective interests deduced a priori from a model of the consequences of different potential trade policies. This model, for the liberal literature on globalization, is economists' neoclassical trade model. In other words, this approach takes as given that policymakers think like economists—understanding the economic benefits of liberalizing trade precisely as economists do. This assumption is clear in political economy studies presenting formal models wherein policymakers act highly rationally in the face of conflicting priorities.[8] The question, then, is the empirical credibility of a one-to-one transposition of economists' trade model into the political world. This transposition assumes, for example, no deviations due to bounded rationality, nationalism, distrust of ethnic outgroups, or concerns about fairness, and it leaves somewhat unspecified the degree to which policymakers possess purely selfish objectives (or seek to maximize social utility).

---

[3] For further details, see Fairbrother 2010.

[4] E.g., Harvey 2005; Rupert 2000.

[5] E.g., Bockman 2011; Mirowski 2013; Sheppard 2005.

[6] E.g., Campbell and Pedersen 2014.

[7] E.g., Ban 2016; Burgin 2012; Christensen 2017; Dezalay and Garth 2002; Helgadóttir 2016; Jones 2012; Slobodian 2018.

[8] Feenstra 2016; Grossman 2016; Grossman and Helpman 1995; Hiscox 2002; see Baldwin 1996 for a discussion.

This chapter elaborates what mainstream, neoclassical economics says about trade and then contrasts that with a second, business-based perspective, which I call mercantilist. After that, it turns to the case of North American free trade and examines the roles played by the neoclassical and mercantilist perspectives. The third section presents economists' own reflections on the differences between these perspectives and articulates reasons why the neoclassical view of trade is, as I show, so marginal. Throughout the discussion, the chapter notes the political implications of different schools of thought with respect to international trade.

Trade and Globalization in the Eyes of Economists

Economists' view of trade rests on the concept of comparative advantage and the proposition that any country can benefit from trading with others, merely because they differ in their productive capabilities. For economists, even a country A that is less efficient than another country B at producing all goods and services can nonetheless benefit from trading with B, insofar as A must be *relatively* less bad at supplying *something*. (And B must be relatively less *good* at something.) From this simple proposition, which famously originates with Adam Smith and David Ricardo, many implications follow.[9]

Trade in Theory

To economists, trade is fundamentally about the welfare of people as consumers: people gain from trade insofar as it widens the range of producers from whom they can acquire some good or service they want. The wider the range, the greater the variety of goods and services available, and the better the chances that someone will be able to supply a given good or service at a lower price. The potential gains from trade, then, are greatest for goods and services that domestic producers are least able to provide. (Iceland has much to gain from the international trade in coffee.) Neoclassical trade theory therefore holds that free-flowing international trade allows countries to specialize in what they do best, leading to a more efficient distribution of productive resources and more wealth for all. If another country can produce something more cheaply than one's own, it makes more sense to import it than produce it at home. Ceasing inefficient production allows the home economy to free up resources (labor, land, machines) it can devote to providing other goods and services, which it can export to pay for imports.

---

[9] See, for example, Feenstra 2016.

It is for this reason that economists regard impediments to trade as damaging. Most of the world's people live near seacoasts and navigable rivers precisely because waterways facilitate trade.[10] Accordingly, intentionally raising the cost of trade is generally self-harm, and countries with impediments to it would be wise to remove them. Contrary to the expectations of many, then, economists recommend that countries liberalize trade unilaterally—not just if other countries do it also.[11] If other nations also eliminate their own barriers to trade, so much the better for everyone involved. But, as Krugman says, "If economists ruled the world, there would be no need for a World Trade Organization," meaning that each country would drop its trade barriers on its own, and an international institution encouraging them to do so would be redundant.[12] From the point of view of mainstream economics countries can benefit substantially from trade liberalization even on a *unilateral* basis—that is, when a country drops its barriers to imports (such as tariffs and quotas) without any other country doing the same.[13] According to mainstream, neoclassical economic trade theory, there is no particular reason why states need to *negotiate* trade liberalization at all. As Clausing puts it, "If policy makers did maximize an economist's perception of social welfare, it is unlikely that they would use tariffs at all."[14]

On the consumption side, in short, economists see trade as a means for expanding people's access to higher-quality and more diverse goods and services. On the production side, economists emphasize the benefits of specialization, with international trade allowing countries to focus on doing what they do well relative to others—whether because of natural geography (Qataris export natural gas for a reason) or accidents of history (the Swiss domination of watchmaking). But, as the typical economist sees it, imports remains the key purpose of trade, while exports are a means to the end of importing.[15]

Given this prioritization of consumer welfare, economists also value trade for the competitive pressures that foreign imports can apply to domestic producers of any given good or service. In an open economy, domestic firms and industries have to be as efficient as their foreign counterparts, and if they wish to keep doing business, they have to match the prices and quality of foreign imports. As a consequence, economists frown on trade restrictions that protect domestic firms, even if some domestic firms or industries stand to suffer or disappear

---

[10] Nordhaus 2006.

[11] Bhagwati 1988; Henderson 1986: 70; Burtless et al. 1998: 27.

[12] Krugman 1997: 113.

[13] See, e.g., Krueger 1990, 1995; Krugman 1991.

[14] Clausing 2001: 694.

[15] As Krugman (1993: 24) puts it, "The need to export is a burden that a country must bear because its import suppliers are crass enough to demand payment." See Taussig 1905: 33 for a similar formulation.

in the absence of such restrictions.[16] In fact, economists think just the opposite: opening up to trade does the most good in sectors where a country's firms are *least* efficient relative to foreign competitors. If that were not true, Bastiat famously asked, why the sun should not be considered an illegitimate foreign competitor to French candle-makers.

But while foreign competitors may replace domestic producers in a given sector, that can never happen in *all* sectors, specifically because of comparative advantage: a free-trading country will export products it produces efficiently relative to other products. In practice, this occurs because of continual adjustments in a nation's currency. When a country's imports expand, the value of its currency falls, and that makes further imports more expensive—while exports become cheaper for foreigners to buy. When the opposite happens—a country's exports increase relative to imports—the currency appreciates, making further exports more expensive and imports cheaper. Trade deficits and surpluses are therefore self-limiting, and rather than sweeping away all domestic production, unilateral liberalization simply reallocates production from relatively inefficient to more efficient producers. For that reason also, economists see little reason to shield any domestic firms or industries from foreign competition.

For economists, nations' trade balances are determined not by trade policies, like tariffs, quotas, and subsidies, but by macroeconomic forces: aggregate savings, investment, spending, and international financial flows.[17] A trade deficit indicates that a country is a net recipient of investment, whereas net senders of investment necessarily run trade surpluses. Erecting trade barriers to reduce a trade deficit (or to increase a trade surplus) simply cannot work.[18] Trade policies can only change the composition of a country's trade (what it exports and imports) and the overall volume of its trade (how much it exports and imports), not the difference between exports and imports.[19] And trade deficits and surpluses are neither causes nor signs of national economic failure or success.[20]

All of the preceding has some further surprising implications.

Trade agreements that include only some countries (e.g. NAFTA) and not all or almost all (i.e. the WTO) are a glass half-full for economists.[21] Economists support nondiscriminatory trade arrangements, and they do not believe it is in countries' best interest to give some countries more access to their markets relative to others. Preferential access of this kind does not allow countries to take

---

[16] Henderson 1986: 67.
[17] Burtless et al. 1998: 104; Krueger 1995: 5.
[18] Henderson 1986: 66.
[19] Congressional Budget Office 2000: 4.
[20] Krugman 1996: 6.
[21] E.g., Bhagwati 2008; Lal 2005.

advantage of their true, underlying comparative advantage. Economists do not support arrangements that help a region's producers to protect themselves from competitors elsewhere.

For economists, trade is a mutually beneficial process, not a competition among nations. The real competition, in the eyes of economists, is *within* countries: among different industries. Protecting one means discriminating against others.[22] The implication of comparative advantage is that producers of different goods and services within each given country will struggle with each other for scarce opportunities to export, while producers of goods and services that can be supplied relatively more efficiently from abroad will eventually go bust—and the latter is not something to fear.[23] Trade protectionism is not therefore something that a *country* can do to benefit itself at the expense of others, though it may benefit select *firms and industries* at risk of being out-competed by foreign counterparts. Trade protection transfers resources from more to less productive sectors.[24] Politically, it is likely that producers that are relatively efficient will favor more opportunities to sell their wares abroad, while producers struggling to compete with imports will not.

Finally, economists do not believe that trade, including the trade balance, has much to do with employment—that is, with the total number of jobs in an economy.[25] Economists' view holds that trade affects the types and quality of jobs in a country, but not their number, the latter being much more a function of macroeconomic factors, aggregate demand and supply, and interest rates. Although imports may close down a domestic industry, sooner or later exports of other kinds of products will inevitably rise, generating new employment opportunities elsewhere in the economy.

Economists' Beliefs in Practice

All that, in any event, is the theory. But we know that economists actually believe it in practice, too, as it is not only what economics textbooks emphasize and try to inculcate in their readers (future economists in training), but also what economists say when surveys ask their views.[26]

---

[22] Krueger 1990: 164.

[23] The extreme version of this is "Dutch Disease," where a boom in exports (such as from the rapid discovery and exploitation of a natural resource) can make other exports uncompetitive.

[24] Krueger 1995: 12.

[25] Burtless et al. 1998; Krueger 1995; Krugman 1996.

[26] Feenstra's (2016) lengthy textbook takes all of two pages to get to comparative advantage. Also, even more anecdotally, Greg Mankiw, one of the world's most influential economists, names "comparative advantage and the gains from trade" as the first of the three most important concepts he would want any economics student to learn (http://gregmankiw.blogspot.com.es/2007/08/top-three-economic-concepts.html).

In the 1970s, Kearl et al. mailed a questionnaire to representative sample of US-based economists, selected from the membership of the American Economic Association.[27] The questionnaire put to the respondents thirty propositions and asked them to agree, disagree, or agree with provisos. Out of the thirty propositions, one addressed trade policy specifically: "Tariffs and import quotas reduce general economic welfare." As it turns out, 81 percent of respondents generally agreed with the statement, 16 percent agreed with provisos, and 3 percent disagreed. A follow-up study in the United States in 1990 found again that 71 percent of US economists agreed that "tariffs and import quotas usually reduce general economic welfare," and another 21 percent agreed with provisos.[28] A third survey, in 1996, found that 89 percent of American economists thought that "trade agreements between the United States and other countries" are "good for the economy."[29] There is then a high level of consensus among American economists about the desirability of free trade.

These results might be taken as proof that economists are fanatical about free markets generally. It is notable, however, that respondents expressed *more* consensus on the issue of trade than on any other question addressed in these surveys. That is perhaps not surprising given that—in the words of probably the most influential Canadian economist ever—"the proposition that freedom of trade is on the whole economically more beneficial than protection is one of the most fundamental propositions economic theory has to offer for the guidance of economic policy."[30] Something else we learn from these surveys is that economists are not really so unified around policies widely perceived as neoliberal.[31] Most economists support a major role for the state in many areas, including the redistribution of income. A majority of the respondents to Frey et al.'s survey, for example, disagreed with weakening consumer protection laws, and significant numbers opposed weakening either public regulatory authorities or labor unions. Only 19 percent disagreed that income redistribution is a legitimate task for the state. We also know from other studies that many more American economists are Democrats than Republicans.[32] In a careful study of the politics of domestic neoliberalism Prasad observes that "most economists rejected the ideas that the Thatcher and Reagan administrations advocated."[33] It

---

[27] Kearl et al.1979.

[28] Alston, Kearl, and Vaughan 1992.

[29] Blendon et al. 1997.

[30] Johnson 1960: 327.

[31] I take "neoliberal" in the sense, per Babb (2007: 128), of "policy prescriptions united by an organizing theme: the liberation of market forces to achieve economic growth and prosperity."

[32] Klein and Stern 2007.

[33] Prasad 2006: 20.

is therefore a caricature to describe economists as beholden overwhelmingly to markets and completely unconvinced about the need for the state to play many roles in economic life. But with respect to trade specifically, there is a high level of consensus on the merits of free markets.[34]

It should also be said that American economists are probably the extreme case; nowhere else are economists so enthusiastic about free markets. There is less survey evidence about the policy ideas and preferences of economists in other countries, but there is some. Frey et al. report results from surveys in Austria, France, Germany, and Switzerland. In all these countries but one, more than 85 percent of economists agreed with the statement about trade barriers reducing welfare.[35] A similar questionnaire put to all members of the Canadian Economics Association in 1986 found that 70 percent of Canadian economists agreed that "tariffs and import quotas reduce general economic welfare," and another 26 percent agreed with provisos.[36] The level of consensus about free trade is not quite so high internationally, then, but still quite strong—and almost as high in some countries as in the United States.

Despite the exceptional consensus among economists, though, what economists think about trade is not what other people think about trade. Economists have always complained that the logic of comparative advantage is little understood or appreciated outside their own circles.[37] Frank Taussig, then president of the American Economic Association, observed glumly in 1905 that "the doctrine of free trade [is] widely rejected in the world of politics."[38] The Nobel Prize–winning economist Paul Samuelson famously argued in 1969 that the subtlety of comparative advantage as a concept "is attested by the thousands of important and intelligent men who have never been able to grasp the doctrine for themselves or to believe it after it was explained to them."

Economists do not see their understanding of trade reflected in contemporary public discourse and policy debates. Instead, if anything, they see mercantilism: the economic doctrine that nations can maximize their wealth and power by increasing exports and minimizing imports. The doctrine emerged in

[34] Gordon and Dahl 2013.

[35] Frey et al. 1984. France was the exception—26.5 percent of economists there disagreed.

[36] Block and Walker 1988.

[37] As Rodrik (1997: 4) notes, with respect to trade there is a "yawning gap that separates the views of most economists from the gut instincts of many laypeople."

[38] Taussig 1905: 65. Taussig (1905: 32) also bemoaned that "the mercantilist view of international trade, exploded though it has been time and again, has a singularly tenacious hold . . . so familiar that probably the immense majority of persons who have never been systematically trained in economics take this point of view as a matter of course."

early modern Europe, when it was widely believed that sales of exports would generate earnings in the form of precious metals, while purchases of imports required the expenditure of such metals. A positive difference between exports and imports would produce a growing stock of gold and silver, which could increase the political and military capacity of the nation-state. The emphasis on the accumulation of precious metals has fallen away in the contemporary world, but the idea that nations gain from exporting much and importing little remains.

John Kay, a leading British economist, cites trade mercantilism as his first example of "do-it-yourself economics," in the sense of "propositions which people who have practical knowledge but no qualifications in economics hold to be self-evident, but which are false."[39] Yet there is a surprisingly strong norm of reciprocity characterizing the practice of trade policymaking, with countries rarely liberalizing trade unilaterally, and this norm reflects explicitly or implicitly a very mercantilist view in which exports are a gain and imports a loss.[40] Mercantilism is almost part of the very constitution of the global trade regime, as the entire organization of the GATT system (see Chapter 2) embodies the expectation that countries will negotiate the reciprocal lifting of trade barriers. And the GATT in turn derived in large part from the US Reciprocal Trade Agreements Act— whose name says it all. Consistent with the mercantilist take on trade, most noneconomists speak as though trade were a win-lose competition among nations. Not surprisingly, then, conversations about trade frequently invoke the concept of "national economic competitiveness." Economists deny that countries compete, and so reject the very validity of the notion of national economic competitiveness. Krugman states plainly that "competitiveness is a meaningless word when applied to national economies" and calls it a "dangerous obsession."[41]

The Mercantilist Foundations of North American Free Trade

We can now return to North American free trade and consider the place of neoclassical and mercantilist ideas in the debates about it in the 1980s and 1990s. How powerful and how prevalent were each of these worldviews at the time? And what arguments convinced noneconomist policymakers to pursue free trade in the first place?

---

[39] Kay 2004: 164.
[40] Finlayson and Zacher 1981; Dam 2005: 712–13.
[41] Krugman 1996: 22, 1994. See also Kliesen 1995.

The Appeal of Free Trade

First, consider how Mexican officials saw NAFTA. In their comprehensive study of the NAFTA negotiations, Cameron and Tomlin argue that the Mexican negotiators "conceded" on many changes to their country's laws and policies that, behind the scenes, they had already decided to make for their own reasons.[42] One of the true-believing Mexican technocrats stated that, had they "been able to, [they] would have negotiated [an agreement] with . . . a much faster movement towards free trade." Another explained how the Mexicans would adopt a mercantilist stance, simply to see if they could win something from the other countries' negotiators: "We would discuss among ourselves: 'We have to go through this process of pretending not to yield to all these things. . . . We should! But okay, let's see what we can get in exchange.'" The Mexican officials' free-trade ambitions were therefore limited more by domestic than foreign opposition. Consistent with the neoclassical theory they knew, the Mexicans believed in the benefits of reducing their country's trade barriers irrespective of whether other countries reciprocated.

That was not the case in Canada, where key decision-makers were elected politicians without (in all but a few cases) any training in economics. To illustrate the point, one former Canadian politician emphatically defended the decision to negotiate free trade in strongly mercantilist rather than neoclassical terms:

> It would take a lot of very hard data to convince me that there wasn't a positive impact [on] employment. . . . Our trade surplus with the United States rose significantly. The amount of two-way trade rose significantly. Exports today are 45 percent of GDP, whereas it was 27 percent when the deal was done. The indirect impact of that on the competitiveness of the Canadian economy . . . You may have an argument as to whether NAFTA or [CUFTA] led to X thousand jobs or Y thousand jobs. But without [CUFTA] we wouldn't be nearly the country we are today.

Articulating a similar view, a Canadian business association representative argued emphatically: "Would we have created the same amount of employment without the free trade agreements that we have? No way. No way."

Suffice to say that Canadian economists saw CUFTA differently. They expected an important benefit of free trade to be its disciplining domestic industry—a productivity-enhancing "cold shower," to use a phrase from one of the academics who contributed to the work of the Macdonald Commission.[43]

---

[42] Cameron and Tomlin 2000: 123.
[43] Winham 1994.

Building on prior studies of the issue, economists argued that free trade would boost productivity by increasing economies of scale within firms. Previously, the 1975 report from the Economic Council of Canada made reference specifically to comparative advantage and even Ricardo (talking about specialization and economies of scale). Recognizing the disruption that comes from trade liberalization, the ECC noted that "the achievement of these benefits would quite clearly imply a considerable reorganization of Canadian manufacturing" and "Some industries would expand and new ones would appear."[44]

On the other hand, the Macdonald Commission also absorbed a range of other arguments that were less consistent with what the academic economists were thinking. To illustrate, in a commentary entitled "The New Face of Canadian Mercantilism," one academic economist remarked afterward that while he applauded the commission's endorsement of free trade with the United States, he objected to its rationale; in his words, "I do not want my students to learn the economics of free trade from the Commission's Report."[45] Elaborating, he summarized acerbically: "The Report reads like an argument that exporting is good and importing is the unfortunate cost which the nation must bear to expand exports. This is classic mercantilism. The Commissioners do not go so far as to argue that international trade is a zero sum game; but they come close."[46] When asked about the mercantilist quality of the Macdonald Commission's report, one bureaucrat involved in writing it explained emphatically that it "was not an economic textbook! It was a report to the government! So you have to put it not in economic terms, but in *political* economic terms!" Consistent with that suggestion, one of the two major studies of the creation of CUFTA argues specifically that Mulroney decided to negotiate a free trade agreement because he was *not* presented with the economists' arguments, which would have led him to see the idea as far too risky.[47] Instead, the more politically benign goal of securing better access to the US market was what motivated him to make the decision.

In the United States, a similar sort of case appears to have convinced Bill Clinton to commit to NAFTA, when—as Chapter 5 explained—he might easily have decided otherwise. Most of the advisers who won him over were generalists, the kind of people who came in for harsh criticism around that time from economists precisely for their ignorance of mainstream trade economics.[48] When Clinton announced he would support NAFTA, while campaigning in October 1992, he articulated a vision of international economics in which the

[44] Economic Council of Canada 1975: 89–90.
[45] Shearer 1986: 58.
[46] Shearer 1986: 57.
[47] Doern and Tomlin 1991: 34.
[48] Krugman 1996.

United States could "compete and win in the global economy." This was a mean-ingless statement from a neoclassical point of view, but it became one of the most common themes in Clinton's advocacy of NAFTA over the course of the following year.

Competition and Competitiveness

Clinton's view was not that different from American business's—even if the fu-ture president combined his mercantilism with a measure of social democracy, looking for ways of ensuring that US competitiveness would not come at the expense of workers' well-being. Like business leaders, Clinton perceived North American integration as a way for the United States to better compete with Asia and Europe. One American business association leader, not trained in eco-nomics, explained:

> The political impetus, the business impetus that gave birth to NAFTA was: How does American business deal with the competitive threat from Japan? . . . The possibility that Japan could use Mexico as a plat-form for selling to the U.S. market scared the bejesus out of a lot of big American companies. . . . So then Bush comes along and proposes this [NAFTA], and they go: "Well! If we had a free trade agreement, and if we had a good one—i.e., one that helped us screw the Japanese—that would be nice!"

None of this distinguishes between the interests of American employers and employees, per se, so this vision of NAFTA's usefulness could appeal as much to Clinton as to American businesspeople.

Much the same sort of case had motivated Canadian businesspeople and politicians to pursue bilateral free trade with the United States back in the 1980s. At that time, Canadian manufacturers began to believe that increasing international integration could *help* them compete; previously, integration had represented more of a threat than an opportunity. But by the 1980s advocates of free trade were manifesting a newfound confidence in Canadian firms' ability to compete internationally.[49] And not only could Canadian business compete successfully, but—this view held—it had no choice but to do so. A Canadian business association official explained this thinking:

[49] Doern and Tomlin 1991: 206.

We had to start rationalizing on at least a regional basis—and by regional, I mean North America—if we ever had a hope in hell of
competing globally.... By being able to rationalize on a North American
basis, you're able to compete globally. Particularly when other trading
blocks were going through similar internal adjustments and structural
changes.

Another Canadian business association official echoed that perspective:

We're not living in an isolated world. Our domestic market has become
everybody else's export market, and it has required our businesses and
our society in general to recognize that we need to be competitive with,
not just John down the street, but with Juan in Monterrey. Or with
Johan in Stockholm.

In their emphasis on international competition, these views diverge substantially from a neoclassical perspective. But in all three countries, as these quotes
show, free trade advocates routinely argued that increased national and regional
competitiveness, derived from an integrated North American market, would
make business more capable of competing against foreigners.[50] That would, they
said, significantly increase their sales in export markets (and protect their existing
shares of domestic markets). In the United States, as explained in Chapter 5, free
trade appealed to businesspeople largely as a means of locking in Mexico's recent
free market policy changes, while giving US firms access to lower-cost labor and
further opportunities for economies of scale. NAFTA would therefore help US
industries consolidate and compete better with other regions, in part by giving
US firms access to geographically proximate cheap labor.

For some firms, on the other hand, competitiveness was not just about exporting into foreign markets—but about staying alive at home. As one Mexican
business association leader explained, from his association's point of view,
"NAFTA's importance was helping us defend ourselves from products from
other continents."

Mercantilism in Trade Negotiations

We can also see how mercantilist perspectives shaped the free trade negotiations.
Describing the NAFTA negotiations as typical of trade negotiations in general,
one Canadian bureaucrat explained bluntly: "There's two sides to every tariff

---

[50] See Sousa 2002.

negotiation. You want to get your export interests *in*, and you want to keep the sensitive products *out*." These priorities reflect that, as noted by a Canadian business association staff person trained in economics, politicians tend to value exports but not imports:

> That's the way the dialogue unfolds, that's the way the politicians talk about it, and that's the way the people in the business community tend to approach it. I'm actually trained as an economist, so I look at it completely differently. The biggest benefit of trade is it allows you to get richer and you can import more.

A congressional staff person in Washington, DC, echoed this argued:

> Too many people in the administration and on the Hill [i.e., politicians and staff in Congress] view trade from a very mercantilist perspective. Exports are good, imports are a political problem. And that's the way they view trade. These agreements, trade is all about expanding markets for US exporters. It's not about helping US importers bring more goods into the US, to the benefit of US consumers.[51]

To reinforce that imports are not a priority, one US negotiator said, when asked about whether NAFTA was useful for reducing US tariffs: "Did we do that because we knew, once that happened, industry X would have to restructure and so on and so forth? No, that wasn't [our] focus." One Canadian interviewee said much the same: "I've never seen a country approach trade negotiations primarily from the point of view of 'How do we make life better for our importers?' as opposed to the exporters."

There is some ambiguity in how government officials think about the source of the mercantilist character of international trade negotiations. On the one hand, some suggested that many trade negotiators who are neoclassical in their worldviews are fully aware that in negotiating trade agreements they up playing a mercantilist game that makes little sense. On the other hand, when asked about the inconsistency between the practice of trade negotiations and what neoclassical economists think about it, one Canadian bureaucrat quipped: "You wouldn't let those guys do a trade negotiation!" And the same interviewee explained, about Canada's foreign ministry, "The people who work there are

---

[51] This was not just a reflection of the situation in recent times. The head of the Council of Economic Advisors in 1979, Charles Schultze, wrote a memo to Jimmy Carter arguing that "the most serious problem which crops up in our trade policy is the low weight often attached to consumer interests . . . as opposed to producer interests."

not economically trained." This was certainly the impression given by another Canadian bureaucrat, who blithely dismissed the importance of import liberalization to consumers: "You put a whole bunch of Canadians out of work, to lower costs to consumers generally. Then you have to look at a cost-benefit ratio. If Canadians are out of work, they can't buy anything."

Some officials who clearly did understand and subscribe to neoclassical trade theory found the mercantilist character of trade negotiations and many negotiators very frustrating—to the point that they conveyed almost physical disgust. One Mexican technocrat stated, bitterly: "I have a very high level of disregard for some [trade] negotiators. They really are destructive. . . . They are *tremendously* mercantilistic." Disputing the picture of the Mexicans as technocratic purists, he elaborated: "A lot of people, I'd say 99 percent, including in the government, they saw the negotiations with the Americans, with the United States and with Canada, as a zero-sum game. They'd say: 'Oh, we got 'em there!'"

Jobs, Jobs, Jobs: Promoting Free Trade to the Public

The public debates about free trade, in each country, were in large part claims and counterclaims regarding employment effects. Advocates often used arguments about jobs in responding to criticisms of the agreements from labor and civil society organizations. In Canada, for example, the corporate campaign association set up specifically to promote CUFTA called itself the Canadian Alliance for Trade and Job Opportunities. American politicians, likewise, promoted NAFTA largely as a job creator; Clinton's main message in promoting NAFTA "could be summed up in three words: 'jobs, jobs, jobs.'"[52] Even years earlier, in 1986, then vice president George Bush stated: "If there is one lesson we can draw from the history of virtually all nations, it is that tariffs produce only unemployment; and that the key to creating jobs is not to be afraid of trade, but to encourage it." While promoting NAFTA during the negotiations, several years later, Bush stuck to this theme, saying: "The argument that it takes American jobs away is just not true. Just in recent history, the exports to Mexico have dramatically gone up, and that's very, very good for American jobs."[53] That same year, campaigning against Bush, Democratic candidate Bill Clinton said much the same: "Changes in Mexico under President Salinas have . . . eliminated the trade deficit we once had with Mexico. . . . Thus, creating jobs here in America." Salinas himself argued for NAFTA as a means of "strengthening our economy, generating more jobs our country, and creating a market of such a size that it has the capacity and

[52] Hufbauer and Schott 2005: 8. See also MacArthur 2000: 277.
[53] Bush 1992.

possibility to compete with the large regional markets being established around the world today."[54]

Many opponents of free trade made a mirror-image argument, saying jobs would be destroyed because their country would import more than export.[55] It was a common assumption of most NAFTA supporters *and* opponents in the United States that the country's trade balance would affect employment, both sides making clearly mercantilist arguments.[56] As one career trade bureaucrat put it, when asked whether he agreed with the argument that NAFTA would have a significant effect on the number of jobs in the United States, "None of the staff here ever did. . . . Politicians decided they would sell it on a jobs basis. Staff tried to keep them as honest as possible."

So while economists did not believe that NAFTA would create jobs in the United States, the politicians did. The US trade representative stated before the House Ways and Means Committee on September 14, 1993, in a presentation entitled "The Administration's Case for NAFTA," that the "vast new market" created by the agreement will make "us more competitive against Europe and Japan and will result in the creation of new jobs. . . . Since we are producing more with fewer workers, opening up new markets is the key to new job creation and economic growth." Evidently, the US trade representative expected that congressional lawmakers would find arguments about net job creation compelling. And one interviewee agreed that, for members of Congress, "what resonated the most with them was if you could convince them that their constituents could benefit directly, in terms of jobs—if you could show that there could be job creation in their districts." This meant only that NAFTA was typical. Surveying the entire sweep of global trade liberalization since World War II, Ethier observes that "governments consistently attempt to 'sell' trade agreements to the public on the basis of the increased exports directly implied . . . (or the jobs devoted to producing those exports), while opponents point to the increased imports directly implied."[57]

The Contradictions between Elite and Folk Economics: Reasons and Consequences

Economists subscribing to neoclassical ideas sometimes felt uncomfortable with the contradictions between how they understood CUFTA and NAFTA

[54] Quoted in Martínez 1990.
[55] Faux and Lee 1993: 237.
[56] Burfisher, Robinson, and Thierfelder 2001: 126; Krugman 1998: 30.
[57] Ethier 2004: 306.

and what they heard about the agreements from other advocates—and even, in some cases, from themselves.[58] They themselves were aware of the contradictions between their views and those of other advocates, and we can consider their later reflections on those tensions. For example, notwithstanding its ubiquity in public discourse, the concept of national economic competitiveness clearly made economists uncomfortable. One of the Mexican technocrats explained apologetically that competitiveness

> was a technically and maybe analytically imprecise term that in the long term creates more confusion, but in the short term had some appeal and was understood in its essence by a lot of people. And that's why that term kept creeping in all the time. Now I'm sorry. As an academic I don't like it. But from a policy point of view, it was a minor price we had to pay.

Another elaborated:

> A country should become more productive in all its industries. Correct. But a country can't be competitive in everything. It's a misnomer. . . . The World Economic Forum, of Davos, speaks of competitiveness—says that a country should be more competitive. This is nonsense. They're using the wrong word. The correct thing would be to speak of productivity, and productivity relative to other countries, such that you're competitive in some industries and not in others. But a country can't be competitive in everything.

A Canadian interviewee agreed that the idea of national economic competitiveness "is nonsense. But it's a good slogan. But it's nonsense from an analytical, policy point of view." Another Canadian official simply described the concept of national economic competitiveness as "economic rubbish."

Trying to explain the popularity of the concept, a Mexican bureaucrat observed:

> Politically, the concept of "competitiveness" has a certain agility. . . . If you said, "We're going to do this to become more productive," that didn't motivate people. But to say, "This will make us more competitive

---

[58] Mexico's trade minister, for example, routinely gave speeches calling competitiveness NAFTA's "essential point" or "essential purpose" ("punto esencial") for Mexico (e.g., Serra Puche 1991).

and will help you defend yourself from competition," that clicked. It was more effective political marketing.

Interviewees agreed that the mercantilist worldview implied by the language of national economic competitiveness was ubiquitous in public and policy discussions about CUFTA and NAFTA. One Canadian interviewee confirmed that even economists who knew better made liberal use of mercantilist arguments in promoting free trade:

> The economics side of it is to go along with it because it meets our model that reduced government interference in business transactions, transactions between individual buyers and sellers, will improve economic performance. That's the business that we're in. So you use the arguments at hand. . . . You sell [trade liberalization] on mercantilist grounds.

Likewise, when asked why he and his colleagues promoted NAFTA in a mercantilist way, a Mexican official replied: "Which other way do you sell a free trade agreement?! It's very difficult to sell a free trade agreement on a theoretical basis because you need people to understand economic theory. So it's easy to sell it on 'We'll have access to the biggest market.' "[59]

Why are public debates about trade policy so mercantilist? Chapter 7 will show how domestic political incentives encourage states to take positions in international negotiations that suggest to observers there are clear international conflicts with respect to trade. But there are also three other reasons why mercantilism is so much more prevalent than neoclassical trade theory in public debate—and why even economists, who know it does not make sense, often find themselves speaking from a mercantilist perspective.

First, comparative advantage is simply very counterintuitive. That one's country might be made better off from exposing itself to *more* competition is not at all obvious. The benefits of trade liberalization are difficult to anticipate ahead of time, and the beneficiaries are not easily identifiable *ex ante*—even to themselves; those who will suffer from additional import competition, on the other hand, are often very aware. Kay therefore proposes that the failure to appreciate comparative advantage is in some part "the result of generalisation in which we mistakenly infer the properties of the whole from our limited experience of a smaller part."[60] People who see imports putting their friends and families

---

[59] Klamer and Meehan (1999) argue in a similar way that economics was "crowded out" in debates about NAFTA.

[60] Kay 2004: 106.

out of work locally do not recognize that a fall in the value of the currency will have impacts elsewhere in the economy. Nor do they recognize, as the neoclassical view holds, that restrictions on imports into a country are simultaneously restrictions on exports from that same country.[61] Mercantilism, by contrast, is very intuitive and resonates with people's lived experience.

Second, mercantilism is particularly resonant with the lived experience of businesspeople. As Krugman puts it, "International trade . . . is an area in which businesspeople seem particularly inclined to make false analogies between countries and corporations," while Kay notes that what he sometimes calls "DIY economics" seems particularly resonant with folk "businessmen's economics."[62] Ethier proposes that exporters only give states political credit for lowering trade barriers abroad, not at home.[63] (And import-competing industries object to the liberalization only of import barriers at home, not abroad.) Seeing countries like firms competing for market share, businesspeople can much more easily value exports over imports. Exports look like sales, and therefore means of making profits.[64] While they appreciate the efficiency emphasized by economists, for them efficiency is less of a goal in itself than a way of running a profitable firm. In some cases, imports give firms access to significantly better inputs, new technologies, and cheaper raw materials, and in that sense they may be desirable. But more often imports just mean increasing competition, and for firms that are less competitive than their foreign rivals that means the risk of being driven out of business.

Third, finally, mercantilism defines away conflicts of interest within countries, which is politically very helpful for advocates of free trade. It downplays that there are inevitably winners *and* losers—an awkward fact that advocates of free trade prefer not to emphasize. In the mercantilist view, there is no contradiction between the competitiveness of firms or industries within a single country; all producers can be beneficiaries of particular agreements, irrespective of sector, industry, or firm size. This perspective also downplays any kind of underlying conflict of interest between workers and employers; nations are taken as the primary units of analysis and communities of common interest. In the economist's view, on the other hand, there are inevitably contradictions—by the basic logic of comparative advantage—and workers and firms can have different interests.[65]

---

[61] See Krueger 1990.

[62] Krugman 1996: 40; Kay 2004.

[63] Ethier 2004.

[64] Kliesen (1995) remarks that "competitiveness enthusiasts believe that the United States competes with Japan or Germany in the same way that Ford competes with Chrysler or General Motors, with presidents and prime ministers playing the role of CEO and profits and losses being measured in terms of trade surpluses and deficits."

[65] Krugman 1996: 123.

In short, mercantilism's nationalist outlook stresses conflicts of interest between nations, while the neoclassical perspective is internationalist.[66]

Despite these differences, the people best positioned to call into question mercantilist ideas—neoclassical trade experts engaged in the policy process—do not do so. Even they promote trade liberalization using mercantilist arguments, finding it easier to appeal to businesspeople and politicians on those terms rather than trying to "teach" neoclassical theory and convince audiences of its veracity. And that is true even though mercantilist ideas are not the ones they themselves believe. As Krugman says, even "people who know that 'competitiveness' is a largely meaningless concept [are still] willing to indulge competitive rhetoric precisely because they believe they can harness it in the service of good policies."[67]

One Mexican negotiator explained, in describing his interactions with business:

> It was hard to say: "Okay guys, this is what's going to happen: A surge of imports is going to come! And then you're going to suffer, and just really—you're gonna really be in bad shape. Some of you are gonna die. Okay?! But others are gonna to start doing a transition, will start to modernize. And overall we're gonna start to export more. And we're just gonna be better—the surviving firms are gonna be stronger, and gonna be able to deal better with the world that's coming." How do you say that?! So you know what we did? "Exports are gonna grow." We never addressed the import issue. . . . The media would come and say: "No, no, no! Emphasize the positive, emphasize the positive!" Well, imports are not negative, I would tell them. Imports are part of—good imports are good! "No, no, no! Imports are bad, imports are bad! Never talk about imports!" It becomes mercantilist.

This approach helped economist advocates of NAFTA in Mexico dodge the awkward talking point that imports from free trade always put some producers under pressure or out of business. In Canada, the man who would become the country's chief negotiator for CUFTA (and who was trained in economics) acknowledged that for "some industries at least, the required changes will be of major proportions . . . on rare occasions a decent burial may be required."[68] His

---

[66] There is some debate among international economists about whether international trade agreements can be understood as the consequence of governments' reciprocal efforts to limit their influence over their terms of trade (e.g., Bagwell and Staiger 2002). But Ethier (2004) and Regan (2015) explain why this argument is not very convincing.

[67] Krugman 1997: 17.

[68] Reisman 1986: 39.

view was consistent with that of the influential 1975 report from the Economic Council of Canada (see Chapter 3), which had openly acknowledged that under free trade some industries would contract—some potentially to a substantial degree.[69]

Though advocates promoted free trade to the general public using mercantilist language, it is not clear that all aspects of that language were actually very appealing. Advocates referring to competitiveness when promoting free trade were probably not making a great choice in their communications; one Canadian survey found that businesspeople supported it as a policy goal significantly more than the general public.[70] As a concept, competitiveness is so elastic that it can serve the purposes of people pursuing many different kinds of agendas.[71] But by many definitions, it suggests to people that things they might otherwise value—good working conditions, high wages, environmental protections—are a burden. To take one example, a 1992 Canadian Manufacturers' Association "Competitiveness Index" listed unit labor costs as one of its key components— just as did one document from the Canadian Department of Finance entitled "Can Canada Compete?"[72] If good wages make a country uncompetitive, it is far from clear why workers should be happy about the need to compete—and much less why they should support their country exposing itself to yet more competition. When business advocates and their friends in government defended North American free trade by reference to its supposed benefits for their nation's competitiveness, then, they were evoking a reality that made more sense to them than to the median voter.

The double-edged character of the concepts of international competition and competitiveness is also clear from a minor scandal that erupted in the United States in late 1991. Vice President Dan Quayle was heading a White House Council on Competitiveness that, it emerged, was largely devoted to a deregulatory, business-driven agenda involving the weakening in particular of health, safety, and environmental programs.[73] The same kinds of people who were promoting NAFTA to American voters were also surreptitiously dismantling environmental protections on the grounds that international competition

---

[69] And with the benefit of hindsight, we now know there were indeed significant costs for some industries in Canada (Larue 2018).

[70] Mendelsohn and Wolfe 2001: 243.

[71] Sousa 2002.

[72] This document explained that progress "made in restraining unit labour costs suggests that Canada is well placed to continue benefiting from international trade" (Department of Finance 1986: 109).

[73] The purpose of the council was specifically to ensure that federal government agencies did not introduce new regulations that would "harm the competitiveness of American business," as a *New York Times* article explained (Hilts 1991: B1).

made them unaffordable. But when environmentalists raised objections to the pathology of doubling down on the kind of competition that was supposedly making deregulation necessary, neoclassical economists denied that the environment had anything to do with trade at all.[74] Whipsawed between business mercantilism and mainstream economics, many environmentalists—and most labor unions—simply gave up on the global economy, and on economists.

Businesspeople's folk mercantilism implied that labor and regulatory costs (including environmental protections or the taxes necessary to pay for encompassing social insurance) were a disadvantage for national economic competitiveness. Different politicians proposed different responses to this dilemma. For example, as Chapter 5 explained, Clinton demanded that NAFTA be supplemented with additional labor and environmental accords that, he argued, would prevent countries from competing by driving down standards in these areas. But while this stance demonstrated the greater value that he and the Democrats attached to labor standards and environmental protection (relative to Bush and the Republicans), Clinton's position implicitly reinforced the idea that countries can be more "competitive" by suppressing labor and regulatory costs. The Canadian government ultimately presented the side-agreements in a similar light, the Canadian trade minister saying in a news release about them that they would ensure "the three NAFTA partners will enforce their environmental and labour laws so that no country gains an unfair competitive advantage." Judging by this statement, high wages for workers (aka labor costs) would be a disadvantage under NAFTA. Given this implicit statement about how trade works, anyone concerned about the well-being of workers or the protection of the environment had little reason to see free trade as anything but a threat. Its opponents erred in taking arguments about competitiveness as mainstream, intellectually legitimate economics. It was not, even if it informed the creation of agreements that most mainstream economists endorsed.

Discussion and Conclusions

> Free trade, one of the greatest blessings which a government can confer
> on a people, is in almost every country unpopular.
> —Thomas Babington Macaulay, 1st Baron Macaulay (1824)

The differences between two books show how differently outside observers can see the role of economic thought: *Interpreting NAFTA*, by Mayer, and *The Making*

---

[74] Bhagwati and Srinivasan 1996; Krugman 1997.

of NAFTA, by Cameron and Tomlin.[75] These two books both present comprehensive studies of the construction—the conceptualization, proposal, negotiation, and ratification—of the North American Free Trade Agreement. Both
rely on numerous interviews with government officials and political staff, and
characterize the outlooks and thinking behind the choices these people made.
Remarkably, however, these books describe two different worlds. Examining
the NAFTA negotiations from the perspective of the international relations literature, which tends to emphasize international rivalry, Cameron and Tomlin
describe competitive struggles among the three countries' negotiators. Theirs
is not really either a liberal or a critical account, as I have labeled them in this
book. In their telling, each team of negotiators fought for the most favorable
outcome as defined by their country's domestic political process—preferences
that Cameron and Tomlin take largely as given, but which amount to as much
access as possible to foreign markets in return for the least possible domestic
liberalization. Mayer's take is different. He says the three countries' negotiators'
underlying goals were the liberalization of their own countries' restrictions on
imports, plus other domestic policy changes they would have liked to enact unilaterally anyway. From Mayer's neoclassical point of view, reducing one's own
trade barriers is not a "concession" that imposes costs on an importing country.[76]
Mayer therefore puzzles over why countries seem to struggle with each other
over policies they should enact in their own self-interest anyway. Cameron
and Tomlin describe the process they saw, while Mayer dwells on the process
he expected to see—starting from the assumption that policymakers are neoclassical thinkers. His expectations went unfulfilled, and despite presenting
a richly detailed (albeit rather Washington-centric) account of the story of
NAFTA, Mayer's account is simply inconsistent with how the vast majority of
policymakers really thought about the choices they made.

The liberal and critical globalization literatures have different takes on the
world, but implicitly one thing they agree on is the power of neoclassical economics in the political processes that have led to globalization. They suggest
economists wield a great deal of influence over public policy, and contributed
to the rise of globalization by disseminating neoclassical ideas and doctrines,
shaping the thinking of other people who played important roles in making
globalization happen—plus perhaps the general public. This chapter has shown
that such a view is unwarranted. Economists have never been very successful
in disseminating the substance of their ideas about international trade. Few
people understand, much less accept, the core of neoclassical trade theory. Most

---

[75] Mayer 1998; Cameron and Tomlin 2000.
[76] Consistent with the views of mainstream trade economists, like, for example, Bhagwati 2008.

noneconomist proponents of North American free trade subscribed to quite different ideas, even if their different worldview did not stop them supporting agreements that economists also endorsed.

Both the critical and (more implicitly) the liberal literatures have taken economists' ideas as more influential than they are. One reason for noneconomist social scientists' fascination with economists may be the tantalizing prospect that people much like themselves can exercise so much influence over policy. But they should be disappointed in practice by the more modest role that economists have actually played in fostering the rise of globalization in the last thirty years. The problem for economists is that their ideas about free trade are inconsistent with the understandings of political and economic elites. As Hirschman and Berman put it: "Every sociologist, anthropologist and political scientist knows that economics is the most politically influential social science. . . . Every economist, on the other hand, knows that such influence is extraordinarily limited."[77]

The divide between neoclassical and mercantilist thinkers can be understood in part as a struggle for authority in the field of economic expertise. In an important study of the political power of intellectual authority, Medvetz has shown how think tanks occupy a middle ground in the United States between academia and government (plus business and the media).[78] The substance of the ideas and policies that think tanks advocate reflects that position. In much the same way, government bureaucrats bridge the divide between the pure land of academic economics and the messier, more practical terrain of trade negotiations in the real world. Consider, for example, the case of Michael Hart. A Canadian civil servant centrally involved in the launching and negotiating of CUFTA, later in his career he became a foreign policy éminence grise, writing about trade issues from the vantage point of an academic post at Carleton University in Ottawa.[79] But despite holding forth on economic policy in an authoritative way, he was trained not as an economist but as a historian—and he never completed his PhD. In a book on Canadian foreign policy, he devalues economic purists in complaining that "academic discussion of foreign policy in Canada is more informed by theoretical considerations than by practical experience. . . . Most practitioners, on the other hand, if they ever knew theory, have learned to rely on experience and precedent."[80] As Medvetz explains, part of the battle in any field is a struggle over the definition of what the field is and what rules apply to it. It

---

[77] Hirschman and Berman 2014: 779–80.

[78] Medvetz 2012.

[79] The social science departments of universities in capital cities tend to operate more like think tanks than those of universities elsewhere. Staff rotate between them and government, for example, and tend to do more applied work.

[80] Hart 2008: x.

suits Hart for practical experience and knowledge to be given more weight as opposed to economic theory and the possession of formal academic credentials. In the acknowledgments of his book, Hart says specifically that his thinking reflects conversations over the years with a list of people including, among others, career corporate lobbyists. On the other hand, in an earlier work, he and his coauthors legitimate the free trade agreement they helped to write by saying that it was "based on one of the most established of economic concepts: that freer trade leads to prosperity while protection undermines it."[81] This chapter has shown that statement is not actually true: trade agreements have been based on a tortured folk view of trade rather than the transposition of mainstream economic theory—even if it can be helpful to advocates to blur the differences between them. Leveraging the authority of academic economics serves the advocates of free trade well, even if they disavow its technical foundations and full implications.

On the other side of the fence from pragmatists like Hart were many of the Mexican bureaucrats who negotiated NAFTA—holders of economics PhDs, not very old at the time of the NAFTA negotiations, and little experienced in the cut-and-thrust of international trade negotiations. One such bureaucrat, speaking about the practical world of trade negotiations, explained: "I'm more of a purist, if you ask me. I always thought we didn't do enough unilateral liberalization. . . . People like me don't survive in that world." In much the same way, Cameron and Tomlin quote a negotiator saying that Mexico "had people with PhDs from Stanford who knew the issues, but had little experience. Although one believes in free trade, [in a trade negotiation] one has to know the protectionist arguments. There were many economists on our team who could not give the protectionist arguments."[82]

Despite the marginalization of neoclassical trade theory in the practical world of trade policy and negotiations, however, there is still some reason to think that economists' support for North American free trade made a political difference. Recognized authorities on a topic can help to legitimate a political agenda and convince other people to support it, even when people have no knowledge or understanding of the technical ideas behind the advice. Economists can in other words play a role simply by virtue of possessing such authority and being recognized as the relevant experts in a policy area. Survey experiments show that simply knowing economists endorse trade openness makes others significantly more likely to support trade liberalization themselves.[83] It is no surprise, then, that US advocates of NAFTA deployed the legitimating firepower of

---

[81] Hart et al. 1994: 368.

[82] Cameron and Tomlin 2000: 123.

[83] Hiscox 2006; see also Mansfield, Mutz, and Silver 2015.

three hundred economists, including a dozen Nobel Prize winners. Likewise, in Canada, the Macdonald Commission benefited from the authority of the academic economists involved, even though many of its arguments were largely inconsistent with neoclassical ideas. One interviewee conveyed the impact of the Macdonald Commission, in paraphrasing Mulroney's response to it: "Here's the best brains in the country, having beavered away for three years about the future of the country, and this is what they say we ought to do. And you know what, I'm going to accept that. I'm politically going to initiate that process." It was easier for Mulroney to do what businesspeople were asking him to do given that credentialed, financially disinterested experts were telling him (and the country) to do the same thing.

Survey experiments also show, however, that it is not the case that economists help win public support for trade liberalization by disseminating their ideas. Core neoclassical arguments for free trade, appealing to people as consumers, simply do not work.[84] Telling survey respondents that freer trade benefits people as consumers actually lowers the probability of their supporting it.[85] So economists' endorsements of liberal economic policies shape people's views, but not the substance of their ideas. More broadly, surveys show that ordinary people simply do not understand many things economists consider basic facts, clinging instead to prejudices that are inconsistent with what makes sense to economists.[86]

---

[84] E.g., Vogel 1999.
[85] Hiscox 2006; Ardanaz et al. 2013.
[86] Caplan 2007.

7

Does Business Exist?

In all three countries, previous chapters have claimed that the business community endorsed and even campaigned for North American free trade. For critics of globalization, this will not be controversial. But from the perspective of the liberal literature, it is surprising that any country's business community could be united in support—and this requires an explanation.

The liberal literature starts from the premise that different firms and industries stand to lose or gain from trade liberalization, and so it should be next to impossible for them to develop a common agenda. In that sense, while businesses may exist, "business" should not. This chapter shows that business does exist—but also that the liberal literature is right to see the formation of a united private sector position on globalization as a challenge. One reason businesspeople can come together is that, as Chapter 6 showed, their folk mercantilist understanding of trade leads them to believe in common interests in a way the neoclassical perspective does not. Advocates can use a mercantilist worldview, and the language of international economic competition, to present free trade as being in the interest of all industries. This chapter shows, however, that it is not just mercantilist ideas that bring businesspeople together with respect to trade policy; it is also the very way that trade negotiations are organized. States can also structure consultations with the private sector in ways that empower business advocates of free trade at the expense of opponents.

These strategies won over potentially unhappy businesspeople in the CUFTA and NAFTA negotiations. As is typical in any trade negotiation, each country sought the most possible access to its export markets: fast, broad-based, and secure dismantling of foreign trade barriers. At the same time, the negotiators often sought to maintain barriers to imports into their home markets. For a small number of industries, that meant complete exclusion from the agreement. For others, it meant long transition periods—since trade barriers can be phased out at variable speeds, and a major focus in the negotiations was the timetable according to which each country's restrictions on imports of different goods and services would be eliminated. Given these possible treatments for different industries, when faced with a government committed to getting a free trade agreement, import-competing producers who might ideally prefer no agreement at all face a choice. They can stand outside the process and attempt to block an agreement entirely; if they do that, though, and an agreement materializes anyway, they lose the opportunity to shape its contents. Alternatively, they can participate, and get their concerns taken into account; but if they choose that strategy, they cannot campaign against the agreement as a whole. If the firms in a particular industry show there is nothing that can change their minds, then the negotiators have no reason to try to give them anything. Being "gettable" is what puts an industry in a strong position to shape the content of an agreement.[1] The opportunity to win better terms than what they might receive otherwise can therefore co-opt potentially hostile business representatives. Comparing an outcome *with* concessions to one *without*, it becomes an easy decision for an industry to participate; but that then means they get engrossed in a struggle for favorable terms rather than in resisting the whole agenda.[2] To avoid the threat of immediate and broad exposure to new foreign competition, protectionist industries mute their own opposition to free trade as a whole.

This chapter shows how the negotiations helped to homogenize business preferences with respect to CUFTA and NAFTA. It describes how opportunities to participate in shaping the negotiations over these agreements, and thereby securing concessions, helped suppress latent business opposition.[3] The organization of these negotiations also further demonstrates the political marginalization of neoclassical economics: there was little about the negotiations, other than the Mexican technocrats' approach to them, that reflected neoclassical thinking. First, though, the chapter begins with a comment about the issue of business unity generally.

The Problem of Hostile Brothers

The critical literature on globalization argues that business plays a central role in driving and promoting agreements like NAFTA.[4] For this perspective, then,

---

[1] This is also shown by the fact that US labor got slightly less favorable terms in the NAALC relative to what environmentalists got in the NAAEC (Evans and Kay 2008). Organized labor decided not to compromise, and it became clear to the Clinton administration that nothing could win them over. Environmental organizations, on the other hand, made a genuine offer to endorse NAFTA.

[2] Sufficiently favorable terms—including lengthy transition periods—may also mean that vulnerable firms can rethink their strategies and make themselves competitive by, for example, eliminating some product lines, building new alliances, or moving some operations abroad (see, e.g., Lusztig 1998).

[3] Some arguments are further elaborated in Fairbrother 2007.

[4] E.g., Bartley 2018; Van Apeldoorn 2000; Robinson 2014; Harvey 2005; Rupert 2000; Sklair 2001; Woll 2008.

it is axiomatic that business coheres with respect to trade liberalization, and most accounts suggest that is because business has much to gain from neoliberal policies, including those that foster globalization.[5] A minority of studies, taking a more sociological approach, also show how business unity rests on a foundation of social ties, by which networks of businesspeople become like-minded about the issue of free trade.[6]

In contrast to the critics, however, most of the liberal literature expects and emphasizes conflicts of interest among different firms and industries. From this perspective, there must always be some producers who are not competitive and will suffer from import competition—as according to the principle of comparative advantage (see Chapter 6). In any given country, the fact that *some* businesses—especially internationally integrated and competitive businesses—support trade liberalization is therefore unsurprising. But other firms should be unable to withstand the additional import competition unleashed by the integration of previously closed markets into international ones, and so are unlikely to be enthusiastic. In fact, it is specifically because it spurs the transfer of resources from some productive activities to others that neoclassical theory expects free trade to generate efficiency gains. The political corollary of this, though, is that the industries where a country has the most to gain economically are also those that are likeliest to oppose free trade.[7] Consistent with this view, some studies of NAFTA have identified differences of opinion and priority across different industries and sectors within each country.[8]

This disagreement in the literature about the stance of business vis-à-vis globalization reflects an even broader debate in the social sciences on the role of business in politics generally. Everything else being equal, investors, business owners, and top managers and executives should have more political influence when they work together than when they do not.[9] Much research has therefore sought to understand the degree to which businesspeople come together as a collective political actor and the conditions under which they are more likely to do so. Businesses are most likely to act collectively when confronted by broad-based efforts by the state to regulate or intervene in the market economy, or when facing positive opportunities to eliminate or scale back existing such interventions.[10] Higher corporate tax rates, labor laws more favorable to unions, or large increases in benefits to the unemployed constrain profit-making by a

---

[5] Harvey 2005; Levitt 2006; McBride 2001; Rupert 2000.

[6] Dreiling 2001; Dreiling and Darves 2011, 2016.

[7] See Rodrik 1994; Watson 1993.

[8] Chase 2003; Martínez and Schneider 2001; Maxfield and Shapiro 1998; Milner 1997.

[9] See, e.g., Mizruchi and Bey 2005; Murray 2017 for discussions.

[10] Smith 2000.

wide range of firms and industries, motivating them to join forces. In contrast, other policy and institutional changes have variable implications for different firms and industries, leading to more conflict than consensus within the private sector. As Vogel quotes one business executive saying: "We don't have a business community. Just a fragmented bunch of self-interested people. When a particular industry is in trouble . . . it fights alone and everyone else turns their back."[11]

From this liberal perspective, unity with respect to trade should be especially hard for business leaders to achieve. Many political economy studies draw on a model of the distributive consequences of trade that predicts significant divisions within business with respect to trade policy.[12] This model, "Ricardo-Viner," starts from the assumption that it costs businesspeople money to transfer assets from one industry or economic activity to another, but that trade liberalization will force some of them—those that cannot compete with cheaper imports—to do so. Workers, similarly, pay a price for having to find new jobs. As a result, import-competing industries—firms and workers—who are vulnerable to new trade competition will oppose liberalization, while export-oriented industries competitive on world markets will support it. Alternatively, models emphasizing increasing returns to scale (IRS) also predict conflict among firms with respect to trade policy. The IRS approach argues that, for many industries, productive efficiency increases significantly with the scope of production, and therefore that smaller producers should not have the same capacity as larger ones to take advantage of the enlarged markets created by trade integration. Again, there are good reasons to expect business to be internally divided.[13]

Even if globalization critics are comfortable speaking of business as a unified actor, with substantial power over public policy, critical social science has classically recognized that the convergence of capitalist firms behind common political projects is not always such a given. Capitalist enterprises are competitors, or, as Karl Marx himself put it, "hostile brothers," whose fortunes do not necessarily rise and fall together. Profitability for one can mean bankruptcy for another. And public policies favoring one industry may be a burden for the rest. Even for much critical social science, then, business unity is fragile and conditional.[14] In North America, as previous chapters have shown, evidence of business hostility to free trade at least at some moments in history shows that business support should not be taken for granted.

---

[11] Vogel 1983: 34.
[12] Hiscox 2001.
[13] Chase 2003; Shadlen 2000; Thacker 2000.
[14] Block 2001.

The potential for business opposition to free markets is also acknowledged in one of the books most frequently invoked in literature on globalization, including from a critical perspective: Karl Polanyi's 1944 book *The Great Transformation*.[15] Polanyi famously proposed a theory of a "double movement"—of market liberalization, on the one hand, and efforts by society to protect itself from the deleterious effects of that liberalization, on the other. Some interpret Polanyi's double movement as a kind of class conflict, with capitalists supporting free markets and subordinate classes of workers and farmers demanding social protections that constrain markets. For example, Polanyi wrote that "industrialists, entrepreneurs, and capitalists" worked to expand the market, while "the traditional landed classes and the nascent working class" sought to defend "the social fabric" against the expansion of the market. But *The Great Transformation*, in several places, also presented business as part of the "society" that actively resists free markets. Social disruption spares no one: "Not human beings and natural resources only but also the organization of capitalistic production itself had to be sheltered from the devastating effects of a self-regulating market." Polanyi therefore says that business stood to gain from certain social protections, including trade protectionism: "Customs tariffs . . . implied profits for capitalists and . . . meant, ultimately, security against unemployment, stabilization of regional conditions, assurance against liquidation of industries." Likewise, "Manufacturers . . . wished to increase their incomes through protectionist action."[16]

So while it is the liberal literature that highlights business disunity, even the critical literature admits the possibility of conflicts about globalization among different firms and industries. Contrary to the expectations of liberals, business can unify in support of globalization. But nor, contrary to the critics, is such unity a given. How then is it possible?

The Organization of the Consultations

Trade negotiations involve huge amounts of private sector consultation. Industry representatives meet regularly with the bureaucrats negotiating over the tariffs and other trade measures that affect them. These meetings give industry people information about what is happening, while allowing them to provide input and therefore shape the process and its outcomes. From the beginning through to the end, they can tell the negotiators what they think their country's position

---

[15] E.g. Dreiling 2001; Harvey 2005; Kuttner 2017; Munck 2002; Adelman 2017.

[16] These quotations from Polanyi 1944 are from pages 155, 132, 154, and 153, respectively.

should be, on any number of issues. The negotiators, in turn, have to weigh these demands against what they hear from their foreign counterparts, whose positions reflect what their own domestic industries and other constituencies are telling them. Trade negotiations are therefore a classic "two-level game."[17]

In the NAFTA negotiations, the organization of these consultations varied somewhat across the three countries. The Mexican officials—despite being the most neoclassical—worked hardest to satisfy their domestic industries. They had to, because Mexican business was initially the most skeptical, as Chapter 4 explained. But while the organization and intensity of the consultations varied somewhat across the three countries, ultimately the negotiators' relationships with their respective private sectors were not that different.

The United States has a formal private sector advisory system comprising dozens of committees and hundreds of advisers. There are three tiers: first, the Advisory Committee for Trade Policy and Negotiations (ACTPN), with forty-five members appointed for two-year terms by the president; second, a small number of trade policy advisory committees on general topics (defense, labor, agriculture, etc.); and third, twenty-six technical, sectoral, and functional advisory committees.[18] These advisers, who are mostly though not exclusively businesspeople, provide input to the executive and legislative branches in the form of testimony at public hearings, written submissions, and private conversations. Industries influence trade negotiations not only directly through their consultations with the officials doing the negotiating, but also indirectly, via Congress. As one interviewee put it, paraphrasing an industry's message to a trade negotiator: "If you want to do what we want—and if you do what we want, we will support it in the Congress—then here is some language for you to use in the agreement." Demonstrating the scope of the private sector input for NAFTA specifically, the chair of the ACTPN testified in September 1992 that the US trade representative and her staff had met with private sector representatives almost a thousand times over the course of the NAFTA negotiations, and that businesspeople "had regular, detailed, substantive input into the process."[19]

Canada uses a similar advisory structure, which includes a top-level committee—called the International Trade Advisory Committee—as well as fifteen sectoral advisory groups on international trade (SAGITs). The SAGITs provided input on more industry-specific issues, like how quickly to reduce different tariffs to zero.[20] As in the United States, trade policy comes predominantly from the bureaucracy, and it is career bureaucrats who solicit business

---

[17] Putnam 1988; Grossman and Helpman 1995.
[18] Huenemann 2002.
[19] Quoted in Dreiling and Darves 2011: 1554.
[20] Dymond and Dawson 2002: 26.

views; the Canadian parliament is less involved than the US Congress.[21] For the CUFTA negotiations, the Canadian government also established a special Trade Negotiations Office reporting directly to the prime minister and his chief of staff.[22] Participating in the advisory structure is regarded as potentially compromising, as shown by the fact that the Canadian Labour Congress flatly refused to participate in the CUFTA hearings.[23]

Mexico created its first formal private sector trade advisory structure specifically for the NAFTA negotiations, the state inviting business leaders to establish something similar to the extant US and Canadian systems.[24] Mexico's system ended up differing, however, in some important respects, and that reflected the exceptional efforts the state had to make to confront potential business opponents. One Mexican negotiator explained that "we had to do [the NAFTA] negotiation with a very protectionist private sector," and that in his view "the internal negotiation was much more difficult than the external one." Another negotiator agreed that, with respect to Mexican business, "there was a very strong opposition. Because of that, we had to work really, really hard at the consultations . . . to convince sectors of the benefits." Another negotiator explained: "We had to be here pushing the private sector, to want more opening." To address the challenge of keeping domestic business supportive, the state made a remarkable commitment, in the words of one negotiator, to "put on the negotiating table the position of the private sector." That is, the state promised not to negotiate anything without first consulting with the industry representatives and considering their views.[25] Their invitation to advise the negotiators was a calculated one. As one of the Mexican technocrats explained: "In the act of consulting, you legitimated the process. . . . It had that double function. . . . The political decision had been made. And [we were looking for] elements to accommodate sectoral interests." Mexican business representatives held meetings and worked exceptionally closely with the government throughout the bargaining process, and ultimately the private sector was pleased by the public negotiators' level of consideration and attentiveness.[26] The negotiations would meet with

---

[21] In previous times, when Canadian business was less positive about free trade, this fact was not always appreciated—presumably because bureaucrats were more consistently committed to free trade than elected politicians. The Canadian Textiles Institute complained in its submission to the Macdonald Commission that "elected representatives have often exhibited a better understanding of the industry and its importance to Canada than civil servants." The Shoe Manufacturers' Association of Canada (1983) agreed that "bureaucrats make most of the decisions affecting an industry such as ours . . . in our view, Canada has drifted a long way from representative government."

[22] Winham 1994: 499.

[23] Doern and Tomlin 1991: 110.

[24] Gallardo 1994.

[25] Alba Vega and Vega Canovas 2002.

[26] Thacker 2000; Schneider 1997.

industry representatives before and after every bargaining session. Private sector representatives even traveled with the Mexican officials to negotiating sessions outside of Mexico and would meet with them in a hotel room near where the negotiations took place, to stay in the closest and most frequent contact possible. This came to be called, semi-ironically, the *cuarto del lado*, or "room next door." The collaboration between the government negotiators and the industry representatives was so tight that Ostry calls the Mexican approach to consultations "the virtual union of government and business in formulating and negotiating trade policy."[27]

When the Mexican government wanted to reach out and invite Mexican business to participate in the country's first private sector trade advisory structure, it was the Consejo Coordinator Empresarial (CCE) that it approached. The CCE, which had in recent years come to be seen as the most encompassing of Mexico's many business associations, in turn created the Coordinadora de Organismos Empresariales de Comercio Exterior (COECE, or Business Coordinating Council for Foreign Trade). Given its origins, COECE's highest authority was the CCE board of directors, constituted by the presidents of the CCE's seven voting members.[28] This is notable given that the CCE's seven member organizations disproportionately represented large, internationally oriented, and financial capital. By extension, COECE too was dominated by large capital; its formal decision-making structure reflected that of its parent organization, the peak business confederation CCE. COECE also over-represented large, internationally oriented business, because to participate in COECE, firms had to fund their own representatives.[29] Smaller business—with fewer resources per firm—could not take part and represent themselves nearly as well as large corporations. While the Canadian and US advisory bodies are government appointed, in the Mexican case, different industries selected representatives of their own choosing.[30] But that largely meant that big-business advocates of free trade got disproportionate influence relative to smaller firms.

While giving industry representatives abundant opportunities to influence the negotiations, COECE also cleverly restricted private sector influence. The Mexican negotiators and COECE agreed not to leak information about the bargaining process, such that for industries to know what was happening they had no alternative but to participate in COECE.[31] COECE also undertook studies that served the government in formulating bargaining positions for each

[27] Ostry 2002: iii.
[28] Puga 1994: 177.
[29] Alba Vega 1997; Johnson Ceva 1998; Thacker 1999; Puga 1994.
[30] Alba Vega and Vega Canovas 2002.
[31] Alba Vega and Vega Canovas 2002; Schneider 2002: 102.

industry, but kept them closely guarded—only a privileged few therefore knew what the likely effects of NAFTA would be.[32]

The Negotiation of Concessions

Trade negotiators know that the more concessions they can extract from their foreign counterparts, the more supportive domestic industries will be. Even negotiators who are neoclassical in their thinking—and believe in the economic benefits of opening up to imports even on a unilateral basis—tend to prioritize the satisfaction of domestic industries; the political benefits of doing so are just too great. As a consequence, trade negotiations become mercantilist, as each country's negotiators resist the others' demands for market access. As one Canadian bureaucrat explained:

> At the end of the day you have to come home and sell the deal you've signed to the public. . . . And if you've sold, supposedly sold, an industry down the drain and that's a strong enough industry, maybe this deal's not going to hold together. So . . . if you have an industry that is at this point in time protected by a tariff, a high tariff, then you hold the line for that industry. You don't play economics at that point.

But the knowledge that the national negotiators *could* "play economics" provides a strong incentive for industry representatives to meet them halfway. In the NAFTA negotiations, hostile industries often started by asking to be excluded from the agreement. The negotiators told them that was impossible. But to get industries not to lobby against the agreement, they provided them with measures that won them over—most notably, long tariff phase-out schedules, as industries liked having as long as possible to prepare for exposure to new foreign competition, rather than right away. One Mexican market access negotiator explained that "the general position of, say, 90 percent of industry was cut the tariffs on my inputs quickly, have the United States and Canada cut their tariffs quickly so I can export, and for imports into Mexico, the longest period possible." An American negotiator elaborated: "We said every commodity is included. So we will negotiate over how long you have to adjust. But at the end of the day there's going to be duty-free trade in X. No quotas, no licensing

---

[32] Pastor and Wise 1994: 480. After the negotiations were complete COECE continued to support the government, by campaigning to promote NAFTA, including inside the business community (Alba Vega and Vega Canovas 2002). COECE also helped organize lobbying in Washington, DC, as Chapter 5 described.

requirements, nothing." And another US negotiator described this whole process in generic form, as a composite conversation he would have with skeptical
private sector representatives:

> You started out with sectors who said: "We're not going to be part of the
> agreement overall. That's our position. We want out." [That shifted over
> time] to "Okay, well, we don't understand why we can't be excluded."
>
> [Negotiator:] "Well, that's the decision, that you're not going to be
> excluded."
>
> [Industry representative:] "We'll oppose this agreement if we're not
> [excluded]."
>
> [Negotiator:] "That's your right." At the end of the day, we got it to
> the point where they would say: "Okay, we may not be happy that the
> United States is negotiating this, but basically we think that, within the
> confines of the negotiation, you have done as well or better than we
> thought we might get in terms of the overall treatment. You worked
> hard with us, and so we're not going to actively lobby against this agree-
> ment." Which, frankly, is important when it comes for passage in the
> Congress.

As this quotation conveys, there were industries that might have rebelled
against the idea of free trade but did not. Some threatened to lobby against
NAFTA in Congress, where the initiative was vulnerable. That they did not do
so, in the end, was due to the negotiators' success in winning them over using
concessionary content in the terms of the agreement.

The next part of this chapter uses a series of industry case studies from the
NAFTA negotiations to show how concessions can win the acquiescence of potentially dissident—if not borderline hostile—business groups. The situations
of these industries—financial services, agriculture, autos, and apparel and
textiles—were all unique in some ways. But each case shows how selective
restrictions on trade helped reduce private sector opposition to free trade in a
politically significant way. These industries are diverse (spanning the primary,
secondary, and tertiary sectors), and in different cases different countries were
asking for protectionist content. These were all industries making demands for
illiberal content in NAFTA, but that is the point: these were all industries that,
in different ways, might have lobbied against free trade, consistent with liberal
political economy theory.[33]

---

[33] In the United States, footwear, glassware, and ceramic tile producers were also industries that
interviewees said threatened to lobby against NAFTA, but ultimately did not (or at least not nearly as
strongly as they originally implied they might).

Mexican Financial Services

It is a truism that developing countries have little capital relative to labor. Consequently, at the start of the NAFTA negotiations, it was clear that the United States would want access to Mexico's banking and financial services sector. US banks would be well able to move in and compete in the Mexican market. Mexico's existing banks, on the other hand, were already in a weak position. As described in Chapter 2, they had been nationalized in 1982 in the context of the country's debt crisis that year. In the spring of 1990, around the same time that Mexico and the United States were initiating talks about NAFTA, the Mexican state announced that it was planning to reprivatize the banks. In 1991 and 1992, as the NAFTA negotiations unfolded, the banks were sold off—though, at that time, only to Mexican buyers and not to foreigners. As this unfolded, the Mexican government had to decide what stance to take in the NAFTA financial services negotiations. Would the government allow foreign banks to set up operations in Mexico? Would foreigners be allowed to purchase existing Mexican banks? And, in general, how fast would Mexico's newly privatized banks be exposed to foreign competition?

There were Mexican officials who believed that more competition in banking would provide other Mexican firms, and consumers, with better financial services, particularly access to more credit at lower interest rates. From this perspective, it would be in Mexico's interest to negotiate a faster opening, with less protection for the domestic industry. This was the view of the SECOFI (Secretaría de Comercio y Fomento Industrial, or Ministry of Trade and Industry), the ministry that was leading the NAFTA negotiations for Mexico. SECOFI was strongly technocratic in character, and had little contact with the banks. On the other hand, SECOFI was not responsible for regulating (and supporting) the country's banks: that was the responsibility of the Finance Ministry (Secretaría de Hacienda y Crédito Público). And the Finance Ministry staff took a very different view. Officials in that agency were strongly committed to maintaining Mexican ownership of the country's banking sector and preferred to demand protections for the sector in the NAFTA negotiations. From their point of view, as one interviewee put it, "It was better to have Mexicans running the Mexican banks and owning the Mexican banks." When asked why, he replied coyly, "It was what I would call the sense of the industry."

The Mexican negotiating position, reflecting a victory for the Finance Ministry (which was given responsibility for the financial services negotiations), became to restrain access to the Mexican banking market. As one Mexican negotiator put it, then, "This negotiation was going to have a defensive character. It was not a negotiation where our interest was access to other markets." In other words, the Mexican negotiators were going to have to push back against their American counterparts' demands for fast, broad access to the Mexican market. The end result of the negotiation was that Mexico committed to allowing foreign participation in its banking sector under NAFTA, but only subject to a number of strict limits and after a transition period during which foreign participation would be very limited.[34] These permanent restrictions and the gradual opening of the Mexican banking sector represented a compromise between US pressures for opening and Mexican efforts to shield domestic firms. Because the Finance Ministry adopted this position on behalf of the banks, the latter raised no strong objections to NAFTA. Some commentators suggested that the state's efforts to restrain foreign competition in the Mexican financial services market were the quid pro quo for receiving rather high prices when selling off the banks—that the state had promised the purchasers a lucrative protected market for years to come.[35] Finance but not SECOFI officials also possessed inside information to the effect that the banks were worth substantially less than they appeared, because of weak regulation of the sector, and because the banks were holding a lot of bad loans. When the banks were sold off, this information was not revealed publicly. At that time, one SECOFI negotiator therefore explained, he "didn't know the size of the mess."

In sum, when negotiating NAFTA's financial services chapter with their foreign counterparts, Finance officials largely expressed the position of Mexico's banks. Their proximity to the industry they were regulating shaped their thinking, and gave the private sector added influence. Where SECOFI would have taken a harder line with the bankers, the Finance Ministry bureaucrats grew sympathetic, and allowed the purchasers of the banks to continue enjoying a more protected market. The banks' new private owners convinced the public sector officials regulating them to delay their exposure to added foreign competition.[36] Given the delayed opening, the otherwise vulnerable Mexican banks acquiesced to NAFTA.[37]

---

[34] Hufbauer and Schott 1993.

[35] Johnson Ceva 1998: 132.

[36] Teichman 2001: 158.

[37] Despite Mexico's protection of its banking sector, in the end Mexico did in fact unilaterally open the sector to more foreign participation—subsequent to the 1994–95 peso crisis. In hindsight, some of the Mexican officials who supported the restrictions in NAFTA said they had made a mistake. They did correctly anticipate, however, the results of such an opening: after the mid-1990s opening, domestic ownership of Mexico's banks plummeted.

Agriculture

There were agricultural producers in all three countries who worried that an unfavorable outcome in the negotiations could be very damaging for them. The issues, and the types of producers vulnerable to freer trade, differed across the three countries.

Canada has long applied an unusual arrangement to its dairy, egg, and poultry producers—a "supply management" system that allocated production quotas to farmers, in principle with the end of maintaining stable prices for both them and consumers. Under this system, producers receive prices for their goods well in excess of what they would command on world markets, and so the system amounts to a form of protection from international competition. US negotiators tried to unpick the system in the CUFTA negotiations, but the Canadian negotiators—knowing that farmers were powerfully organized around the issue—rebuffed those attempts. The Americans came away with little other than some reductions in Canadian agricultural tariffs. In the NAFTA negotiations, US negotiators tried again—one negotiator said they "beat and beat and beat" on Canada over supply management—but again ended up empty-handed. US-Canada agricultural trade remained subject to the provisions negotiated under CUFTA. In the end, then, Canadian negotiators simply avoided a confrontation with producers operating under the supply management system, by excluding them completely. Canadian agricultural groups were not very happy even about the tariff reductions. But the Canadian Egg Producers Council, for example, stated in 1987: "We are very appreciative, and I cannot stress this enough, that supply management has been maintained."

Mexico obtained very long transition periods for producers of corn and beans—the country's key subsistence crops, grown by millions of very poor and often indigenous peasants on small plots of marginal land. US producers had better land for growing these crops, better and more machinery, and large government subsidies—making them much more competitive than the small producers in Mexico. Being very numerous, however, producers of corn and beans were a potentially politically explosive force, and Mexican officials were somewhat divided on this issue, with some preferring no opening at all. In the end, Mexico's trade barriers against imports of these products were phased out over fifteen years—the longest possible transition period under NAFTA.

The leverage of the agricultural sector was clearest of all, however, in the case of the United States. NAFTA presented a threat to a number of agricultural groups in the United States—particularly those in climatic regions similar to Mexico. These groups, producing things like sugar, orange juice, peanuts, avocadoes, and many fruits and vegetables, made their objections known about NAFTA right away. The Florida citrus industry, for example, convinced several

Florida counties to pass resolutions calling for the exclusion of citrus fruits from NAFTA. These resolutions were then brought to the attention of the Bush administration by representatives of county commissioners and via local members of Congress.

Nevertheless, the agreement as negotiated in 1992 did not restrict access for these products sufficiently to appease the producers. When the NAFTA negotiations were concluded, some producer groups remained angry. Setting out a series of demands, the Florida Fruit and Vegetable Association (FFVA) for example warned it would fight: "NAFTA, as currently written, fails to satisfy [us]. The agreement must be amended to include the following provisions, or FFVA must oppose its ratification by the United States Congress."[38] In the fall of 1993, with the ratification vote on NAFTA getting closer, the Clinton administration realized that the Florida citrus industry might persuade several congressional representatives to vote against the agreement—potentially endangering the political viability of NAFTA as a whole.

Clinton warned Salinas that without some last-minute changes to the agreement in this area, NAFTA might not pass in Congress. While the Mexicans were unhappy, they knew Clinton was right. In hopes of mollifying the opposition, then, US and Mexican negotiators worked out an agreement whereby if citrus or tomato imports began to hurt American producers, tariffs would be automatically reimposed. The US trade representative explained that the Mexicans "agreed with us to put price-based safeguard mechanisms in NAFTA . . . to ensure there is no disruption of those industries in the United States."[39] At the same time, separately, the Clinton administration promised the citrus producers that it would protect citrus products in the Uruguay Round of GATT negotiation, and not give foreign citrus producers additional access under either the Generalized System of Preferences or Caribbean Basin Initiative. Given all these concessions, the FFVA withdrew its opposition to NAFTA in November 1993, just before the ratification vote in Congress.[40]

Much the same happened with sugar. In the fall of 1993, the US sugar industry pledged to campaign against NAFTA if its demands were not met.[41] The United States was protecting its sugar industry by maintaining the price of sugar in the domestic market well above the world price. In the NAFTA negotiations, Bush administration officials would have liked to see that protection eliminated, but unsurprisingly the sugar industry was opposed, and its geographical concentration gave it a lot of influence over the votes of members

---

[38] Florida Fruit and Vegetable Association 1992: 6.
[39] Quoted in Ross 1993.
[40] Orden 1996.
[41] Orden 1996: 368.

of Congress from Florida, Louisiana, Minnesota, Colorado, and California. As one US negotiator put it, "The sugar industry potentially had enough votes to kill the NAFTA." US negotiators therefore had to find some way of appeasing the industry. Fortunately for them, Mexico was not a competitive sugar producer, so US sugar-*using* industries were not demanding access to Mexican sugar. Officials eventually resolved the conflict by devising a formula according to which Mexico could only export its surplus sugar (sugar produced beyond that consumed in the country). Given that Mexico was a net importer anyway, this proposal did not seem threatening to US producers: Mexico would not export any more sugar than it already was, and that was not much at all. Just in case, though, the last-minute agreement on sugar even included a restriction preventing the importation of sugar in case food manufacturers in Mexico began substituting high-fructose corn syrup, thereby liberating surplus sugar for export.[42] In effect, Mexico agreed never to export sugar to the United States.

Because of these groups' intransigence, they ultimately managed to obtain a variety of special concessions.[43] Some members of Congress were willing to base their entire votes on how NAFTA would affect major agricultural producers in their districts, so US officials had to seek extra protections for them from potential Mexican competitors. The US negotiators themselves did not necessarily believe that extracting these concessions was even in the US national interest, but they believed that doing so was necessary to make the agreement politically feasible. The political costs of confronting protection of these producers would be too high. Indefinite import restrictions, along with transition periods, won the consent of potential opponents.[44]

Autos

Antiliberal producers could also be found among large, internationally integrated firms. The case of autos demonstrates the importance of trade-restrictive concessions even for a major manufacturing industry that was already highly integrated across the three nations of North America.[45] In this case, the industry's

---

[42] Ross 1993.

[43] Some agricultural sectors were more supportive of NAFTA, including producers of grains, oilseeds, and livestock, as well as processing and supply industries (Orden 1996).

[44] Orden (1996: 378) also identifies dairy and cotton as US agricultural producers who only endorsed NAFTA once determining it would include favorable (for them) rules of origin, in the sense that users of their products would not be able to choose competing inputs from outside of North America.

[45] This subsection draws heavily on Mayer (1998) and Thacker (2000).

concerns were more with competition from outside rather than within the region.

The CUFTA negotiations established free trade in automobiles, including the rule that for a vehicle to count as North American—and therefore to be free of import duties—it had to contain at least 50 percent value added from within North America. This "rule of origin" was not especially contentious in the CUFTA negotiations, especially given that the 1965 Auto Pact had already fostered binational rationalization of the industry. But events after the implementation of CUFTA led the governments of the United States and Canada to better appreciate the importance of clearly defining regional and nonregional products. In 1991, after an investigation, the US Customs Service ruled that some Honda cars assembled in Canada and exported to the United States had, contrary to Honda's assertions, not met CUFTA's threshold for being defined as North American. This meant they were not entitled to duty-free access to the American market. Canada disputed the US decision, and the conflict led the NAFTA negotiators to try to make the new agreement's rules clearer and less ambiguous.

For background, rules of origin are the criteria according to which a good is judged to be "originating" (i.e., produced within a free trade zone) or "nonoriginating." Originating goods are free-tradable within the free trade zone—that is, they benefit from preferential treatment vis-à-vis goods produced outside the zone. "Loose" rules of origin allow goods to benefit from an agreement despite containing substantial nonregional value-added, while "tighter" rules establish a lower limit on this share of the good's total value. Rules of origin are often specified as the minimum share of a good's total value that must have been added within a free trade zone in order for it to be considered originating. Without rules of origin, goods produced outside the region might be imported into one country and then shipped tariff-free to another, thereby circumventing the latter's tariffs and other barriers to imports on goods originating outside the free trade zone. Strict rules of origin discourage the importation of component parts or raw materials from outside of a free trade area, thereby helping to protect regional producers of these inputs and materials.

In all three countries, the auto industry was dominated by the American "Big Three" manufacturers: GM, Ford, and Chrysler. Though based in the United States, the Big Three all had plants in Mexico and Canada and did substantial intraregional trade. (Autos and auto parts trade represented a large share of all intraregional trade.) The US autos negotiators wanted little except to satisfy the Big Three, while the preferences of the Big Three were slightly less important for the Canadian and Mexican negotiators, because other auto producers—from Asia and Europe—represented larger shares of the motor vehicle industries in those countries. That is, firms such as Volkswagen, Toyota, Nissan, and Honda held preferences that differed from those of the Big Three and so the Canadian and Mexican objectives differed somewhat from those of the United States. In the NAFTA negotiations, the Big Three recommended a rule of origin stricter than the one negotiated for CUFTA—62.5 percent North American value added. They made clear the source of this request:

> The Mexican government has indicated that its major interest in the NAFTA automotive negotiations is to encourage investment and production in its domestic motor vehicle manufacturing and parts industry. It is critical that the United States government immediately make clear to Mexico that a NAFTA agreement cannot allow Mexico to establish itself as a platform for major new automotive capacity from third country producers for export to the U.S. market.[46]

The strict rule of origin would therefore protect the Big Three from foreign competition: just the opposite of what economists want free trade to do.[47] The Big Three's broader aim was to use NAFTA to further integrate production on a continental basis, while relying on the strict rule of origin to protect them against non–North American competitors, who would be more reliant on nonregional inputs and components. The Big Three would have the easiest time satisfying a strict rule of origin, because they were already using the most North American parts.

The US negotiators adopted the Big Three position as their own and advocated the new, strict rule.[48] The Mexican negotiators, being free traders, were more sympathetic in principle to the arguments for a looser rule (such as Nissan's and VW's preference for a 50 percent rule). Moreover, a loose rule might encourage investment in vehicle assembly by allowing manufacturers to use more inputs imported from outside North America. But the Mexicans were also interested in attracting more investment to the auto sector in Mexico, and they believed that a strict rule would encourage foreign firms to manufacture more parts in Mexico to serve the US market. Given this mix of concerns, Mexico's position on the rules of origin fell in between those of the United States and Canada, and the conflict was primarily between the two latter countries. In the end, they settled on a 62.5 percent rule—substantially stricter than what they had agreed on under CUFTA.

---

[46] Chrysler Ford General Motors 1991.

[47] E.g., Krueger 1995: 95.

[48] Like the Big Three, manufacturers of auto parts in all three countries wanted a strict rule (a high percentage).

Another way in which the auto industry sought antiliberal content was with respect to the phaseout of Mexico's "Auto Decrees" (see Chapter 2)—performance requirements with respect to domestic content and trade balancing. Under the decrees, in order to import, an auto company had to export and had to meet a minimum domestic content requirement. The Auto Decrees were therefore designed to encourage investment in Mexico—firms had to produce in Mexico in order to sell in Mexico. The United States wanted the performance requirements eliminated quickly, but not in every way, as the Big Three wanted the Mexican vehicle market opened for themselves, but not other producers. The US-based firms had made costly investments in Mexico in order to meet the requirements of the Auto Decrees, and they did not want new—that is, nonregional—firms to be able to come in to Mexico, build new plants, and not have to meet the old performance requirements, thereby gaining an advantage over firms that had already invested there. Consequently, the United States demanded protections against new plants rushing in to Mexico before existing ones had time to recoup their costs under the old auto rules, though also a fast elimination of the requirement for existing producers to buy Mexican parts.

The Mexican negotiators conceded on this. They were worried that the end of the decrees—and their trade-balancing and domestic content requirements—would mean the departure of some producers from Mexico, and thought that the Big Three might abandon some older plants if foreign firms were allowed to export there immediately, without restriction.[49] Their departure would also harm their local suppliers: Mexican parts producers. While the Mexican officials did agree to the elimination of the trade-balancing and domestic content requirements, then, they only agreed to phase out those measures over time. The Big Three and US negotiators, though, wanted other countries' producers to have to meet the old performance requirements during that transition period. The transition periods—including the continued requirement for US firms to do some sourcing in Mexico—would also give parts manufacturers time to adjust to new competition.

Given the size of the Big Three, their adamant demands for strict rules of origin show that even large, internationally integrated firms prefer some kinds of protection, rather than the free markets favored in economic theory.[50]

---

[49] CUFTA did much the same thing for Canada's auto production as NAFTA did for Mexico's. In the Canadian case, auto production had been governed by the 1965 bilateral Auto Pact—which provided for duty-free two-way trade, but also allowed Canada to maintain trade-balancing requirements, meaning firms had to produce a certain amount in Canada. CUFTA eliminated that arrangement.

[50] The debate about the rule of origin in the NAFTA negotiations was so vicious that in November 1992 the Big Three expelled Honda from the US Motor Vehicle Manufacturers Association (Levin 1992). Honda had advocated a looser rule of origin, and the Big Three were so resentful that the MVMA redefined its membership criteria in such a way as to exclude Honda.

Apparel and Textiles

In the case of apparel and textiles, as for autos, strict rules of origin were central to the organization of business support—both in Mexico and in the United States. In this case, unlike for autos, the discussion of rules of origin led to a split between industries at different stages of the supply chain. The textiles and apparel industries in the United States had historically been opposed to trade liberalization, as these were products in which other countries had grown competitive over the course of the postwar period. The US apparel sector was heavily protected, and studies expected it to contract under NAFTA.[51] Accordingly, US producers looked for ways of limiting their exposure to competitive imports. Mexican firms were also concerned about foreign competition, though Mexican producers felt they stood a better chance in an integrated market with the United States.

In the CUFTA negotiations, Canada and the United States agreed on a "fabric-forward" rule of origin for apparel. That is, to be considered originating, a product would have to be made of fabric produced inside North America— but the fabric could be made of imported yarns or fibers. US industry would have preferred a "yarn-forward" rule under CUFTA, according to which even the yarns or fibers would have to be North American-made to benefit from free trade. They did not get that rule, but that was not a great loss for them, as they did not see Canada as much of a threat. Canadian firms were competitive only in some niche markets, like men's suits. Those suit makers, concentrated in Quebec, relied heavily on wool fabrics imported from Europe—inputs on which the United States was charging a higher tariff than Canada, such that the Canadian producers had an advantage.

At the opening of the NAFTA negotiations, and facing the prospect of added competition from Mexico, the US apparel and textile industries took conflicting positions with respect to the rules of origin. The president of the American Apparel Manufacturers Association wrote to the US negotiators that "there should be a double transformation rule of origin on apparel, similar to the one in the US-Canadian Free Trade Agreement."[52] The Knitted Textile Association, on the other hand, demanded a stricter rule, "so that all textiles and textile products accorded . . . preferential treatment, from fiber forward, must be of true NAFTA origin."[53] Crucially, the textile producers made their support or at least acquiescence to NAFTA explicitly conditional on the rule of origin: "We are prepared to work with your Administration on the development of a mutually beneficial

---

[51] International Trade Commission 1992; Aguilar 1993.

[52] Boswell 1991.

[53] Arnold 1991.

North American Free Trade Agreement, but we must be assured on this essential issue."[54]

Confronting these conflicting positions, the US negotiators decided to pursue the more restrictive rule. The Mexican negotiators were of two minds about the issue, as in principle they favored open markets and therefore a loose rule, but on the other hand that was not what the industry in Mexico wanted. Their textiles and apparel producers were, as in the United States, divided on the question of the rules of origin, with producers of fibers and textiles asking for a stricter rule. Because textile producers were more concentrated, however, their preference carried more weight than that of the apparel producers, who also tended to be smaller firms. The Canadian negotiators favored a loose rule of origin—a continuation of the rule established under CUFTA. Commenting on the difference of national priorities, one of the Canadian negotiators explained that "the drive for more restrictive rules was more from the United States, which makes sense . . . we rely more on imported inputs."

In the end, Canada lost out, as the less liberal preference of the US and Mexican industries for a stricter rule ended up getting written into the agreement. The United States and Mexico outnumbered Canada on the issue and made a deal: the United States would quickly open up its market—lowering its tariffs and getting rid of quota limits on apparel imports from Mexico—while Mexico would support a US demand for strict rules of origin.[55] The US and Mexican industries formulated this proposal together and their respective governments followed suit. Though apparel producers would face the disadvantage of restrictions on the use of imported materials, the Mexican negotiators expected NAFTA to lift wages in Mexico, and higher wages would mean Mexico would not stay competitive in the apparel industry for very long.

In the United States, having obtained the restrictive rule of origin that they wanted, the fiber and textiles industries endorsed NAFTA. The support of the American Textile Manufacturers Institute (ATMI) was a surprise to some, since it had previously been opposed to trade liberalization.[56] Members of Congress from North Carolina, the biggest textile-producing state, had voted nine to two against the principle of negotiating NAFTA in 1991, but eight to four in favor of it in the end.[57] They, like the ATMI, decided to support NAFTA specifically given

[54] Arnold 1991.

[55] The textiles and apparel trade liberalization under NAFTA was a major change. Previously, Mexico's apparel and textiles exports to the US market were constrained by quotas, which NAFTA converted immediately into tariffs. And those tariffs would eventually be phased out. The rules of the GATT prohibit quantitative restrictions in general, but quotas for apparel and textiles were given a pass (under the Multi-Fiber Agreement governing world trade in such goods).

[56] Ostroff 1991.

[57] Destler 1995: 227.

the strict rules of origin.[58] Apparel manufacturers were more internally divided, though some—particularly larger firms—saw in NAFTA a new opportunity to move their production to Mexico. Some quantitative research codes both the apparel and textiles industries in the United States as anti-NAFTA and protectionist, reflecting comments by their representatives in congressional hearings.[59] But the key industry associations ultimately endorsed NAFTA, demonstrating their support for the agreement in its final form—with trade-restrictive rules of origin helping to reduce opposition to NAFTA from industries that might otherwise have fought it. Canadian apparel manufacturers were less enthusiastic. But they felt there was little more their negotiators could have done for them—and Canada did negotiate some favorable exemptions to the general rules, which amounted again to a kind of concession for the industry.

Conclusion

> We are, by and large, incrementalists here, in that pure economic theory of any particular stripe doesn't matter, unless it gets implemented. So our focus is always on what is the best that we can bring home.
> —US trade negotiator

> There was a very large element of practicality. You may say we should have certain things from a trade policy principle. But if they are going to have a very serious impact on an industry, based on how that particular thing was going to be implemented, we wanted to have the practical feedback from companies who were there.
> —Canadian politician

> At no time were there any impositions; there were never impositions. All issues were always discussed. And, in the end, we reached a consensus.
> —Mexican industry representative

Market access, including the deadlines for phasing out tariffs on different products, was not the only focus of the CUFTA and NAFTA negotiations. As explained in Chapter 5, a major reason the United States wanted these agreements was to include governance content appealing to American firms—most notably investor and intellectual property rights.[60] The priority for Canadian firms was,

---

[58] See American Banker-Bond Buyer 1991.

[59] Chase 2003.

[60] The inclusion of these rights added to the private sector support for NAFTA in the United States. American demands for them led to divides among the three countries, however, as the Mexican and particularly the Canadian negotiators were less enthusiastic. The investor and

in contrast, security of access to the US market, so their top focus was a dispute settlement procedure capable of constraining American antidumping and countervailing duties. Mexican businesspeople, likewise, wanted secure export access to the United States. In these terms, CUFTA and NAFTA presented at least some firms in all three countries with content that was appealing to them, making it easy for them to support the agreements. But that was not enough to build the broad private sector consensus that Chapters 3, 4, and 5 described in each country. That consensus required that firms and industries likely to lose out from free trade not fight it as hard as they might have, or even to drop their objections completely. This chapter has shown how the negotiations gave them reasons to do that.

The negotiators' main goal was to bring home an agreement that satisfied, as much as possible, domestic industries. They knew that if they could provide skeptical businesspeople with meaningful concessions, they could win them over. For that reason, even when authority over trade policymaking rested in the hands of officials with clearly neoclassical outlooks, in practice all three countries adopted mercantilist positions in the negotiations. That meant CUFTA and NAFTA provided for long transition periods or strict rules of origin for some industries, and outright exclusions for others. Economists dislike these measures, seeing them as deviations from their free trade ideals, to the point that some economists were even lukewarm about NAFTA.[61] One of the Canadian negotiators commented, wryly: "When I read the NAFTA the first time, I must say, I looked at the rules-of-origin chapter and wondered how we could call this a free trade agreement!" But, as another negotiator explained: "You face the reality of the politics. You can get an industry to agree to go into zero tariffs eventually over a ten- or whatever year period. But their price is, 'But we've got to have some content in the rules of origin.'"

All of this shows that broad-based business support for free trade is not a given. But the liberal globalization literature has, for the most part, ignored how support from business can be constructed, with the organization of the negotiations themselves playing a key role. Public officials set the parameters, but then step back and mediate between domestic and foreign industry demands, giving individual industries considerable influence over the negotiations. Irrespective of national differences and their own ideas, trade negotiators therefore behave very similarly, working in principle to achieve the most liberal agreements possible, but in practice readily including lots of trade-restrictive, antiliberal content. The

---

intellectual property protections sought by large American firms were not something that Canadian or Mexican businesspeople were much interested in.

[61] E.g. Bhagwati 2008; Galbraith 1993; Henderson 2001: 95; Lal 2005.

concessions mute criticism even among those businesspeople who start out hostile to the basic principle of free trade, rejecting free trade in principle or ask for their sector specifically to be excluded or treated in some exceptional way. In the interest of winning domestic political support, then, negotiators act pragmatically and do not hold out for what most of them consider an optimal—most liberal—agreement.

The mercantilist character of trade policymaking makes little sense, from economists' perspective.[62] It also contradicts the expectations of the critical literature, which provides little reason to think trade should be internationally contentious. (Why should governments struggle so much to reconcile their divergent preferences, if the powers that be in all countries are so strongly committed to free markets?) From a neoclassical point of view, in a sense trade restrictions should not work to build business support, insofar as any restriction on imports is also a discouragement to exports. Politically, any potential benefit of an import restriction should be offset by its corresponding costs. But that does not happen, as the owners, managers, and employees of firms with the potential to take advantage of new export opportunities do not know who they are. Because of the mercantilist way in which people think about trade, concessions work to build business support—even if they create conflict internationally. Conversely, the conflicts convey to casual observers that the biggest conflicts of interest are among nations supposedly competing in global markets—reinforcing mercantilist understandings of international economics.

Critics of globalization have long complained about a deficit of democracy in the processes by which it has been established. Trade negotiations tend to be organized in rather secretive ways, which has not helped build trust in the end results. Not only radical activists feel this way; even scholars broadly supportive of free trade, liberal investment policies, and institutional foundations for the global economy sometimes acknowledge that states have not always achieved these ends through very inclusive policymaking means.[63] As Stiglitz and Charlton put it, "A fair agreement is unlikely to be produced through an unfair process."[64] Behind closed doors, negotiators write agreements that are awkward and hard for legislators to reject later on. The inclusion of investor and intellectual property rights in international trade agreements is a case in point. This content reflects private sector representatives' access to the negotiators—and negotiators' receptiveness to their arguments—which tends to be far better than the access granted to other voices. Given the access they enjoy, representatives can convince negotiators to compromise with their positions.

---

[62] See Regan 2015.

[63] E.g., Nye 2001.

[64] Stiglitz and Charlton 2005: 8.

Insofar as trade negotiations reflect competitive struggles among nations (as from the mercantilist point of view), it would seem that doing things behind closed doors makes sense. Why give away your strategy to the other team? But the consequence of such thinking has been the denial of access to most constituencies, while a select few enjoy inside information and privileged opportunities to influence the process. Larry Summers, the former president of Harvard University and éminence grise of Democratic Party centrist economics, agrees that public skepticism of international economic integration has been largely a consequence of perceptions that are "not wholly unwarranted, that it is a project carried out by elites for elites with little consideration for the interests of ordinary people."[65] It is hardly surprising that negotiations held in secret and resulting in business-friendly content have given rise to such concerns.

[65] Summers 2016.

8

Conclusions

With many countries becoming more open and inclusive in their politics, the late twentieth century was a pretty good time for democracy.[1] The 1980s and 1990s were also a period of rapidly deepening international economic integration, and it is no exaggeration to say that rising "economic and political liberalism was the defining feature of the late twentieth century."[2] To some, the simultaneity of these trends may not come as a surprise, as astute commentators have long noted their association. Karl Popper, one of the more celebrated philosophers of the twentieth century, observed in the 1940s that one hallmark feature of a closed, undemocratic society is economic autarky.

But while there is clearly a statistical association between democratization and globalization, as Chapter 1 explained, there is little reason to think that the association reflects a causal relationship running from the one to the other. North America got free trade not because of public demand, but because elites grew enthusiastic for their own reasons. Business advocates perceived an opportunity to gain an advantage, as they saw it, in world markets. Intellectually, politicians followed their lead—except in Mexico, where economists in government seized an opportunity to implement the economics they had studied and to which they adhered on principle.

This chapter sums up the core claims of the previous chapters, and identifies some implications of the book's arguments for the academic literatures on international political economy and the role of ideas in politics more broadly. After that, it compares the cases of Canada, Mexico, and the United States with those of other countries, highlighting differences and similarities in the ways globalization unfolded in different places in the late twentieth century. The chapter then closes with a discussion of the prospects for globalization generally, particularly in light of events since 2016, as the mercantilist foundations of globalization are now coming back to destabilize it.

---

[1] Lindberg et al. 2014.
[2] Simmons, Dobbin, and Garrett 2006: 781.

Elites and the Rise of Globalization

The power of elites is a classic concern of the social sciences, but it has perhaps never again received as much attention as it did in the mid-twentieth century, after the publication of C. Wright Mills's classic work *The Power Elite*.[3] Mills's thesis was that, at least in the America of his day, a close-knit network of political, military, and corporate elites were exercising such power over public life that it called into question the democratic character of the US government. The book made a significant impact, including outside academic circles, though the response it received from some influential social scientists was critical and even dismissive.[4] Mills's argument that an identifiable, coherent network of elites was systematically determining key policy outcomes, indeed ruling the country, was considered untenable, too extreme, and it was largely rejected. Some scholars continued to document ties among powerful elites, but they were few.[5]

Now, however, elite theory of a kind is thriving, and is even becoming mainstream. A number of empirical studies find the elite theorists had a point: at least based on US data, public opinion can influence government decisions, but to a remarkable degree it is only the opinions of the rich that matter.[6] Taking advantage of new and more advanced methods and data, this literature shows that when the preferences of elites contradict those of the median voter, policy outcomes reflect far more the former.

The case studies presented in this book are not evidence enough to conclude that economic elites rule America or anywhere else. But they do speak to the question of which political forces constructed the global capitalism we have today. Mid-twentieth-century social science was skeptical about elite theories largely because there was evidence of important divides within elite circles; it did not appear that elites were united enough to rule. But the story of North American free trade shows that high levels of elite coalition-building are possible, at least with respect to the policy decisions that have made globalization happen. Contrary to the expectation that businesspeople can never unite on the issue of trade, in fact they can. Previous chapters have identified why: the ubiquity of mercantilist ideas; business-friendly governance content; trade-restrictive concessions; internal leadership by internationalist firms and industries; and, depending on the context, state control of the institutional channels by which business can either dissent or acquiesce.

---

[3] Mills 1956.

[4] E.g., Parsons 1957; Dahl 1958.

[5] E.g., Domhoff 2010.

[6] Barabas 2016; Bartels 2008; Druckman and Jacobs 2015; Gilens 2012; Gilens and Page 2014; Page and Bouton 2007.

The liberal literature on globalization places the median voter at the center of its causal interpretation of the statistical association between democracy and globalization. But surveys do not find much evidence that public opinion is even what the theory presumes, and this book has shown that public opinion was, in any event, largely irrelevant for the rise of globalization. The impressive elegance of the theory of democracy's impacts notwithstanding, the liberal literature takes it too far. Today's globalized world economy does not rest on democratic foundations, at least in the sense that governments pursued globalization because of the public's preferences with respect to international economic policy.[7]

Economists and Ideas in International Political Economy

The book has also shown that globalization has not been a project resting on the technical ideas of economists. Endorsements by economists have helped to make free trade, including real-world CUFTA and NAFTA, politically viable. But that does not mean that the architects and advocates of agreements like NAFTA actually subscribed to, or even understood, economists' technical ideas about trade. Unless they were themselves economists, they did not, and those ideas were not their motivation. Rather, the ideas behind the rise of globalization were those of business. This fact is more than just an academic curiosity. If the ideas of disinterested, intellectually autonomous experts were behind globalization, in most people's eyes that would make it more legitimate. Advocates would *like* globalization to be seen as deriving from the deliberations of neutral experts weighing logic and evidence in a disinterested way. It is specifically the autonomy of the science that gives it a chance of identifying valid propositions about the world.[8] But globalization did not derive from the ideas of academic economists; ironically, some of the strongest critics of agreements like NAFTA have therefore failed to see quite how shaky the intellectual foundations of such agreements really are. In treating such agreements as the products of mainstream economic ideas, critics have indirectly exaggerated their legitimacy, and thereby

---

[7] This is not to say, however, that the rise of globalization has necessarily been inconsistent with democracy by every definition. In some conceptions, it is not a requirement that the leaders of democracies must obey the public's policy preferences—rather, what matters is that the electorate can remove leaders who fail to satisfy people's basic interests and values. Gilens and Page (2014) call this an "electoral reward and punishment" perspective. But this conception is less relevant here, as the liberal literature specifically links democracy to globalization insofar as it expects politicians to recognize, respect, and pursue voters' trade policy preferences.

[8] Bourdieu 1975.

strengthened them politically. Advocates, it is safe to say, are less keen to have globalization seen as a corporate project resting on the preferences and folk ideas of economic elites.

The combination of mainstream economics and the folk mercantilism of business was difficult for free trade's critics to deal with. Defenders of the interests of workers and the environment faced economists saying globalization was good, and business mercantilists saying that globalization meant competition—which in turn required deregulation and a leaner, meaner society. When anyone asked why globalization was such a good thing if it meant that kind of society, economists responded that it presented no threat at all to workers and the environment, and that critics should stop talking about those things.

The pervasive influence and importance of mercantilist ideas points to a generalized limitation of the broader field of international political economy (IPE), of which the liberal globalization literature is a part. Many studies in IPE rely on stripped-down models of objective interests and self-interested, rational action—devoid of cognition, identity, morality, and culture.[9] As Chapter 1 explained, parsimonious theories of this kind—their obvious simplifications of reality notwithstanding—are satisfying insofar as they make predictions sufficiently close to observable reality. But this book has shown that they describe a world of globalization that does not exist.[10]

The liberal IPE literature needs ideas. Research in behavioral economics has shown that people make all kinds of decisions based on cognitive shortcuts. It is also clear that public attitudes toward trade have at least as much to do with nationalism and identity as with economics.[11] We need to make sense of relevant behaviors—and the institutions that follow from them—by thinking about people's lived experience of economic processes. Many influential scholars have remarked on the limits of minimalist, interest-based explanations of policy outcomes, and highlighted how important political actors (including the mass public) can be convinced to perceive their interests in ways that outside academic observers find puzzling.[12] Even Helen Milner, perhaps *the* central figure in the democracy-centered globalization literature, recognized earlier in her career that the ideas of policymakers matter and consequently that "the preferences of interest groups and voters are less

---

[9] See Simmons and Elkins 2004.

[10] IPE is the name given to a field of research born in the 1970s with the first scholarly efforts to understand international economic integration. One of its central goals has always been to identify the political determinants of globalization, but members of the field concede it "has proved to be much better at asking questions than at providing answers" (Cohen 2008: 169; Lake 2006: 758).

[11] Mansfield and Mutz 2009, 2013.

[12] E.g., Bates and Krueger 1993; Simmons and Elkins 2004; Woods 1995; Schneider 2004; Woll 2008.

important in determining trade policy than are those of the policy makers themselves."[13] Even minimalist studies of trade policymaking, based on rational choice models, have made implicit assumptions about the ideas to which policymakers subscribe. Such studies tend to assume that policymakers think like economists; this book has shown they do not.

Globalization around the Globe

The argument of this book leaves a puzzle: If there is no causal relationship between democratization and globalization, why do statistical studies find them to be associated?

There are at least two possible reasons why there could be a spurious, rather than causal, relationship between democratization and globalization. One is that democratization is endogenous to future economic policy changes. Businesspeople may be more likely to accept a transition to democracy if they do not fear it will mean unwanted new policies or other changes undermining their power.[14] So when elites are confident that a potential government under democracy is likely to be reasonably market-oriented, which a technocratic government will be, they will accept the transition. Even if they do not love free trade specifically, they will appreciate the kinds of political leaders who favor and pursue it.

A second possible reason is that both democratization and globalization are more likely to occur in countries with greater exposure to a world culture sympathetic to political and economic liberalism.[15] One key means by which world culture is transmitted is epistemic communities, or groups of recognized experts.[16] The relative population of such experts varies from country to country, as does experts' freedom to travel or study abroad, and thereby to absorb norms and ideas that they may import back home. The same nondemocracies that come to be governed by technocrats—highly educated individuals exposed to foreign expertise and ideas—are also those exposed to the democratic ideas and norms that make a transition to democracy more likely. Technocrats themselves transmit the influence of education, whose affinity with both political and economic liberalism is well established. People who are more educated tend to be more supportive of free trade, and also of democracy, while countries with higher levels of

[13] Milner 1999: 98.
[14] Greenwood 2008.
[15] Finnemore 1996.
[16] Simmons, Dobbin, and Garrett 2006.

education are also more likely to democratize.[17] The educational level of political leaders tends to be higher in democracies than nondemocracies, even controlling for many other differences between the two groups of countries.[18] Individuals educated in democracies tend to promote democracy at home, and democratization is likelier in countries that allow more emigration to democracies.[19] So while technocracy is more characteristic of nondemocratic contexts, technocrats may nonetheless believe in the value of democracy and be likelier to introduce it compared to other kinds of leaders (such as the "dinosaurs" one hears about in many countries). Technocrats may also be less likely to use violence in repressing popular demands for democracy, setting technocratic nondemocracies apart from other, more intellectually *and* economically autarkic nations. If political and economic liberalism is diffused via global mechanisms like non- and intergovernmental organizations, in short, then differences in countries' connectedness to flows of global culture should make a difference to both simultaneously. Countries' connectedness certainly varies, potentially explaining why the kinds of developing countries that globalize also tend to democratize.[20]

We can see this happening using comparisons to the experiences of other developing and democratizing countries, the task to which I will turn next. I will briefly examine the pathways by which four countries outside North America opened their economies: Japan, Australia, Thailand, and Chile. In these two high-income democracies and two developing countries, levels of international trade integration grew noticeably in the late twentieth century. In the latter two cases authoritarian regimes also gave way to democracy. Clearly these four cases do not exhaust the range of possible variants. But they do roughly illustrate the diversity of pathways by which different countries globalized in the late twentieth century, and in all four cases we can see some intriguing similarities to and differences from the experiences of the three countries of North America. They largely substantiate the two-pathway model of globalization described in Chapter 1 and demonstrate the systematically limited role for public opinion in politicians' decisions to open their countries' economies. They also show how the ingress of liberal world culture—often absorbed in the course of an education overseas—contributes to both globalization and democratization.

[17] Alemán and Kim 2015; Hainmueller and Hiscox 2006; Wike et al. 2017.
[18] Besley and Reynal-Querol 2011.
[19] Docquier et al. 2016; Spilimbergo 2009.
[20] See Torfason and Ingram 2010.

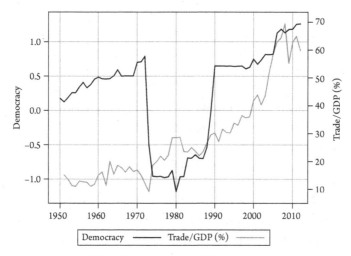

Figure 8.1 Democracy and Trade Openness in Chile, 1950–2012. Sources: Pemstein et al. 2010 (release 2014); Penn World Table 9.0.

Chile

Chile is a legendary case of globalization by technocracy. At least outside of East Asia, Chile became the first developing country to substantially open its economy to world markets. Before that, it had always had high tariffs, and despite being a founding member of the GATT, Chile adopted an import-substitution industrialization (ISI) strategy that kept international markets at bay—see Figure 8.1.[21]

In the mid-twentieth century, unlike most developing countries, Chile was fortunate to enjoy a long period of uninterrupted democracy. That came to an end, infamously, in 1973, with a military coup d'état against democratic socialist president Salvador Allende. The coup represented a backlash by Chile's elites against Allende's efforts on behalf of subordinate social groups, Chilean society being marked—as typical for Latin America—by very high inequality. Elites' hostility to Allende's state-interventionist and redistributive policies, and the economic and political turmoil that hostility engendered, led the army's newly appointed commander-in-chief, Augusto Pinochet, to seize power.

Initially, the new regime adopted only modest economic policy changes, seeking largely just to return Chile to the status quo prior to Allende's election in 1970. But in the mid-1970s, Pinochet granted substantial control to the "Chicago Boys"—a cohort of economists who had taken advantage of US scholarship funding to study at the University of Chicago in the 1950s. Unlike the technocrats in Mexico, the Chicago Boys had not fought their way up inside the

---

[21] Coatsworth and Williamson 2004.

state hierarchy; they were, instead, university professors and researchers in think tanks. Reflecting what they had learned in the United States, they were strong believers in the merits of free markets, and they developed a policy agenda to which Pinochet proved receptive.[22] Using the substantial control they enjoyed between 1975 and 1981, they implemented what would later be regarded as the world's first neoliberal revolution. Among other actions, they substantially opened the economy. By 1979, Chile had a flat 10 percent tariff—a very low rate by the standards of the day.[23]

But even if the technocrats only got their chance because of the power of Chile's elites, it is important to recognize that they were not, in fact, closely tied to business. Nor were some of the policies they introduced very well received by the business class. For the most part, the Chicago Boys dismissed input from businesspeople and the country's major business associations, and they simply went about doing as they saw fit.[24] The policy of opening the Chilean economy, in particular, was not greatly appreciated by Chile's economic elites.[25] Some businesspeople were supportive, but many were not, and the latter had to be compensated for the costs of declining tariff protection by other appealing measures, such as labor repression.[26] In the end the Chicago Boys were ultimately pushed out, as an economic crisis in the early 1980s shook the confidence of the business sector, and Pinochet sought to rebuild it using, among other things, a substantial increase in tariffs.[27] Pinochet reallocated power over economic policy back to business, though technocrats retained some role.[28]

The technocrats were empowered by the absence of constraints on the actions of the executive branch, and in the case of Chile under the Chicago Boys trade liberalization followed after a coup, not democratization—the opposite of what the democracy-centered globalization literature says has been the norm. But as Figure 8.1 shows, in the later 1980s and through the 1990s, Chile once again embraced economic opening, and this time in the context of growing levels of democracy, such that the case of Chile over the whole period is partly consistent with the liberal theory.[29] It is also only partly consistent with critical perspectives

---

[22] Fourcade-Gourinchas and Babb 2002.

[23] Wacziarg and Welch code Chile as open starting in 1976.

[24] Silva 1998.

[25] Bianculli 2017.

[26] Lederman 2005: 125.

[27] Stallings and Brock 1993.

[28] Pop-Eleches 2009; Gilson and Milhaupt 2011.

[29] Chile's democratization was possibly endogenous to the entrenching of free markets under the technocrats. A constitution adopted under Pinochet in 1980 included some economic rules that were written specifically to be hard to alter later (Gilson and Milhaupt 2011: 257–58). Though the constitution was amended in some ways after the end of the dictatorship, the economic provisions were not.

suggesting that neoliberal policies are rooted in the interests and preferences of economic elites. The business community was on the whole lukewarm at best about the exposure of the country to international trade flows, much as in the case of Mexico, where business regarded some kinds of neoliberal policies—like trade liberalization—less positively than others.

Australia

Across the Pacific, Australia's embrace of economic opening came somewhat later, and in different political circumstances, but it also reflected policymakers' past educations in economics.

Relative to other high-income democracies, Australia maintained exceptionally high trade barriers until late in the twentieth century—probably the most restrictive in the developed world, along with New Zealand.[30] After World War II, investment poured into Australia (largely from the United States and United Kingdom), initially to get behind the country's tariff wall and later to mine Australia's abundant mineral resources.[31] In response, Australia limited foreign investment using a screening process introduced in 1972. The Australian case therefore presents several parallels with the Canadian.

Australia joined the GATT, but used high tariffs as part of an import substitution strategy similar to those of the developing nations, to the point of allying with them on many issues.[32] None of the country's major political parties questioned the tariffs, and both manufacturers and organized labor supported them, even if Australia's small community of economists grew increasingly critical.[33] In 1991, trade as a share of GDP was still only 29 percent, not much different than it had been in 1950 (at 23 percent). Over the next twenty years, though, that share would more than double, as trade protection fell substantially. Australia's tariff on passenger motor vehicles, for example, declined from 57.5 percent at the start of the 1980s to 17.5 percent by the end of the century.[34]

The state played an active role in directing the Australian economy in the postwar period, and it was also state leadership that led to the country's economic opening.[35] The agents of the cuts were the Labor governments of Prime Ministers Bob Hawke and Paul Keating. Their decision to open the economy was not the result of interest group lobbying; business was internally divided

---

[30] Pomfret 2000.
[31] Ville and Withers 2014.
[32] Brown 1950; Leigh 2002; Capling 2001; Pincus 1995.
[33] Leigh 2002; Millmow 2005.
[34] Lloyd 2008.
[35] Bell 1993; Capling and Galligan 1992.

on the issue of tariff cuts, while labor unions were opposed.[36] The cuts appear to have been instead the product, to a large degree, of Hawke's own thinking and that of his cabinet and advisers. Because of his studies in economics both abroad (at Oxford with a Rhodes Scholarship) and in Australia (at the University of Western Australia), Hawke described himself as "intellectually a free trader from my earliest thinking days."[37] Though it would be a stretch to call Hawke or his government technocratic, he was clearly motivated to pursue trade liberalization even in the absence of proactive pressure from outside. Hawke believed Australia's trade barriers were protecting inefficient industries, and he saw their removal as a way of stimulating the manufacturing sector, explaining that protection had "dulled the entrepreneurial spirit and reduced the competitive pressures for high performances by a number of Australian manufacturers."[38] Hawke's agenda was also supported by economists within the state, who had been trained in American-style economics; over time Australian economics had become very critical of the tariffs protecting the country's industrial sector.[39]

Public opinion was favorable to trade restrictions throughout the postwar period, and there is little reason to think that electoral considerations played any notable role in the decisions to liberalize the country's trade flows.[40] Trade liberalization was "treated with suspicion by much of the population."[41] That Hawke decided to avoid talking about economic opening until after the 1983 election suggests he did not think the policy was a vote-winner. Polls also showed that restrictions on inward foreign direct investment had been popular when they were introduced in the 1970s, but the Hawke government relaxed those too.[42]

Why did the Hawke and Keating governments liberalize trade so decisively, contrary to Australian tradition, and in the absence of proactive support from business, labor, or voters? Given that the policy change reflected the changing substance of Australian academic economics, and the election of a new government more sympathetic to free trade, Australia's pathway to globalization was therefore more like that of a developing country. This is understandable given that even in the 1980s Australia's circumstances were in some respects much like those of a developing country. Australia still had much less outward than inward FDI.[43] In Canada by then that was no longer the case, and there were Canadian multinational enterprises keen on opening and ready to campaign for it within

[36] Bell 1993; Leigh 2002.
[37] Quoted in Leigh 2002: 500.
[38] Quoted in Leigh 2002: 501.
[39] Garnaut 2002; Goldfinch 2000; Pusey 1991.
[40] Garnaut 2002; Leigh 2002.
[41] Pomfret 1995: 1.
[42] Pokarier 2017.
[43] Department of Foreign Affairs and Trade 2014.

the business community and beyond. Australia's opening was therefore the project of a strong state populated by leaders and economists motivated to take action without business leadership.

Japan

Compared to Australia, Japan's economic opening was more rooted in the preferences of the private sector.

Japan heavily regulated its trade after World War II, with exchange quotas, restrictions on foreign investment, tariffs, and other measures keeping the economy closed. These measures enjoyed the full support of business and the country's influential farm lobby.[44] That began to change in the 1950s, particularly as the United States made large purchases from Japanese suppliers during the Korean War. Japan acceded to GATT in 1955 and began liberalizing imports in the 1960s. Still, many restrictions were maintained, as bureaucrats sought to use them in reconstructing industries that had been destroyed in the war. The redevelopment of Japanese manufacturing was famously successful; as just one sign of the speed of the transformation, machinery and transport equipment increased from one-quarter of Japan's exports in the early 1960s to more than three-fifths by the mid-1980s.[45] By the 1970s, manufactured goods from Japan were competing with those from the United States and other Western countries, and Japanese firms were starting to invest in factories overseas to serve local markets. Although in 1980 only 2 percent of the production of Japanese corporations took place offshore, compared, for example, to 10 percent for US firms, this share rose substantially in the following years.[46]

As a consequence, foreign trade grew more important to business leaders.[47] Multinational firms and business associations lobbied for trade and investment liberalization, particularly given concerns about protectionism abroad—some of which was a consequence of resentment about Japanese restrictions on access to its own market.[48] Bureaucrats acceded to the changed preferences of industry and further opened the Japanese economy, for example, by negotiating bilateral and regional trade agreements in the 2000s.[49] These agreements were also the product of demands coming from Japanese business leaders, who saw them as means of facilitating investment overseas and making foreign markets

---

[44] Vogel 1999.
[45] World Trade Organization 2013.
[46] Calder 1988: 539.
[47] Yoshimatsu 1998a.
[48] Yoshimatsu 1998b.
[49] Manger 2005.

(including China) safe for Japanese firms.[50] Reducing the tariffs applied to intermediate goods would help Japanese firms consolidate and organize production on a regional basis. But while seeking to open markets abroad, and despite the increasing influence of American economics, Japan's negotiators still worked to protect uncompetitive industries at home—for example, excluding rice and many service sectors from a trade agreement with Thailand.[51]

There are clear parallels, then, with the situation in North America, with Japan playing a dominant role in its region, much like the United States in North America. In another sense, Japan was more like Canada: not so keen on international trade until a critical mass of outwardly oriented, multilateral firms felt confident about their prospects in international markets. As firms develop multinational operations, they appear to become more positive about trade liberalization.[52] As in the United States, Japanese business leaders began seeking protection for their investments in nearby developing countries, seeing them much as the Americans saw Mexico—as a host for production facilities with lower labor costs. Even Mansfield and Milner note that in Japan business campaigning seems to have been an important impetus to the start of trade liberalization, a notable acknowledgment coming from two leading contributors to the democracy-based literature on globalization.[53]

Thailand

Technocracy has a storied history in Thailand. Unlike most of the globe, Thailand never became a European colony, and one major reason was that at an early stage Thai rulers embarked on a program of administrative modernization that included sending Thais to Western countries to study.[54] Ever since then, foreign-educated policymakers and administrators have been central to public life in Thailand.

For a developing country, by the standards of the time, Thailand had relatively liberal trade policies in the post–World War II period.[55] Nevertheless, import substitution dominated and, as Figure 8.2 shows, until the 1980s there was limited economic opening. That was the preferred arrangement of Thai bureaucrats, who exercised substantial control over economic policy.[56] In the

---

[50] Zhang 1998.
[51] Ikeo 2014.
[52] Yoshimatsu 1998a, 2000.
[53] Mansfield and Milner 2012: 60.
[54] Mead 2004.
[55] Bowie and Unger 1997; Sachs and Warner 1995.
[56] Laothamatas 1988, 1992.

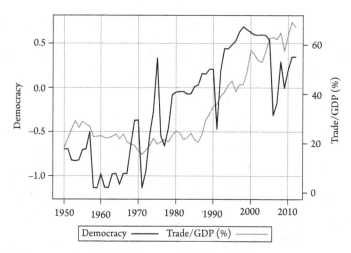

Figure 8.2 Democracy and Trade Openness in Thailand, 1950–2012. Sources: Pemstein et al. 2010, Penn World Table 9.0

early postwar period, the bureaucrats were mostly trained in Europe. Over time, though, they were replaced by officials educated in the United States, and the latter were significantly more convinced about the merits of free markets.[57] In the 1980s, and through the early 1990s, the US-trained technocrats grew in influence.[58] They negotiated Thailand's accession to the GATT in 1982, and taking advice from advisers at the World Bank, they substantially redirected industrial policy from import substitution to export-oriented industrialization.[59] Like other countries in southeast Asia, Thailand began attracting substantial foreign investment.[60] Japanese investors entered the market in force, building facilities for manufacturing passenger vehicles, electronics, and other products.[61]

As Figure 8.2 shows, Thailand's politics have oscillated between democracy and authoritarianism, and in February 1991 the military once again forced out an elected government. Military leaders appointed a caretaker prime minister, Anand Panyarachun, a businessman and former career diplomat. Anand committed to serving as Thailand's leader only until fresh elections the following year. During his brief tenure, he and a cabinet of academics, technocrats, and businessmen further opened the Thai economy, cutting tariffs and deregulating capital flows.[62] Anand's administration liberalized the rules on inward FDI and

[57] Phongpaichit and Baker 2014; Lao 2015.
[58] Phongpaichit and Baker 2014.
[59] Baker and Phongpaichit 2005.
[60] Tabb 1995; Yoshimatsu 2002.
[61] Baker and Phongpaichit 2005.
[62] Bowie and Unger 1997; Phongpaichit and Baker 1997.

relaxed regulations that had previously all but banned the importation of passenger vehicles.

Anand's government was by all accounts competent and uncorrupt. His team maintained friendly relations with the private sector, who appreciated that Anand had appointed a number of businessmen to his cabinet and that he had previously headed a major Thai business association.[63] The political influence of business expanded substantially in Thailand over the course of the post–World War II period. As in much of Southeast Asia, the business community in Thailand was initially dominated by ethnic Chinese, who—wishing to avoid any trouble—kept a low profile.[64] Businesspeople mostly sought to influence policy though informal, personalistic means, including bribery and invitations for policymakers to join corporate boards. Eventually, though, businesspeople grew to be a more powerful influence on Thai policy, and some accounts suggest the business community supported the country's economic opening.[65] The case of Thailand may, then, be one in which the public and private sectors both came to support policies favorable to opening—though the channeling of American economic ideas into the bureaucracy appears to have been the decisive factor.

The case of Thailand shows how the globalization of developing countries has been heavily influenced by foreign-educated officials importing new policy ideas. Thailand, like Mexico, experienced a substantial rise in trade/GDP after taking steps toward greater political democracy—consistent with the liberal literature. But while it might seem from Figure 8.2 that democratization was the impetus to trade liberalization, the literature explains how the real force was a team of economic technocrats—as in Chile under the Chicago Boys. In these countries, policy changes that substantially opened the economy had little to do with democracy, even if, for the most part, they were not about the preferences of business either.

Democratization unfolds largely through socialization, where elites and the public begin to subscribe to a liberal-rational world culture. Anand was not the only foreign-educated Thai technocrat who took a stand for democracy and human rights.[66] Another relevant instance of this was Puey Unghakorn, the longtime governor of the central bank, and the holder of a PhD in economics from the London School of Economics. After leaving the Bank of Thailand to become the head of Thammasat University in Bangkok, in 1976 he took the side of his pro-democracy students as they protested against a coup d'état returning their country to military rule. As a consequence, he ended up going into exile and

---

[63] Abbott 2002.

[64] Laothamatas 1988; MacIntyre and Jayasuriya 1992.

[65] Laothamatas 1988, 1992; Phongpaichit 1992.

[66] Girling 1994; Lynch 2006.

living abroad for the rest of his life. In ways like this, technocrats can contribute to both economic and political liberalism.

Democracy and the Future of Globalization

> Hidden in NAFTA was a new set of rights—for business—that poten-
> tially weakened democracy throughout North America.
> —Joseph Stiglitz, Nobel laureate in economics

This book has shown that the rise of globalization in the late twentieth century was predominantly a top-down, elite-driven process. But even studies that have correctly identified globalization as a project of elites have been flawed.

One kind of critical account, especially common from Canadian and Mexican perspectives, suggests that continental free trade was in some sense an American imposition.[67] This book has belied nationalist takes like these. Elites in Mexico and Canada came to believe in free trade for their own reasons; both countries held out successfully on many contentious issues in the negotiations; and both made the United States wait many years before agreeing to negotiate in the first place. In the Mexican case, it is true the state sought assistance from the United States and US-dominated international financial institutions in the 1980s, and that dependence contributed a lot to the reshaping of Mexican politics and economic policies. But there is no evidence that external actors directly imposed free trade on Mexico (or Canada). There is also a certain symmetry between these perspectives and those of some American critics, insofar as both talk up the loss of employment, which they present as a direct consequence of growing trade deficits.[68] As explained in Chapter 6, these concerns are part of a folk mercantilist economic worldview that reinforces the nationalist vision of trade as a win-lose competition among nations.

Critics should think carefully about whether this is really a perspective they want to perpetuate. Aside from the fact it contradicts mainstream economics, the mercantilist view of trade has recently had consequences with which many critics of globalization are probably uncomfortable. Now that the promised benefits of globalization have failed to trickle down, as ordinary people had been told to expect they would, a populist backlash is endangering many kinds of international integration. The form of the backlash is hardly sympathetic to the perspectives of the civil society alliances that challenged North American free trade back in

[67] E.g., Calderón and Arroyo 1993; Barlow and Campbell 1993.
[68] E.g., Faux and Lee 1993.

the 1980s and 1990s. Some people who know better—economists—bear some responsibility for failing to challenge nationalist ideas, instead making a Faustian pact with mercantilists in endorsing agreements like NAFTA.[69] But while mercantilism may have helped make globalization politically feasible, it has done so at the cost of strengthening nationalist understandings of trade that are now coming back to bite.[70] In recent years, the vote share of neonationalist parties in Western Europe has correlated with exposure to Chinese imports.[71] Such parties have turned the social disruption of globalization into a nationalist populist movement against it.

In fairness, economists are now more circumspect in advocating for agreements like NAFTA. Since the height of free market fundamentalism in the 1980s and 1990s, the discipline of economics has grown more balanced in its assessment of the capabilities and limitations of free market policies, including free trade. Some humbling experiences—the Asian financial crisis of 1997, the global financial crisis of 2008 and after—have forced a rethink, as has the rather disappointing track record of agreements like NAFTA, as this book's afterword will explain. It is also because, in recent years, economics has taken a turn toward harder, more rigorous empirical tests of economic theory—the "credibility revolution"—and this work has revealed the limitations of what previously might have been taken as no-brainer policies.[72] Many mainstream economists sympathize with at least some of the criticisms of neoliberalism that were formerly associated much more with the voices of radicals; even IMF staff concede that policies they used to think would do a lot of good have proven disappointing in practice.[73] This kind of acknowledgment has allowed for some constructive détente between them and their erstwhile critics, some of whom have also turned toward a middle-ground view that markets can work, if governed well. Economists have also grown warier of agreements like NAFTA because of the investor and intellectual property rights provisions they contain.[74]

---

[69] Krugman (1997: 115) explained this decision by saying that "if economists are sometimes indulgent toward the mercantilist language of trade negotiations, it is . . . because they have found that in practice this particular set of bad ideas has led to pretty good results."

[70] Rodrik 2018a, 2018b.

[71] Colantone and Stanig 2018.

[72] Angrist and Pischke 2010.

[73] Howse 2017; Ostry, Loungani, and Furceri 2016.

[74] There is no need for trade agreements to contain these things; the U.S.-Australia agreement, for example, does not include investor-state dispute settlement (ISDS) procedures. The "new NAFTA" negotiated at Donald Trump's insistence has actually eliminated ISDS, in most respects. Paul Krugman (2018) says he was against the Trans-Pacific Partnership, though "not because I want a return to protectionism: the trouble with TPP was that it wasn't about trade at all, it was mainly about intellectual property (e.g. pharma patents) and dispute settlement (giving corporations more

If globalization cannot claim the legitimacy of resting on democratic foundations, what are its future prospects? Though I have argued that the public has not been very supportive of globalization, the converse is also true: public opinion is not, overall, all that hostile to it. Popular support for North American free trade increased in Canada and the United States after its implementation, and, recent events in the United States notwithstanding, getting rid of it is not a political priority of many people in any of the three countries.[75] Economic elites, meanwhile, have never shown signs of being less enthusiastic than they were at the time of NAFTA's creation. So, as elsewhere, free trade in North America is not going away anytime soon. But given the current ambivalence of the United States and popular skepticism about international integration elsewhere too, globalization may not deepen in the years ahead as much as some advocates would like.

Dani Rodrik holds that any two—but only two—of political democracy, national sovereignty, and deep economic integration are possible.[76] The European Union has, for example, achieved deep integration while protecting democracy, but only at the expense of pooling national sovereignty—which has not sat well with many, as shown in the extreme by Britain's vote to leave in 2016. Ruggie famously argued that domestic social protections were part and parcel of the postwar period's "embedded liberalism"—albeit, ironically, just before the advent of international liberalism on a scale Ruggie did not anticipate.[77] In his view, what makes globalization palatable to the public are measures for cushioning the negative effects it cannot but impose on some people. Many countries chose to trim such measures at just the same time they embraced free trade, and somehow the winners never quite managed to compensate the losers, as many economists said they needed to for globalization really to serve the interests of the many. Arguably, at least in the absence of adequate social protection, globalization sows the seeds of its own democratization, inevitably—as Karl Polanyi predicted—fostering social movements that challenge it. If so, then sooner or later the only real choice will be between national sovereignty, on the one hand, and a more democratic, humane form of globalization, on the other.

As of 2019, North America has had free trade for twenty-five years. The arrangement has been controversial for all that time. Back in 1999, one of NAFTA's more notable opponents explained why he had always been against it to the popular American television host Larry King. The charismatic New York

---

power)." Public opposition to ISDS has also threatened to undermine public acceptance of free trade, such as between the European Union and the United States (Bollen, De Ville, and Orbie 2016).

[75] Ipsos 2017; Rankin 2004.

[76] Rodrik 2011.

[77] Ruggie 1982.

businessman said: "I'm not an isolationist. What I am, though, is I think that you have to be treated fairly by other countries. If other countries are not going to treat you fairly, Larry, I think that those countries should be—they should suffer the consequences."

That was, of course, Donald Trump. As in many other interviews over the years, Trump talked about problems confronting America, his ambitions for a possible Trump presidency, and in particular his views of international trade. Now, twenty years later, the world is getting to see the full implications of his zero-sum, mercantilist outlook.

Just a few weeks after Trump's appearance on *Larry King Live* in 1999, the issue of international trade—not usually one for the front pages—hit the news in a big way. Fifty thousand protesters descended on Seattle during a Ministerial Conference of the World Trade Organization. Amid scenes of chaos, "Teamsters and Turtles," a mix of labor and environmental and other civil society and radical protestors, disrupted what would otherwise have been a staid meeting of trade professionals, diplomats, and politicians. Economists watching what the activists quickly dubbed the "Battle of Seattle" were alternately bemused and outraged, and extremely dismissive of the concerns motivating the protests. Attending the Ministerial, though, US president Bill Clinton expressed some sympathy. He said he wanted to see labor and environmental concerns better incorporated in future WTO agreements, and that ultimately he favored "a system in which sanctions would come for violating any provision of a trade agreement."

In many ways, Trump and Clinton are polar opposites in their perspectives on the world economy. The one sees only a zero-sum world of hard bargains, cheats, and chumps; the other looks for cooperative arrangements in which every country wins. But this book has shown how Trump and Clinton—and even most of the protestors in the streets of Seattle, like the opponents of North American free trade years earlier—have thought about the global economy, in some important respects, the same way. That way of thinking is highly misleading, flies in the face of mainstream economics, and has done serious damage to the world—indeed, it continues to do serious damage today. Mercantilist ideas have been propagated by people who had no idea they were so wrong, but also by some who knew better. Nonspecialists often think of mercantilist ideas as validated by the minds and research of serious, independent experts.

In reality, the experts—economists—see trade very differently. Mercantilism, however, has the advantage of being intuitive; it makes much more sense given people's, especially businesspeople's, lived experience. For this reason, politically, mercantilist ideas are useful. They have given us nothing less than the global economy we have today, obscuring conflicts of interest that might otherwise have gotten in the way of the policy decisions and international agreements that have made globalization happen. Amazingly, even critics seeing globalization as an elitist project contrary to the interests of most ordinary people have failed to recognize mercantilist ideas for what they are. Critics have not noticed the differences between mercantilism and the ideas of economists. But the critics are not alone: even scholars on the other side of the debate, who study and believe in globalization, have also overlooked the prevalence and power of mercantilist ideas.

It matters that so many people subscribe to the idea that nations compete because it prevents many good, important things from happening. From a folk mercantilist perspective, protecting the environment and helping workers or the poor is a problem. It is economically costly. And it is largely for this reason that defenders of labor and the environment dislike globalization: they know that powers that be in their societies will say international competition makes environmentalism and social democracy unaffordable. It turns out that this is economic nonsense, but economists have done little to correct the misconception—often because they believed in globalization, and thought a little mercantilist rhetoric was a price worth paying to achieve it.

Afterword

The Legacies of North American Free Trade

This is a book about the origins of globalization, not its consequences. But it's hard to have any kind of conversation about globalization, or free trade in North America specifically, without addressing the impacts. This afterword therefore addresses what we know about the legacies of free trade in North America. It reports the results of studies that have been done, statistics that have been collected, and commentaries that have been made about the major questions in the debates over CUFTA and NAFTA back in the 1980s and 1990s. With the benefit of hindsight, which of the predictions made back then by free trade's advocates and critics were right, and which were wrong?

Whole volumes could be written about this. The discussion that follows provides a summary, and though I will review the literature on globalization in general where it seems helpful to do so, in the main I will focus on CUFTA and NAFTA specifically. Assessing claims about the impacts of free trade is further complicated by the impossibility of knowing how exactly the world would have evolved in the absence of these agreements. With many other things changing at the same time, it is difficult to know for certain which changes and trends have really been due to CUFTA or NAFTA. Still, we can consider findings from studies that try to control for important confounding factors, like the breakneck expansion of China's economy and its integration into world markets; the rise of the internet and digital technologies; and the expanded concerns about security in the aftermath of September 11.

One event in particular requires a special mention: the Mexican peso crisis that began suddenly in December 1994, just less than a year after NAFTA went into effect. The crisis was unleashed when—in a desperate attempt to confront massive capital flight, a growing current account deficit, and rapidly declining foreign reserves—the Mexican government unpegged the peso from the dollar. Suddenly allowed to float, the peso plunged, and for several months so did the Mexican economy, with real GDP shrinking 8 percent between 1994 and 1995.

The origins of the crisis are debatable, but it certainly followed the accumulation of dollar-denominated debt by the Mexican government in the course of making large public expenditures in 1994—a typical practice for the ruling party in election years. Partly because of the dramatic political events that year (described later in this afterword), many investors began withdrawing from the country, shrinking the reserves of the central bank, and putting downward pressure on the peso. Can NAFTA be blamed for any of this? Views are mixed. To some, the collapse seemed to follow suspiciously soon after the agreement's implementation. Others, in contrast, say the crisis was the consequence of macroeconomic mismanagement that had little to do with trade. Fortunately, though the fall was hard, recovery was swift; economic growth resumed by 1996. Still, Mexicans felt the impact of the crisis for several years afterward, and statistics about the rest of the 1990s need to be considered in light of it.

Parts of the discussion that follows will also note relevant outcomes of the recently concluded negotiations over the new NAFTA (also known as USMCA, CUSMA, or T-MEC). As of the middle of 2019, it appears that NAFTA—in name, if not in substance—will soon be no more. But it is also entirely possible that Congress will reject the new agreement, and NAFTA will live on. Alternatively, though it is unlikely, a showdown between the US executive and legislative branches could lead the United States to withdraw from NAFTA without replacing it. Overall the old and the new agreements do not differ that much. But in discussing the existing NAFTA I will comment on aspects of it that will change if the new one does in fact get implemented.

Trade and Investment Flows

CUFTA and NAFTA were meant above all to expand cross-border flows of trade and investment within North America; this was the first objective specified in the NAFTA text (Article 102). On this issue there is little disagreement: free trade in North America certainly led to rising flows of goods and capital, and to a lesser extent trade in services, among the three countries. Within ten years after the implementation of CUFTA, Canada-US trade roughly doubled, while US-Mexico trade tripled within six years after NAFTA went into effect.[1] On the other hand, Canada and Mexico still don't do much trade with each other; NAFTA didn't change that. Nor did free trade eliminate the effects of national borders. An influential study by Helliwell showed that even several years after the implementation of CUFTA Canadian provinces traded significantly more

---

[1] Villarreal and Fergusson 2017: 14.

with each other than with US states of equivalent size and distance.[2] And it is certainly the case that a significant part of the trade increases would have happened even without NAFTA.[3]

A number of studies have modeled and attempted to determine the effects of CUFTA or NAFTA alone, net of all other influences. While the exact magnitude of the trade growth due to the agreements is up for debate, it's definitely not small. Caliendo and Parro, for example, estimate that intra–North American trade increased 118 percent for Mexico, 11 percent for Canada, and 41 percent for the United States because of NAFTA.[4] Cipollina and Salvatici agree that NAFTA had major impacts on trade flows—they put the effect at something like 131 percent for the region as a whole.[5] Clausing estimates that, within five years, CUFTA expanded United States imports from Canada by 26 percent.[6]

There is also a general consensus that cross-border investment grew massively after the implementation of NAFTA. Especially as Mexico consolidated its status as an export platform to the rest of North America, the stock of American FDI in Mexico grew from $15 billion in 1993 to more than $100 billion in 2012.[7] NAFTA increased FDI flows to Mexico by something like 40 to 60 percent.[8]

There is little doubt that North American free trade succeeded in knitting the three economies together, and adding substantially to cross-border economic flows. As Figure 1.1 shows, especially for Canada and Mexico the enactment of the two agreements was followed by large increases in trade as a share of GDP. Those increases include the substantial growth of intrafirm trade and the reflect the formation of regional supply chains in many industries.

Economic Growth and Incomes

Transnational economic flows are not ends in themselves; they are means to higher living standards. Did all the increased trade and investment engendered by CUFTA and NAFTA actually lead to higher incomes and economic growth? The typical view among economists ex ante was that CUFTA and NAFTA would produce modest benefits for the US economy

[2] Helliwell 1998.
[3] Congressional Budget Office 2003.
[4] Caliendo and Parro 2015. This is for NAFTA alone, not including CUFTA.
[5] Cipollina and Salvatici 2010.
[6] Clausing 2001.
[7] Villarreal and Fergusson 2017: 20.
[8] Cuevas, Messmacher, and Werner 2005; Waldkirch 2003.

and more substantial ones for Canada and Mexico. Influential studies predicted gains for the Canadian economy on the order of 7 to 10 percent of GNP—especially through productivity gains.[9] An analysis by Sobarzo foresaw aggregate benefits to Mexico in the form of 9.9 percent GDP growth and 21.7 percent wage growth.[10] A series of studies summarized by the US International Trade Commission predicted Mexico's GDP would increase by up to about 11 percent.[11]

Relative to these predictions, North American free trade in practice has been pretty underwhelming.[12] Economic analyses do not show large gains for growth (though nor do they show any notable reductions). One recent analysis, by Caliendo and Parro, concludes that NAFTA, despite substantially expanding trade flows, raised welfare by just 1.31 percent in Mexico and 0.08 percent in the United States, and *reduced* welfare in Canada (net of CUFTA) by 0.06 percent.[13] This state-of-the-art study attended to an impressive diversity of issues, including sectoral heterogeneity, intermediate goods, and sectoral linkages. Likewise, based on an analysis of fine-grained commodity trade data, Romalis concludes that no country experienced welfare gains from NAFTA, because the agreement caused substantial trade diversion, driving out imports to North America from elsewhere.[14] Conconi et al. agree that NAFTA had substantial consequences for trade diversion, as its strict rules of origins reduced imports of intermediate goods from third countries.[15] Under the potential new NAFTA, this diversion is likely to intensify, as the rules of origin for some industries are even stricter.

To put the three countries' circumstances in perspective, between 1993 and 2014 Mexico's real GDP per capita grew about 50 percent—the second least out of nineteen large Latin American economies. By comparison, in the twenty-one-year period from 1960 and 1981 (before the onset of the debt crisis and the lost decade of the 1980s), Mexico's real GDP per capita grew about 123 percent, which was the fourth most out of the same nineteen economies. For Canada, GDP per capita more than doubled in the twenty-five years prior to CUFTA (1963–88), but in the first twenty-five years after CUFTA (1989–2014) GDP per capita grew only 36 percent. The corresponding figures for the United States were 85 percent before CUFTA and 44 percent after, or, comparing twenty years

[9] Harris and Cox 1984; Wonnacott and Wonnacott 1967.
[10] Sobarzo 1994.
[11] International Trade Commission 1992.
[12] Hufbauer, Cimino, and Moran 2014.
[13] Caliendo and Parro 2015.
[14] Romalis 2007.
[15] Conconi et al. 2018.

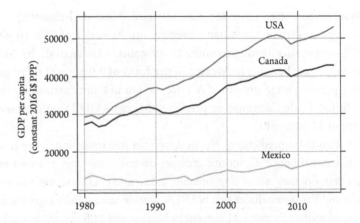

Figure A.1 National Economic Output Per Capita, 1980–2015. Source: IMF World
Economic Outlook Database, October 2017, gross domestic product per capita, constant prices, PPP,
2011 I$.

before and after NAFTA, 42 percent versus 34 percent.[16] The age of free trade
has not therefore been an age of booming growth rates.

To be sure, these aggregate comparisons do not rule out that growth might
have been even slower without the agreements. To investigate that possibility,
the best we can do is turn to the small number of studies that attempt to control for other influences. For the United States, such studies conclude that any
growth or GDP effects from North American free trade were certainly small.[17]
An assessment by the US Congressional Budget Office put the GDP benefits of
NAFTA to the American economy by the year 2000 at 0.1 percent at most.[18] The
US International Trade Commission estimated the total effects of *all* bilateral
and regional trade agreements in force in 2012 as having only a +0.21 percent
effect on US real GDP.[19] Researchers at the Peterson Institute for International
Economics, a Washington think tank that has generally championed free trade,
estimate that Americans gained $400 per person because of NAFTA—which
would not be trivial for a much poorer country, but for the United States means
less than a 1 percent gain.[20]

We can also compare well-being based on microdata, rather than national accounts figures.

---

[16] I calculated these figures using data from the Penn World Table, version 9.0. They are based on
expenditure-side real GDP at chained purchasing-power parity. Figure A.1 shows similar series from
the IMF, for comparison.

[17] International Trade Commission 2016.

[18] Congressional Budget Office 2003.

[19] International Trade Commission 2016: 127.

[20] Hufbauer, Cimino, and Moran 2014.

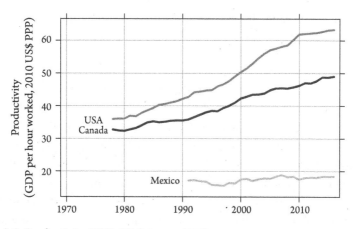

Figure A.2 Productivity, 1978–2016. Source: OECD 2018.

For the United States, the 2015 Caliendo and Parro study mentioned earlier estimated that NAFTA raised real wages in the United States by 0.11 percent. Another study, modeling the effects of NAFTA on local labor markets using census data for 1990 to 2000, concludes that while NAFTA had little impact on "the" US labor market, it had big impacts on some specific local labor markets.[21] The wages of blue-collar workers in some industries and communities suffered substantially, depending on their vulnerability to competitive imports from Mexico. Less-educated workers in particular suffered substantial wage losses if their industry or community of residence was hit by import competition unleashed under NAFTA, and this held even for workers in nontradable industries. The reason for the spillover is that workers in tradable industries who were displaced by imports put downward pressure on wages for all jobs in their community. (So a waitress in a restaurant down the road from a factory shut down by NAFTA could suffer along with people working in the factory.)

Those who argued that free trade would have substantial economic benefits generally made their case on the basis of productivity gains, through competitive pressures on inefficient industries, and by enhancing market access for exports. The gains were expected to be meaningful for Canada and Mexico, but not the United States. In their classic treatment, Wonnacott and Wonnacott went so far as to take as given that Canadian productivity would converge with that of the United States under a free trade arrangement.[22] But in practice, according to OECD data, multifactor productivity in Canada did not just fail to catch up to the United States—it fell further behind, as shown by Figure A.2. In Mexico, the

[21] Hakobyan and McLaren 2016.
[22] Wonnacott and Wonnacott 1967.

story is much the same. In real terms, the productivity of the average Mexican worker in fact failed to increase for thirty years.[23]

Inequality, Distribution, and Poverty

So much for averages. One of the major objections leveled at NAFTA during its creation was that, even if it generated additional output per capita, that would redound to the benefit of the few and not the many. How then have the fruits of free trade been apportioned? While it was critics who were most focused on distribution, some free trade advocates also talked about it and argued there would be distributional benefits in terms of reduced inequality.[24] Assessing the distributional effects of free trade requires controlling for other secular trends in recent decades, as many studies suggest that inequality has been rising because of unrelated factors. In particular, new technologies have been making more difference to the productivity and therefore wages of highly educated workers ("skills-biased technological change"). Theory would predict growing inequality in developed countries that increase trade with developing countries (recall Heckscher-Ohlin from earlier chapters), and the empirical record is generally consistent with that expectation.[25] In developing countries, by contrast, theory would predict trade integration with richer countries to reduce inequality, but that does not appear to have happened, for the most part.[26] Inequality has increased in both contexts, though in some cases not by very much.

In Canada, Townsend finds that CUFTA increased interindustry wage inequality in the tradable goods sector, as workers in industries previously protected by the highest tariffs against US imports experienced substantial wage declines relative to others.[27] Other studies conclude in contrast that free trade did not contribute to rising income inequality in Canada.[28] Overall some of Canada's moderately increased inequality since 1988 may have been due to free trade, but not much.[29]

In the United States, NAFTA contributed slightly to a growing divide between the wages of skilled and unskilled workers, and therefore to wage inequality.[30]

---

[23] Remes 2014: 31.

[24] E.g., García Rocha and Kehoe 1991.

[25] E.g., Forbes 2001.

[26] Goldberg and Pavcnik 2007.

[27] Townsend 2007.

[28] Trefler 2004.

[29] It is a somewhat separate question, addressed subsequently, whether free trade encouraged changes in public policy with regressive distributional impacts, as some critics predicted.

[30] Audley et al. 2004: 12.

There is evidence that growing import competition has suppressed the wages of workers in exposed occupations—on the order of 12 to 17 percent.[31] The impact of NAFTA should not, however, be exaggerated, as the upward trend in US wage inequality predated NAFTA by decades, especially in the upper half of the wage distribution.[32] And while rising trade with developing countries, including Mexico, may have contributed some part of the rising inequality in the United States in recent decades, it can explain at most a minority share—and NAFTA by itself can only explain a part of that.[33]

In Mexico, the story is a little more complex. Inequality was growing in Mexico before NAFTA (Goldberg and Pavcnik 2007), and in the 1990s, the wages received by more educated workers grew faster than those received be less educated workers.[34] The education premium appears to have stopped growing precisely when NAFTA went into effect, however, and between 1996 and 2006, the Gini coefficient of income inequality fell from 0.543 to 0.498.[35] Esquivel, Lustig, and Scott explain the decline, most of which occurred after 2000, as a function largely of policy changes, as the Mexican government increased its spending on education for the poor.[36] (More on this later.)

Still, that improvement made a small dent at most in the stark divide between the "two Mexicos": traditional and modern, less and more productive sectors of the economy, the Mexican workforce being characterized by a very large informal sector. According to the World Bank's $5.50 per day poverty line, the proportion of poor Mexicans rose from 43.3 percent in 1984 to a peak of 58.7 percent in 1996, and then declined to 32.8 percent by 2004—since which time the poverty rate has changed little.[37] For indigenous people specifically, the poverty rate has remained higher.[38] And inequality in Mexico has a geographical dimension: Hanson shows that incomes in northern Mexican states generally increased in the 1990s, while those in the south declined.[39] The northern states that enjoyed larger FDI inflows also saw greater decreases in income inequality.[40]

In sum, the distributional consequences of free trade in North America have likely been regressive, but credible studies do not suggest that it has caused

[31] Ebenstein et al. 2014.

[32] Autor, Katz, and Kearney 2008.

[33] Krugman 2008; Lawrence 2008.

[34] Hanson 2004.

[35] Robertson 2004; Esquivel, Lustig, and Scott 2010. See also OECD 2011.

[36] Esquivel, Lustig, and Scott 2010: 210.

[37] The $5.50 per day benchmark is what the Bank considers most appropriate for upper-middle-income countries like Mexico.

[38] Hall and Patrinos 2005.

[39] Hanson 2007.

[40] Jensen and Rosas 2007.

much of the increased inequality seen in the three countries—and especially the United States.

Employment

Probably the most famous soundbite from the whole debate about North American free trade, in any of the three countries, was Ross Perot's warning of a "giant sucking sound" of jobs moving across the border from the United States to Mexico. Though Perot was correct that US officials expected NAFTA to help American firms invest in Mexico, economists were always skeptical that the agreement would affect US employment. The relative sizes of the economies alone ensured that integration with Mexico would make little impact on the huge US labor market. Even more generally, though, as explained in Chapter 6, economists do not believe that trade has much impact on employment.[41] Still, noneconomist advocates in the United States and Canada promoted free trade as a jobs machine. The business campaign group for CUFTA in Canada had, after all, called itself the "Canadian Alliance for Trade and Job Opportunities." Did free trade affect the number of jobs in any of the three countries?

Consistent with economists' expectations, the empirical record shows no effect of free trade on the number of jobs in either the United States or even in the smaller Canadian economy. In the United States, the middle to late 1990s were a period of tremendous job creation. However, serious investigations conclude NAFTA had effectively no impact on US employment.[42] In Canada, similarly, as Trefler points out, the percentage of Canadians in employment was the same in April 2002 as it was in April 1988—about 62 percent—so it seems unlikely that CUFTA did much to influence it.[43]

There is more to be said about the issue of employment, however, if we consider the cases of specific sectors. Manufacturing is the sector that tends to attract the most attention, though it is important to keep trends in manufacturing employment in perspective: such jobs have been gradually disappearing worldwide in recent decades.[44] They are not just moving from country to country,

---

[41] As Stiglitz (2004) puts it, "To most economists there was little basis for [worries about employment] in the first place [since they believe] maintaining full employment is the concern of monetary and fiscal policy, not of trade policy."

[42] Burfisher, Robinson, and Thierfelder 2001: 130; Audley et al. 2004: 12.

[43] Trefler 2004. Given the large size of the informal sector in Mexico, credible and meaningful employment statistics are hard to come by there.

[44] International Labour Organization 2015.

but being replaced through automation. With that in mind, it is remarkable that Mexico added around a half-million manufacturing jobs in the first eight years of NAFTA, and the share of manufactures in Mexico's exports increased substantially—from about 37 percent between 1980 and 1993 to more than 80 percent between 1994 and 2002.[45]

In the United States, manufacturing employment has been in decline for decades. In 1970, 26 percent of US jobs were in manufacturing (including mining and construction), while by 2010 the share had declined to 10 percent. Though this change has been dramatic, the importance of trade should not be overstated; Autor, Dorn, and Hanson estimate that only about one-quarter of manufacturing job losses between 1990 and 2007 were due to rising import competition.[46] And the most important trade effect in recent decades has not even come from Mexico, or the Americas as a whole—despite the scale of North American trade. Rather, the major influence has been China. So in the years since NAFTA's implementation, US job losses in manufacturing have not meant American jobs moved south to Mexico—rather, if anywhere, they went predominantly to Asia.[47]

NAFTA did have some impacts, which varied somewhat depending on the region of the country; according to some studies, the Northeast, for example, gained jobs from trade with Canada.[48] But aside from the question of the total number of manufacturing jobs in the United States, questions about the impacts of rising trade have led to sophisticated econometric studies drawing increasing attention to the costs—both economic and social—of job displacement. As discussed earlier, such studies show that overall figures can mask harsh local realities, as even workers who find a new job suffer a wage penalty for being forced to change occupations because of trade displacement.[49] A recent study by Autor, Dorn, and Hanson shows how local plant closures can leave behind a high local unemployment rate for some time, with substantial local social impacts—slow adjustment in local labor markets and a long-lasting depression in wages and labor-force participation.[50]

In Canada, in the years immediately after CUFTA went into effect, manufacturing firms shed about four hundred thousand jobs, or one-fifth of all the jobs in the sector nationally.[51] That contraction was probably more due,

---

[45] Audley et al. 2004: 6; Kose et al. 2005: 52.

[46] Autor, Dorn, and Hanson 2013.

[47] Acemoglu et al. 2016.

[48] Logan 2008.

[49] Ebenstein et al. 2014.

[50] Autor, Dorn, and Hanson 2016.

[51] Breau and Rigby 2010.

however, to macroeconomic conditions at the time.[52] The adjustment costs were borne disproportionately by low-paid workers in industries that had previously been protected by relatively high tariffs.[53] But in the longer run, Canadian manufacturing employment actually proved stronger than in most other OECD countries—growing 9.1 percent between April 1988 and April 2002, while such employment fell 12.9 percent in the United States.[54] Within a decade, Canada had as many manufacturing jobs as before CUFTA's implementation, though manufacturing employment began falling again in the early 2000s.[55]

Finally, another sector that deserves close consideration is Mexican agriculture, as a large share of North America's poorest and most marginalized people are Mexican campesinos. NAFTA's impact on them has been a topic of intense disagreement, and it may be the case that out of all outcomes, this is the one about which there is the least consensus. Even before the agreement's enactment, some warned this could be painful for the roughly one-fifth of Mexicans working in the agricultural sector, and that the displacement of maize production could lead to increased migration to cities in Mexico. Small corn farms in Mexico were certainly always going to struggle against subsidized American competitors, though it should also be recalled that subsidies lower the price of corn to the benefit of consumers, including many urban residents in Mexico who are not as poor as the campesinos, but still far from well off.[56] Mexican agriculture certainly suffered substantial displacement after NAFTA, but some of that was due less to US competition than agricultural reforms within Mexico, including privatization of traditional communal lands (*ejidos*) and the removal of subsidies and price controls.[57] Audley et al. claim Mexico's agricultural sector lost more than a million jobs after NAFTA went into effect.[58] On the other hand, official statistics indicate that Mexican corn production grew rather than fell after the enactment of NAFTA, a fact that is hard to square with claims that American production substantially disrupted the sector.[59] Moreover, there has been substantial growth of some fruits and vegetables exports from Mexico to the United States, which have generated some new agricultural employment.

---

[52] Gaston and Trefler 1997.
[53] Trefler 2004.
[54] Trefler 2004: 879.
[55] Audley et al. 2004: 12.
[56] Stiglitz 2004.
[57] Villarreal 2010.
[58] Audley et al. 2004: 6.
[59] Hufbauer and Schott 2005.

Labor Rights and Standards

Setting aside the number of jobs, did free trade affect the *quality* of jobs in any of the three countries, through its effects on labor rights and standards? US labor unions complained that Mexican labor standards would drag down the quality of American jobs and make it harder for US workers to win good pay and conditions. The concern was that international competition (or at least its appearance) would incentivize states to suppress the rights of workers and use dubious means to restrain wages, in the pursuit of investment and trade. There was some irony in US unions' demands for better conditions in Mexico, as Mexico's labor law is actually very generous to workers (and US labor law is quite antiworker compared to other high-income democracies). The Mexican constitution specifies working hour limits, a six-day workweek, a minimum wage, and equal pay (by race or gender) for equal work, and grants workers the right to organize, bargain collectively, and strike. Of course, the implementation of Mexican labor has long been another story, and American employers have used the threat of relocation against their workers, in efforts to resist unionization and restrain demands for better wages and working conditions. Similarly, Canadian employers have sometimes used comparisons with conditions in the United States to threaten their workers, and to convince Canadian governments not to enact stronger labor laws.

Changes in unionization and labor market institutions certainly contributed to rising inequality in many countries in recent decades.[60] But it is less clear that those changes were driven in any sense by rising flows of trade and international investment, and it is hard to argue that the problems of labor in any of the countries are the fault of any of the others. Minimum wages, for example, have not risen in the United States, but it is hard to blame free trade for that, as they have fallen below Canada's (Figure A.3)—despite Canada's lower standard of living. The American labor movement has struggled, then, but that has less to do with free trade than with the generalized political weakness (or suppression) of labor in domestic US politics. Comparing union density, Canada's rate of unionization has declined only modestly over time (by about ten percentage points, down to about 26 percent currently), while unionization in the United States has collapsed, with only about 10 percent of workers in unions by 2016, down from a level similar to Canada's in the mid-twentieth century. Baldwin models the decline of union membership in the United States from 1977 to 1997 and, at least in that period, concludes that rising trade had little to do with it.[61] Neumayer

---

[60] E.g., Lemieux 2008.
[61] Baldwin 2003.

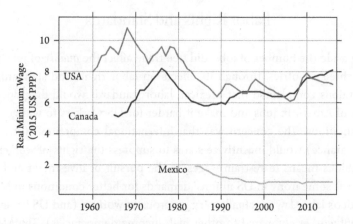

Figure A.3 Real Minimum Wages, 1960–2016. Source: OECD. Real minimum wages, hourly, in 2015 constant prices at 2015 USD PPPs.

and De Soysa find no evidence that trade openness and FDI penetration drive down labor standards generally (in the sense of free association and collective bargaining rights).[62]

On the other hand, NAFTA did lead to the signing of the North American Agreement on Labor Cooperation and the establishment of a trinational Commission for Labor Cooperation. As explained in Chapter 5, unions had pretty low expectations of the NAALC. But it has ended up making some impact, with the NAALC's citizen-petition mechanism providing nontrivial opportunities for labor advocates to draw attention to their concerns and gain judicial support for their campaigns.[63] Because of the way the mechanism works—requiring a complaint originating in a partner country—it has fostered constructive cross-national union collaboration that would not have materialized otherwise.[64]

The potential new NAFTA also includes additional labor-related content, committing each country to respect a number of core labor rights as defined by the International Labour Organization. These include measures on union recognition and rights to collective bargaining. The new agreement also stipulates that a minimum percentage of the value of an automobile must be made by workers earning at least $16 per hour, for it to be eligible for duty-free trade in North America. If the new NAFTA becomes a reality, the implications for labor could be surprisingly positive.

[62] Neumayer and De Soysa 2006.
[63] Graubart 2008.
[64] Kay 2011.

Environmental Protection and Quality

So much for labor. What about the environment? Back in 1993, this was the other main area of concern among civil society actors in the United States. Some advocates of NAFTA argued that the agreement would positively contribute to better environmental outcomes, by raising incomes in Mexico.[65] Critics, pointing to obvious environmental problems in poorly planned industrial areas in Mexico's northern border zone, claimed on the contrary that NAFTA would simply provide US firms with an opportunity to flee to Mexico as a dirty "pollution haven."[66] The debate about NAFTA's likely environmental effects actually spawned a large literature in environmental economics on the relationship between trade, development, and the environment more generally.[67]

The pollution havens hypothesis has led to a lot of statistical research on the relationship between globalization and the environment generally, and particularly the degree to which firms are sensitive to jurisdictions' environmental obligations when choosing where to site their facilities. The general conclusion of such research is that environmental costs play a very small role.[68] There is not much evidence that the costs of complying with environmental regulations have much impact on firms' decisions about where to invest, or that interjurisdictional competition leads to a race to the bottom with respect to environmental standards. While there are identifiable social and economic factors that predict better or worse environmental performance—such as membership in many kinds of intergovernmental organizations—trade openness and foreign investment are not among them.[69] There is also little evidence that FDI flows per se have negative environmental impacts.[70] All this implies that policymakers would do well to disregard objections to stricter environmental policies on competitiveness grounds.

NAFTA actually did some good, in environmental terms, by setting the precedent of including explicit protections for the environment in a trade agreement.[71] Since 1994, moreover, it has been common for trade agreements to commit all parties to enforce their own environmental laws. One of the earliest legal experts on the relationship between trade and the environment, Dan Esty, wrote recently of "a new consensus that promoting free trade without careful

---

[65] Bhagwati 1993.
[66] Daly 1993.
[67] Grossman and Krueger 1993.
[68] Gallagher 2004; Neumayer 2001.
[69] Spilker 2012.
[70] Cole, Elliott, and Zhang 2017.
[71] World Trade Organization 2013: 245.

attention to other public policy priorities, including environmental sustainability, risks endangering the public's health and welfare."[72]

The NAFTA debate also changed environmental politics in Mexico, insofar
as the Mexican environment (and particularly the weak enforcement of laws
protecting it) became an issue outside the country for the first time. NAFTA
advocates had to respond to the agreement's critics, and while Mexico's environmental spending initially dipped during the Salinas *sexenio*, in its second
half it increased substantially. That was largely because the trinational NAFTA
debate increased scrutiny of Mexico's environmental policies and practices.[73]
Salinas took measures like closing the oil refinery in Mexico City, which yielded
substantial benefits for the city's air quality. Likewise, while the environmental
conditions of the border region still leave much to be desired, the environmental
impacts of new developments since NAFTA have certainly been much more benign than the rapid unplanned expansion of earlier times.

Still, the story is not all positive. The investor-state dispute settlement (ISDS)
process established under NAFTA's investment chapter (Chapter 11) has led
to some egregious lawsuits by firms claiming expropriation, when the measures
said to have expropriated them were environmental in nature. In perhaps the
most infamous case (Metalclad), an American waste management firm successfully sued the Mexican government for more than $15 million, with a NAFTA
arbitration panel concluding that a local government had illegitimately rejected
the company's application to operate a hazardous waste facility. Metalclad's view
was that the Mexican authority's decision was de facto appropriation of an asset,
and that it had denied the company fair and equitable treatment.

Though the number of cases like Metalclad—and where the foreign investor's
suit proved successful—has been small, their effect has nonetheless been one
of "regulatory chill," with the threat of lawsuits by foreign investors making it
even harder for governments and public authorities at all levels to regulate for
environmental protection.[74] NAFTA certainly makes it easier for firms to sue for
"regulatory expropriation." than for environmental organizations to take a government to court for failing to adequately protect the environment.

When asked about controversy over ISDS, the Mexican and Canadian investment negotiators said that cases such as Metalclad were not what they had
anticipated seeing under Chapter 11. Their intention was for the mechanism to
be used only in very clear-cut cases of expropriation—such as where a government completely nationalized an industry. But on the other hand one Canadian
did acknowledge negotiators had foreseen that ISDS might get exploited for

---

[72] Esty and Salzman 2017: 125–6.

[73] Hogenboom 1998.

[74] Barenberg and Evans 2004; Stiglitz 2004.

other purposes. "Did we think about regulatory expropriation? Absolutely! Absolutely! We looked at the investor-state, and said: 'Well, you know, the Americans are litigious and if you put a tool in place, they will use it. And we can't say exactly how they are going to use it.' And that's in fact happened." For their part, the Mexicans originally objected to the inclusion of ISDS in NAFTA, because they said it contravened Mexico's constitution in giving foreign investors more legal options than domestic firms, the latter having recourse only to Mexico's domestic courts. Though the Mexican negotiators eventually found a way around that legal impediment, it is telling that ISDS was a problem for a constitutional provision requiring that foreign capital enjoy no special privileges.

Overall, though, if NAFTA has had an impact on environmental protection in North America, the effect has not been large, and certainly much smaller than many other decisions the three countries' government have made in the intervening years. Canada's rapid development of its tar sands and the US decisions to withdraw from the Kyoto Protocol and Paris Agreement, for example, have certainly been much more consequential. Also, as of 2019, the new NAFTA has eliminated ISDS. If the new version of NAFTA in fact gets ratified and replaces the old one, the removal of ISDS will be a significant improvement relative to the status quo.

Migration

NAFTA advocates said increased economic development and improved conditions in Mexico would reduce emigration to the United States, particularly undocumented migration. Carlos Salinas promised that with free trade Mexico would "export goods, not people." Was he proved right?

Statistics are inexact, given that much of the migration across the Mexico-US border is undocumented, but surveys can still tell us a great deal. Above all, we know the peso crisis in 1994–95, coupled with a robust American labor market, propelled the extraordinary growth of migration in the middle and later 1990s.[75] By the peak, roughly one-tenth of the Mexican population was living in the United States, and the United States had not seen an influx of this size since the nineteenth century.[76] This increase came despite substantial tightening of US border enforcement, which ironically worked more effectively to keep Mexicans in the United States than to discourage them from coming in the first place.[77] So there is no question that, contrary to what Salinas promised, migration from

[75] Massey, Durand, and Pren 2014.
[76] Hanson 2006.
[77] Massey, Durand, and Pren 2014.

Mexico to the United States increased substantially after NAFTA's implementation. On an annual basis, the number of people moving from Mexico to the United States doubled between 1990 and 2000. But most commentators do not think NAFTA had much to do with the increase.[78]

In more recent years, as the demand for labor has declined in the United States, the net flow of Mexicans northward came to a halt.[79] From 2009 to 2014, 140,000 more Mexicans left the United States than entered.[80] The decline reflected lower demand for workers in the United States, especially in sectors that employ a large percentage of Mexican-born workers, such as construction.[81]

Dispute Settlement and North American Cooperation

Advocates of free trade said it would contribute to better cooperation and coordination among the three countries, above all by establishing more predictable and reliable mechanisms for resolving conflicts about trade and investment among the three countries. For Mexico and especially Canada, one of the top reasons for negotiating free trade with the United States in the first place was to establish rules-based trading relationships protected by formal institutions strong enough to constrain the actions of their hegemonic neighbor. The goal was a dispute settlement procedure capable of curtailing US trade remedies actions (antidumping and countervailing duties). Was the system created under CUFTA and NAFTA able to do that?

Examining the early effects of CUFTA, Gagné argues that the agreement did increase the security of Canadian exporters' access to the US market, even if it did not deter American trade remedy actions completely.[82] The telling comparison is that the United States used trade remedies against Canada less in the years after CUFTA went into effect than before; and Canada was more successful with the CUFTA panel mechanism than other countries were with US courts in appealing antidumping and countervailing duty determinations. From 1989 to 1993, one-third of the cases in US courts ended up being settled in favor of the foreign exporters, while two-thirds of the cases considered by CUFTA's binational panels went the way of Canadian complainants.

---

[78] Audley et al. 2004: 7.
[79] Passel, Cohn, and Gonzalez-Barrera 2012.
[80] Gonzalez-Barrera 2015.
[81] Villarreal 2014.
[82] Gagné 2000.

On the other hand, there have been cases that have shaken the confidence of both Canada and Mexico in the power of CUFTA and NAFTA to constrain US actions. Canada has been frustrated by a very long-running case with respect to softwood lumber.[83] That conflict (which has been ongoing in various guises since before the CUFTA negotiations even started) revolves around a US interpretation of the fees Canadian lumber companies pay for the trees they cut down on public ("Crown") land. The US logging industry considers the Canadian fees unjustifiably low, and therefore a de facto subsidy. Some NAFTA panels have rejected the US industry's case, but US administrators have then ignored the ruling of the panels. The most frustrating conflict in Mexico's case was over trucking. NAFTA was supposed to liberalize the American market in commercial truck and cargo shipping services, but the US government ended up substantially delaying the opening—ostensibly out of safety concerns. Mexico won a formal NAFTA dispute over the issue in 2001, but it still took the United States another decade to open the market.

These cases aside, in other ways relations among the three countries have been reasonably good since free trade went into effect. Mexico used to want to limit its dealings with the United States, but turned into the source of many new and constructive ideas about North American cooperation.[84] For the United States, improved relations with Mexico generally was perhaps the greatest benefit of NAFTA.[85] The United States got a more friendly southern neighbor, and one that, over the course of the 1990s, and very contrary to its history, turned into a very outward-looking nation. Mexico proceeded to build on NAFTA by signing a series of bilateral and regional trade agreements with other countries, in both the developing and developed worlds.[86]

For Mexico, conversely, NAFTA may have helped by increasing America's goodwill at a crucial moment—specifically, very soon after the agreement went into effect, in the context of the peso crisis. Seeking to help contain the crisis, in early 1995 Bill Clinton authorized a $20 billion loan to Mexico—in the face of substantial congressional opposition. This was a remarkable outcome in terms of demonstrative commitment on the part of the US executive branch (even if the legislative branch's indifference was less encouraging). So although Mexico experienced a severe economic crisis almost immediately after implementing NAFTA—suspiciously soon in the eyes of some—the fallout from the crisis would arguably have been even worse, had NAFTA not been in place. It is telling

---

[83] Gagné and Paulin 2013.
[84] Pastor 2011: 48.
[85] Hufbauer, Cimino, and Moran 2014: 23.
[86] Ortiz Mena 2004.

that while Mexico's GDP fell further in the peso crisis than it did in the recession of the early 1980s, it recovered to its precrisis peak in less time.[87]

Much of the goodwill built up through cooperation such as this, however, has recently evaporated. The election of Donald Trump has completely undone a trend toward more positive feelings on Mexicans' part toward the United States. Between 2008 and 2016, Mexicans' feelings gradually grew more positive, but then in late 2016 they took at sharp turn for the worse.[88] The Mexican populace's distrust of the United States rose from 31 to 84 percent in just three months after the election of Donald Trump as US president.[89] The way President Trump has gone about imposing a renegotiation of NAFTA has substantially alienated both Mexicans and Canadians.

Democracy, Human Rights, and the Rule of Law in Mexico

Advocates argued that NAFTA would strengthen democracy, human rights, and the rule of law in Mexico. Critics, on the other hand, predicted that NAFTA would help sustain the PRI's rule and cronyism and would reinforce authoritarianism in Mexico.[90]

Early indications of NAFTA's impact on political life in Mexico were not encouraging. Famously, on the very day NAFTA went into effect—January 1, 1994—indigenous insurgents in the southern state of Chiapas launched a lightly armed revolt against the state. The Ejército Zapatista de Liberación Nacional (Zapatista Army of National Liberation) argued that NAFTA was a further assault against the rights and well-being of indigenous peoples in Mexico, who were already suffering from five hundred years of displacement, oppression, and neglect. Though the rebellion's practical impacts were modest, the movement attracted substantial interest and sympathy internationally, and was probably not the first association that the Mexican government would have wanted for NAFTA—especially with a presidential election scheduled for later that year, on July 1.

Worse was yet to come, however. In the spring of 1994, on March 23, Salinas's designated successor as the PRI's candidate for the election was gunned down and killed in Tijuana. The case was never solved. Then, on September 28, the

---

[87] Kose et al. 2005: 42. Contrary to what members of Congress had feared, the United States eventually got back all the money it sent Mexico's way.

[88] Ortiz-Mena 2017: 26.

[89] Chavez 2017, citing a poll by the Americas Barometer.

[90] Aguilar Zínser 1993: 203–15.

PRI's secretary-general—and Salinas' brother-in-law—was also killed. The two assassinations rocked the Mexican political world, and it seemed that Mexican politics was spinning out of control. By the end of 1994, as the peso crisis began to plunge the Mexican economy into chaos, things were not going well at all.

But in some ways, as the years went by, life did get better. Most importantly, the election of 2000 ended decades of single-party rule, as the PRI finally lost the presidency—and agreed to accept the result. Prior to that, there were also other important steps on the long road to democracy in Mexico (as explained in Chapter 4), most notably the PRI's loss in 1997 of both its absolute majority in the federal congress and of the mayoralty of Mexico City. Some commentators have speculated that the NAFTA debate in Mexico indirectly contributed to these events. Openly repressive suppression of domestic criticism was not an option for the PRI in the early 1990s, as it would have further damaged the political viability of the agreement in the United States. And while the power of the PRI was still able to constrain public criticism of its rule and its policies, the debate about NAFTA encouraged the emergence of civil society and political opposition forces that arguably played a role in the subsequent liberalization of Mexican politics.[91]

After NAFTA went into effect, Mexicans began to enjoy some notable improvements in the country's level of social development, even if some of the trends predated free trade. The country's literacy rate, for example, increased from 83 percent in 1980 to 90 percent in 2000. Life expectancy, likewise, rose from 66.6 years in 1980 to 74.4 years in 2000, and is now more than 77 years (according to the World Bank's World Development Indicators database). The peso crisis meant the poverty rate (using a $1.90 a day cutoff, at 2011 PPP) rose from 6.6 percent of the population in 1994 to 11.2 percent in 1996, but since then has fallen to 2.5 percent as of 2016. As all of these things have improved, Mexico's score on the Human Development Index has risen. Improvements under NAFTA may have been disappointing, then, but there have been some improvements. These modest signs of progress, along with the slight drop in inequality discussed earlier, reflect changes in public policy, and are a sign that democratization has had real benefits for ordinary people. In the 1990s and 2000s, public spending on education, health, and nutrition expanded and grew more equitably distributed across the population; Esquivel, Lustig, and Scott argue this "state-led redistribution was a top-down process led by enlightened technocrats."[92]

[91] Cameron and Wise (2004) suggest, though, that this argument should not be taken too far. They see more of a role for increasing public frustration with the failures of the grander promises of the economic liberalizers.

[92] Esquivel, Lustig, and Scott 2010: 213.

Mexico even became an influential innovator in the area of policies for poverty reduction, helping to launch a worldwide revolution in "conditional cash transfer" (CCT) programs. Under Mexico's 1997 Progresa program (Programa de Educación, Salud y Alimentación, later renamed Oportunidades, and then Prospera), households would receive cash payments conditional on children's school attendance and health checkups. By 2004, transfers were being paid to five million beneficiary households, initially only in rural and semiurban areas, but later in cities too. The program was, furthermore, rolled out using random assignment, such that researchers were able to evaluate its impacts in a rigorous way—and given the program's demonstrable effectiveness, dozens of countries subsequently introduced variants of it. The program contributed to the reduction in income inequality in Mexico, and systematic reviews show that CCTs generally lead to lower rates of child labor and improved school enrolment and attendance.[93] Progresa/Oportunidades, which where possible paid out transfers specifically to mothers, generally also helped narrow some gaps in well-being between indigenous and nonindigenous children.[94]

More negatively, since the 2000s, Mexico has suffered a tremendous surge of drugs-related violence. Though Mexico has long been home to significant levels of organized crime, the scale of the activity expanded significantly in the years after NAFTA's implementation, especially as Mexico took over some of Colombia's old role in the international cocaine trade. President Felipe Calderón (2006–12) ordered the military to assist police in targeting major drug traffickers in Mexico, but this accomplished little except to instigate a horrendous surge in violence—with gangs fighting both the authorities and each other, leading to many deaths on all sides.[95]

NAFTA: A Balance Sheet

Looking dispassionately at the track records of CUFTA and NAFTA, it is clear that both the advocacy and the opposition were overblown.[96] North American free trade has not been a disaster, even if it has not been a great success either.[97] The two agreements failed to generate a significant boom in economic output, the main mechanism by which free trade was supposed to benefit ordinary people. But nor did free trade do the most serious harms that opponents argued it would.

[93] Kabeer and Waddington 2015; Soares et al. 2009.
[94] Hall and Patrinos 2005.
[95] Dell 2015.
[96] Hufbauer, Cimino, and Moran 2014.
[97] Audley et al. 2004; Pastor 2011.

In Canada, critics worried that economic integration with the United States would bring heavy downward pressures to bear on the more regulated, egalitarian, and social democratic features of Canadian capitalism (more generous social spending, universal healthcare, better labor rights, and so on). In practice, evidence that free trade made much of an impact of this kind is scarce: CUFTA has also not undermined Canada's formal political autonomy, nor its national identity, and Canadians' attitudes on many topics have not converged with those of Americans.[98] Canadian political economy evolved over the course of the 1990s, in the years after CUFTA and NAFTA went into effect, but that was probably more due to the post-1993 Liberal government's efforts to cut the federal deficit. That said, from the perspective of 2019, there is some irony that the man who led the CUFTA negotiations for Canada once warned of an "ever-present danger that a sudden shift in U.S. trade policy . . . could severely affect Canada's total economy."[99] CUFTA critics agreed, claiming that free trade with the United States would exacerbate Canada's dependence on the United States. That warning has been proved correct, as Donald Trump's aggressive threats in 2018 to withdraw the United States from NAFTA meant that Ottawa had little choice but to renegotiate the agreement; it would be much costlier for Canada than the United States if the two countries had to unscramble the egg.

In Mexico, the lives of ordinary people are in many ways better today than they were in 1993. But the amount of improvement has been disappointing. Without active efforts by the state to make globalization more broadly beneficial, research shows it tends to have few benefits for the poor in developing countries.[100] Such efforts are far from a given, as the poor typically struggle to assert their preferences politically. NAFTA has not helped Mexico to close the gap with the United States and Canada in terms of the rule of law and freedom from corruption, though conceivably things could have been even worse without the agreement. Nor have Mexican incomes converged on those of the United States or Canada; since 1993, GDP per capita has grown slower in Mexico than in the other two countries, and indeed than in most other Latin American countries. Some might argue that Mexico's earlier, more closed economic policy mix was unsustainable, but the fact remains that the Mexican economy grew much faster before the 1980s than it has under the new economic regime. The decision to sacrifice policy space (to use Robert Wade's phrase)[101] in return for access to the US market was questionable. That decision was motivated largely by the pursuit

---

[98] Adams 2003.
[99] Reisman 1986: 39.
[100] Rudra and Tobin 2017.
[101] Wade 2003.

of foreign investment, the benefits of which have proven underwhelming for growth.[102]

NAFTA's greatest downsides have probably been its highly dubious governance content and the reinforcement of some damaging misconceptions about supposed economic competition among nations. From the point of view of democratic governance in all countries, investor rights provisions like those in NAFTA transfer power from elected governments to private firms.[103] Still, shady corporate lawsuits aside, free trade has not undermined social and environmental protection. NAFTA established a precedent for incorporating environmental and labor standards in international trade agreements—albeit in a weaker way than intellectual property and investor rights.[104] NAFTA also fostered a debate that put the PRI on the defensive about its hitherto poor record on the environment and its less than democratic character—arguably contributing to important political reforms thereafter, and improvements in environmental and social policy. Had the Mexican state not put itself in a position to be subjected to scrutiny by an alliance of civil society groups, both abroad and at home, some of those important improvements in public administration might never have happened, or at least taken much longer.

[102] Howse 2017.

[103] Barenberg and Evans 2004; McBride 2006.

[104] Intellectual property rights do have some benefits—to the holders of the rights. The US International Trade Commission estimates that rising foreign patent protections between 1995 and 2010 raised US intellectual property receipts 12.6 percent by the end of that period (International Trade Commission 2016: 76).

Appendix A

LIST OF INTERVIEWEES

United States

Askey, Thelma, Minority Trade Counsel, House Ways and Means Committee

Autor, Erik, International Trade Counsel, Senate Finance Committee

Barreda, William, Deputy Assistant Secretary for Trade and Investment, Department of Treasury

Biel, Eric, International Trade Counsel, Senate Finance Committee

Brosch, Kevin, Deputy Assistant General Counsel for International Affairs, Office of the General Counsel, US Development Agency

Collins, Paula, Director of Government Relations, Business Roundtable

Condon, Leonard, Deputy Assistant USTR for Agricultural Affairs

Craft, William, Division Chief, Special Trade Activities, Office of Multilateral Trade Affairs, Department of State

Dunathan, Amy, Legislative Assistant to Senator Chafee (R-RI)

Dunn, Alan, Assistant Secretary for Import Administration, International Trade Administration, Department of Commerce

Fisher, Robert, Director, Mexico, USTR

Gaines, Robin, International Trade Specialist, International Trade Administration, Office of Auto Industry Affairs, Department of Commerce

Gorlin, Jacques, Director, Intellectual Property Committee

Haverkamp, Jennifer, Director for Environmental Policy, USTR

Huenemann, Jon, Deputy Assistant USTR, Latin America

Kantor, Mickey, United States Trade Representative

Kyle, Robert, Chief Trade Counsel, Senate Finance Committee, US Congress

Lamb, Deborah, International Trade Counsel, Senate Finance Committee

Lande, Stephen, President, Manchester Trade, Ltd.

Levy, Charles, Partner, Wilmer Cutler Pickering LLP

McNiel, Dale, Senior Counsel, Office of the General Counsel, US Development Agency

Melle, John, Deputy Director, Generalized System of Preferences, USTR

Miller, Marcia, Professional Staff Member, Senate Finance Committee

Morici, Peter, Professor, University of Maine

Morton, Colleen, Executive Director, US Council, Mexico-U.S. Business Committee, Council of the Americas

Otero, Jack, Deputy Undersecretary of Labor for International Affairs

Pastor, Robert, Professor, Emory University (also Director, Latin American Program, Carter Center)

Price, Daniel, Principal Deputy General Counsel, USTR

Pumphrey, David, Director, Office of International Market and Policy Analysis, Department of Energy

Samuel, Bryan, Deputy Assistant USTR for North America

Self, Richard, Deputy Assistant USTR for Investment and Services

Shapiro, Ira, General Counsel, Office of the USTR

Shoyer, Andrew, Assistant General Counsel, USTR

Simon, Emory, Deputy Assistant USTR for Intellectual Property

Skud, Timothy, Deputy Director for Tariff and Trade Affairs, Treasury

Sorini, Ronald, Chief Textiles Negotiator, USTR

Sweeney, Jack, Financial Attaché, US Embassy in Mexico

Workman, Willard, Vice President, US Chamber of Commerce

Canada

Barrett, Dave, NDP Member of Parliament, Trade Critic, member of the Standing Committee on External Affairs and International Trade

Bleyer, Peter, Executive Director, Council of Canadians

Boutziouvis, Sam, Staff, Business Council on National Issues

Bradford, Meriel, NAFTA services negotiator, External Affairs and International Trade

Burney, Derek, Canadian Ambassador to the United States

Cameron, Duncan, President, Canadian Centre for Policy Alternatives (also Editor, *Canadian Forum*; head, Action Canada Network analysis team; and Professor of Political Science, University of Ottawa)

Campbell, Bruce, Research Fellow, Canadian Centre for Policy Alternatives (also Senior Economist, Canadian Labour Congress)

Clark, Bob, NAFTA Deputy Chief Negotiator, External Affairs

Clarke, Tony, Director, Social Affairs Commission, Canadian Council of Catholic Bishops (also Chairperson, Action Canada Network)

Close, Patricia, NAFTA market access negotiator, Finance Canada

Dillon, John, Research Coordinator, Ecumenical Coalition for Economic Justice

Dymond, William, Minister Counsellor (Commercial), Embassy of Canada to the United States, Washington

Finlayson, Jock, Vice President of Policy and Research, Business Council on National Issues

Foster, John, staff, North-South Institute

Grey, Rodney de C., Chief Negotiator, Kennedy Round, Department of Finance

Griffin Cohen, Marjorie, Professor of Political Science, Simon Fraser University

Hart, Michael, Director of Economic Analysis, Policy Planning Bureau, External Affairs and International Trade Canada

Hecnar, David, Director of International Policy, Canadian Chamber of Commerce

Kube, Arthur, Director of Special Projects, Canadian Labour Congress (also member, Action Canada Network)

MacKenzie, Denyse, GATT division, External Affairs and International Trade Canada

MacLaren, Roy, Liberal Caucus Trade Critic (also Minister of International Trade)

May, Elizabeth, Executive Director, Sierra Club of Canada

Moore, Jim, Vice President–Policy, Canadian Exporters' Association

Moroz, Andrew "Sandy," NAFTA Rules of Origin and Customs Procedures negotiator, External Affairs and International Trade Canada

Morpaw, May, Director of Special Projects, Strategic Policy Branch, Dept of Labour Canada

Myers, Jayson, Chief Economist, Canadian Manufacturers' Association

Page, Tim, Senior Vice President–International, Canadian Chamber of Commerce

Phillips, Roy, President, Canadian Manufacturers' Association

Rebick, Judy, President, National Action Committee on the Status of Women

Sorensen, Sandra, Executive Director, Canadian Centre for Policy Alternatives (also member, Common Frontiers)

Swenarchuk, Michelle, staff, Canadian Environmental Law Association

Thibault, Laurent, President, Canadian Manufacturers' Association

Thomas, Chris, Senior Policy Advisor to the Minister for International Trade

Traynor, Ken, member, Common Frontiers

Turk, Jim, Chairperson, Ontario Coalition for Social Justice

Van Houten, Steve, President, Canadian Manufacturers' Association

Verdun, Emmy, Assistant Chief Negotiator for Investment, Investment Canada

Wilson, Michael, Minister of Industry, Science and Technology and International Trade

Mexico

Amigo Castañeda, Jorge, Director General of Foreign Investment, SECOFI

Antebi, Karen, Deputy Director, Free Trade Agreement Negotiating Unit, SECOFI

Beltrán, Ulises, Technical Advisor, Office of the President

Carreño Carlón, José, Public Relations Director, Office the President

Cevallos Gómez, Jesús, President, CONCAMIN

Cohen, Aslan, Director General for Rules of Origin, SECOFI

Cruz Miramontes, Rodolfo, Industry Sector Coordinator, COECE (also President, Trade Committee, CONCAMIN)

de la Calle, Luis, Counsellor, SECOFI (NAFTA office in Washington, DC)

Espinosa, Enrique, Director General of North American trade relations

Fernández, Arturo, Coordinator, Deregulation Unit, SECOFI

Flores Ayala, Jesús María, Chief of Staff to the Chief Negotiator, Free Trade Agreement Negotiating Unit, SECOFI (energy negotiator)

González Fisch, Carlos, member, Canacintra's capital goods division

Gurría, Angel, Undersecretary for International Financial Affairs, Secretaría de Hacienda y Crédito Público

Gutiérrez Haces, María Teresa, Professor, National Autonomous University of Mexico

Heftye, Fernando, Technical Secretary, National Foreign Investment Commission

Hurtado López, Carlos, Director General of Economic and Social Policy, Secretaría de Programación y Presupuesto

Jasso Torres, Humberto, Director of Tariff Negotiations, Free Trade Agreement Negotiating Unit, SECOFI

Leycegui, Beatriz, Director of Legal Affairs, Free Trade Agreement Negotiating Unit, SECOFI

Madero, Enrique, President, Mexican Business Council for International Affairs

Márquez, Héctor, Director General, SECOFI (autos negotiator)

Noyola, Pedro, Chief of Staff to the Secretary of Trade and Industry

Ojeda Gómez, Mario, President, El Colegio de México (member of the Consejo Asesor)

Ojeda, Lucía, Director of Legal Analysis, Free Trade Agreement Negotiating Unit, SECOFI

Ortiz Mena, Antonio, Director of Legislative-Executive Branch Relations, Free Trade Agreement Negotiating Unit, SECOFI

Ortiz Muñiz, René, Chairperson, Bilateral Relations Committee, Canacintra

Patiño Manffer, Ruperto, Coordinator of Legal Advisors, SECOFI

Provencio, Marco, Director General of International Financial Affairs, Secretaría de Hacienda y Crédito Público

Ramos, Eduardo, Director of Information, SECOFI

Rivera, Adán, founding member, ANIT

Rodríguez Sánchez, Leopoldo, Director, Girsa S.A. de C.V. (also chemical industry representative to COECE)

Ruíz Sacristán, Carlos, Undersecretary, Finance (government procurement negotiator)

Ruíz Sacristán, Federico, President, National Chamber of the Electronics and Electric Communications Industry (also Vice President, CONCAMIN; Rules of Origin Coordinator, COECE)

Salas, Fernando, Director General for Financial Services, SECOFI

Serra Puche, Jaime, Secretary of Trade and Industry

Solís, Eduardo, Director General of Agriculture and Agro-Industry Negotiations

Suárez Mler, Manuel, Minister for Economic Affairs, Mexican Embassy in the United States

Ten Kate, Adriaan, temporary entry negotiator, Free Trade Agreement Negotiating Unit, SECOFI

Ubbelohde Rosaldo, Edgar, Government Procurement Coordinator, COECE (also Vice Chairman of the Government Procurement Committee, CONCAMIN)

Villarreal Gonda, Roberto, Director General of Technological Development, SECOFI (IPRs negotiator)

Appendix B

ARCHIVES CONSULTED

Ronald Reagan Presidential Library, Simi Valley, CA
Jimmy Carter Library and Museum, Atlanta, GA
George Bush Presidential Library and Museum, College Station, TX
US National Archives and Records Administration in College Park, MD
Canadian Manufacturers and Exporters (formerly Canadian Manufacturers'
    Association), Ottawa
Mexican Confederation of Chambers of Industry (CONCAMIN),
    Mexico City
Library and Archives Canada, Ottawa
Centro de Estudios Internacionales, El Colegio de México, Mexico City
Centro de Investigaciones Sobre America del Norte, Universidad Nacional
    Autónoma de México, Mexico City (held by Elisa Dávalos)

Personal Papers

Adán Rivera, Asociación Nacional de Industriales de la Transformación,
    Mexico City
John Foster, North-South Institute, Ottawa
Peter Bleyer, Council of Canadians, Ottawa

Several libraries held useful unpublished documents: Canada's Department of
Foreign Affairs and International Trade, the Centro de Investigación y Docencia
Económicas, and the Instituto de Investigaciones Económicas at the Universidad
Nacional Autónoma de México.

REFERENCES

Abbott, Jason P. 2002. *Developmentalism and Dependency in Southeast Asia: The Case of the Automotive Industry*. New York: Routledge.

Abelson, Donald E. 2002. *Do Think Tanks Matter? Assessing the Impact of Public Policy Institutes*. Montreal : McGill-Queens University Press.

Abrams, Elliott. 1988. "Some Thoughts about U.S. Interests in Post-election Mexico, Information Memorandum (8/16/88) to the Secretary, from the Bureau of Inter-American Affairs." Robert S. Pastorino Files, Box 92350. Ronald Reagan Presidential Library.

Acemoglu, Daron, David Autor, David Dorn, Gordon H. Hanson, and Brendan Price. 2016. "Import Competition and the Great US Employment Sag of the 2000s." *Journal of Labor Economics* 34: S141–S198.

Achen, Christopher H., and Larry M. Bartels. 2016. *Democracy for Realists: Why Elections Do Not Produce Responsive Government*. Princeton, NJ: Princeton University Press.

Adams, Michael. 2003. *Fire and Ice: The United States, Canada and the Myth of Converging Values*. Toronto: Penguin.

Adelman, Jeremy. 2017. "Polanyi, the Failed Prophet of Moral Economics." *Boston Review*, May 30. http://bostonreview.net/class-inequality/jeremy-adelman-polanyi-failed-prophet-moral-economics.

Adler, Emanuel, and Peter M. Haas. 1992. "Conclusion: Epistemic Communities, World Order, and the Creation of a Reflective Research Program." *International Organization* 46[1]: 367–90.

Advisory Committee for Trade Policy and Negotiations. 1992. "Report on the North American Free Trade Agreement." OA/ID CF01116 (NAFTA). George H. W. Bush Presidential Library.

Aguilar Zínser, Adolfo. 1992. "El Tratado de Libre Comercio, Dimension Política." Pp. 159–72 in Bárbara Driscoll de Alvarado and Mónica C. Gambrill, eds., *El Tratado de Libre Comercio: Entre el Viejo y el Nuevo Orden*. Mexico City: UNAM.

Aguilar Zínser, Adolfo. 1993. "Authoritarianism and North American Free Trade: The Debate in Mexico." Pp. 205–16 in Ricardo Grinspun and Maxwell A. Cameron, eds., *The Political Economy of North American Free Trade*. New York: St. Martin's Press.

Aguilar, Linda M. 1993. "NAFTA: A Review of the Issues." *Federal Reserve Bank of Chicago Economic Perspectives* 17[1]: 12–20.

Alba V., Carlos, and Gustavo Vega C. 2002. "Trade Advisory Mechanisms in Mexico." Pp. 55–65 in *The Trade Policy-Making Process: Level One of the Two Level Game. Country Studies in the Western Hemisphere*. Occasional Paper 13. New York: Inter-American Development Bank.

Alba Vega, Carlos. 1997. "La COECE: Un Caso de Cooperación entre los Sectores Público y Privado en México." *Comercio Exterior* 47[2]: 149–58.

Alemán, Eduardo, and Yeaji Kim. 2015. "The Democratizing Effect of Education." *Research and Politics* 2[4]: 1–7.

Alston, Richard M., J. R. Kearl, and Michael B. Vaughan. 1992. "Is There a Consensus among Economists in the 1990's?" *American Economic Review* 82[2]: 203–9.

American Banker-Bond Buyer. 1991. "Textile Trade Groups Seek NAFTA Protections." *North American Report on Free Trade* 1[45]: 6.

Amigo Castañeda, J. 1991. "Regulación y Proyectos de Inversion Extranjera en México." *El Mercado de Valores* 7: 3–7.

Angrist, Joshua D., and Jörn-Steffen Pischke. 2010. "The Credibility Revolution in Empirical Economics: How Better Research Design Is Taking the Con out of Econometrics." *Journal of Economic Perspectives* 24[2]: 3–30.

Appel, Hilary, and Mitchell A. Orenstein. 2018. *From Triumph to Crisis: Neoliberal Economic Reform in Postcommunist Countries.* New York: Cambridge University Press.

Ardanaz, Martin, M. Victoria Murillo, and Pablo M. Pinto. 2013. "Sensitivity to Issue Framing on Trade Policy Preferences: Evidence from a Survey Experiment." *International Organization* 67[2]: 411–37.

Arnold, Richard. 1991. "Letter from the President of KTA to President Bush." August 19. TA005, WHORM, 263562. George H. W. Bush Presidential Library.

Aspe, Pedro. 1990. "Mexico: Foreign Debt and Economic Growth." Pp. 123–34 in D. S. Brothers and A. E. Wick, eds., *Mexico's Search for a New Development Strategy.* Boulder, CO: Westview Press.

Audley, John J., Demetrios G. Papademetriou, Sandra Polaski, and Scott Vaughan. 2004. "NAFTA's Promise and Reality: Lessons from Mexico for the Hemisphere." Carnegie Endowment for International Peace. http://carnegieendowment.org/files/nafta1.pdf.

Autor, David H., David Dorn, and Gordon H. Hanson. 2013. "The China Syndrome: Local Labor Market Effects of Import Competition in the United States." *American Economic Review* 103[6]: 2121–68.

Autor, David H., David Dorn, and Gordon H. Hanson. 2016. "The China Shock: Learning from Labor-Market Adjustment to Large Changes in Trade." *Annual Review of Economics* 8: 205–40.

Autor, David H., Lawrence F. Katz, and Melissa S. Kearney. 2008. "Trends in U.S. Wage Inequality: Revising the Revisionists." *Review of Economics and Statistics* 90[2]: 300–323.

Ayres, Jeffrey M. 1998. *Defying Conventional Wisdom: Political Movements and Popular Contention against North American Free Trade.* Toronto: University of Toronto Press.

Babb, Sarah. 2001. *Managing Mexico: Economists from Nationalism to Neoliberalism.* Princeton, NJ: Princeton University Press.

Babb, Sarah. 2007. "Embeddedness, Inflation, and International Regimes: The IMF in the Early Postwar Period." *American Journal of Sociology* 113[1]: 128–64.

Babb, Sarah. 2009. *Behind the Development Banks: Washington Politics, World Poverty, and the Wealth of Nations.* Chicago: University of Chicago Press.

Babb, Sarah. 2013. "The Washington Consensus as Transnational Policy Paradigm: Its Origins, Trajectory and Likely Successor." *Review of International Political Economy* 20[2]: 268–97.

Baccini, Leonardo. 2012. "Democratization and Trade Policy: An Empirical Analysis of Developing Countries." *European Journal of International Relations* 18[3]: 455–79.

Backhouse, Roger E. 2010. "Economics." Pp. 38–70 in Roger E. Backhouse and Philippe Fontaine, eds., *The History of the Social Sciences since 1945.* New York: Cambridge University Press.

Bagwell, Kyle, and Robert W. Staiger. 2002. *The Economics of the World Trading System.* Cambridge, MA: MIT Press.

Baier, Scott L., and Jeffrey H. Bergstrand. 2001. "The Growth of World Trade: Tariffs, Transport Costs, and Income Similarity." *Journal of International Economics* 53: 1–27.

Baier, Scott L., and Jeffrey H. Bergstrand. 2007. "Do Free Trade Agreements Actually Increase Members' International Trade?" *Journal of International Economics* 71: 72–95.

Bailey, Norman A. 1988. "Bridge Loan to Mexico: Bailing Out the Lenders?" *Los Angeles Times*, December 28. http://articles.latimes.com/1988-12-28/local/me-788_1_bridge-loan.

Bak, Daehee, and Chungshik Moon. 2016. "Foreign Direct Investment and Authoritarian Stability." *Comparative Political Studies* 49[14]: 1998–2037.

Baker, Andy. 2005. "Who Wants to Globalize? Consumer Tastes and Labor Markets in a Theory of Trade Policy Beliefs." *American Journal of Political Science* 49[4]: 924–38.

Baker, Chris, and Pasuk Phongpaichit. 2005. *A History of Thailand*. New York: Cambridge University Press.

Balassa, Bela. 1983. "Trade Policy in Mexico." *World Development* 11[9]: 795–811.

Baldwin, John R., and Guy Gellatly. 2005. "Global Links: Long-Term Trends in Foreign Investment and Foreign Control in Canada, 1960 to 2000." Statistics Canada, Canadian Economy in Transition Series. Ottawa: Minister of Industry.

Baldwin, Richard E. 1997. "The Causes of Regionalism." *World Economy* 20[7]: 865–88.

Baldwin, Robert E. 1996. "The Political Economy of Trade Policy: Integrating the Perspectives of Economists and Political Scientists." Pp. 149–73 in Robert C. Feenstra, Gene M. Grossman, and Douglas A. Irwin, eds., *The Political Economy of Trade Policy: Papers in Honor of Jagdish Bhagwati*. Cambridge, MA: MIT Press.

Baldwin, Robert E. 2003. "The Decline of US Labor Unions and the Role of Trade." Washington, DC: Peterson Institute for International Economics. https://piie.com/bookstore/decline-us-labor-unions-and-role-trade.

Baldwin, Robert E., and Christopher S. Magee. 2000. "Is Trade Policy for Sale? Congressional Voting on Recent Trade Bills." *Public Choice* 105: 79–101.

Ban, Cornel. 2016. *Ruling Ideas: How Global Neoliberalism Goes Local*. New York: Oxford University Press.

Barabas, Jason. 2016. "Democracy's Denominator: Reassessing Responsiveness with Public Opinion on the National Policy Agenda." *Public Opinion Quarterly* 80[2]: 437–59.

Barenberg, M., and P. Evans. 2004. "The FTAA's Impact on Democratic Governance." Pp. 755–89 in A. Estevadeordal, D. Rodrik, A. M. Taylor, and A. Velasco, eds., *Integrating the Americas: FTAA and Beyond*. Cambridge, MA: Harvard University Press.

Barlow, Maude. 1998. *The Fight of My Life: Confessions of an Unrepentant Canadian*. Toronto: HarperCollins.

Barlow, Maude, and Bruce Campbell. 1993. *Take Back the Nation 2: Meeting the Threat of NAFTA*. Toronto: Key Porter.

Bartels, Larry M. 2008. *Unequal Democracy: The Political Economy of the New Gilded Age*. Princeton, NJ: Princeton University Press.

Bartley, Tim. 2018. "Transnational Corporations and Global Governance." Annual Review of Sociology 44: 145–65.

Basáñez, Miguel. 1995. "Winners and Losers: A View from Mexico." Pp. 49–64 in Brenda McPhail, ed., *NAFTA Now! The Changing Political Economy of North America*. Lanham, MD: University Press of America.

Bates, Robert H., and Anne O. Krueger. 1993. "Generalizations Arising from the Country Studies." Pp. 444–72 in Robert H. Bates and Anne O. Krueger, eds., *Political and Economic Interactions in Economic Policy Reform: Evidence from Eight Countries*. Oxford: Blackwell.

Bauer, Raymond A., Ithiel de Sola Pool, and Lewis Anthony Dexter. 1963. *American Business and Public Policy: The Politics of Foreign Trade*. New York: Atherton.

Beaulieu, Eugene, and Christopher Magee. 2004. "Four Simple Tests of Campaign Contributions and Trade Policy Preferences." *Economics and Politics* 16[2]: 163–87.

Bélanger, Éric, and François Pétry. 2005. "The Rational Public? A Canadian Test of the Page and Shapiro Argument." *International Journal of Public Opinion Research* 17[2]: 190–212.

Bell, A., and Jones, K. 2014. "Explaining Fixed Effects: Random Effects Modeling of Time-Series Cross-Sectional and Panel Data." *Political Science Research and Method* 3: 133–53.

Bell, Stephen. 1993. *Australian Manufacturing and the State: The Politics of Industry in the Post-war Era*. Cambridge: Cambridge University Press.

Bennett, Tim. 1986. "Memorandum to the Files, Subject: Yeutter-Hernandez Bilateral of August 14." August 27. Latin American Affairs Directorate, NSC Records, Box 91063. Ronald Reagan Presidential Library.

Bergesen, Albert J., and John Sonnett. 2001. "The Global 500: Mapping the World Economy at Century's End." *American Behavioral Scientist* 44[10]: 1602–15.

Bermingham, Finbarr. 2014. "TTIP: Opponents Attack Negotiations as Undemocratic and Lacking Transparency." *International Business Times*, May 21. http://www.ibtimes.co.uk/ttip-opponents-attack-negotiations-undemocratic-lacking-transparency-1449406.

Besley, T., and M. Reynal-Querol. 2011. "Do Democracies Select More Educated Leaders?" *American Political Science Review* 105: 552–66.

Bhagwati, Jagdish. 1988. *Protectionism*. Cambridge, MA: MIT Press.

Bhagwati, Jagdish. 1993. "The Case for Free Trade." *Scientific American* 269: 42–49.

Bhagwati, Jagdish. 2008. *Termites in the Trading System: How Preferential Agreements Undermine Free Trade*. New York: Oxford University Press.

Bhagwati, Jagdish, and T. N. Srinivasan. 1996. "Trade and the Environment: Does Environmental Diversity Detract from the Case for Free Trade?" Pp. 1:159–223 in Jagdish Bhagwati and Robert E. Hudec, eds., *Fair Trade and Harmonization: Prerequisites for Free Trade?* Cambridge, MA: MIT Press.

Bianculli, Andrea C. 2017. *Negotiating Trade Liberalization in Argentina and Chile: When Policy Creates Politics*. New York: Routledge.

Blendon, Robert J., John M. Benson, Mollyann Brodie, Richard Morin, Drew E. Altman, Daniel Gitterman, Mario Brossard, and Matt James. 1997. "Bridging the Gap between the Public's and Economists' Views of the Economy." *Journal of Economic Perspectives* 11[3]: 105–18.

Bleyer, Peter. 1997. "Coalitions of Social Movements as Agencies for Social Change: The Action Canada Network." Pp. 102–17 in William K. Carroll, ed., *Organizing Dissent: Contemporary Social Movements in Theory and Practice*. 2nd ed. Toronto: Garamond Press.

Block, Fred. 2001. "Using Social Theory to Leap over Historical Contingencies: A Comment on Robinson." *Theory and Society* 30: 215–21.

Block, Walter, and Michael Walker. 1988. "Entropy in the Canadian Economics Profession: Sampling Consensus on the Major Issues." *Canadian Public Policy* 14: 137–50.

Blonigen, Bruce A. 2011. "Revisiting the Evidence on Trade Policy Preferences." *Journal of International Economics* 85[1]: 129–35.

Blyth, Mark. 2002. *Great Transformations: Economic Ideas and Institutional Change in the Twentieth Century*. New York: Cambridge University Press.

Boas, Taylor C., and Jordan Gans-Morse. 2009. "Neoliberalism: From New Liberal Philosophy to Anti-liberal Slogan." *Studies in Comparative International Development* 44[2]: 137–61.

Bockman, Johanna. 2011. *Markets in the Name of Socialism: The Left-Wing Origins of Neoliberalism*. Stanford, CA: Stanford University Press.

Bockman, Johanna. 2015. *Markets in the Name of Socialism: The Left-Wing Origins of Neoliberalism*. Stanford, CA: Stanford University Press.

Bockman, Johanna, and Gil Eyal. 2002. "Eastern Europe as a Laboratory for Economic Knowledge: The Transnational Roots of Neoliberalism." *American Journal of Sociology* 108[2]: 310–52.

Bollen, Yelter, Ferdi De Ville, and Jan Orbie. 2016. "EU Trade Policy: Persistent Liberalisation, Contentious Protectionism." *Journal of European Integration* 38[3]: 279–94.

Bombardini, Matilde, and Francesco Trebbi. 2012. "Competition and Political Organization: Together or Alone in Lobbying for Trade Policy?" *Journal of International Economics* 87: 18–26.

Boswell, G. Steward. 1991. "Letter from the President of AAMA to John H. Sununu, Chief of Staff, EOP." August 27. TA005, WHORM, 266240. George H. W. Bush Presidential Library.

Bothwell, Robert, Ian Drummond, and John English. 1981. *Canada since 1945: Power, Politics, and Provincialism*. Toronto: University of Toronto Press.

Boughton, James M. 2001. *Silent Revolution: The International Monetary Fund, 1979–1989.* Washington, DC: International Monetary Fund.

Bourdieu, Pierre. 1975. "The Specificity of the Scientific Field and the Social Conditions of the Progress of Reason." *Social Science Information 14:* 19–47.

Bourgault, Jacques, and Stéphane Dion. 1990. "Canadian Senior Civil Servants and Transitions of Government: The Whitehall Model Seen from Ottawa." *International Review of Administrative Sciences 56*[1]: 149–69.

Bowie, Alasdair, and Danny Unger. 1997. *The Politics of Open Economies: Indonesia, Malaysia, the Philippines, and Thailand.* New York: Cambridge University Press.

Bradford, Neil. 1998. *Commissioning Ideas: Canadian National Policy Innovation in Comparative Perspective.* Toronto: Oxford University Press.

Breau, Sébastien, and David L. Rigby. 2010. "International Trade and Wage Inequality in Canada." *Journal of Economic Geography 10*[1]: 55–86.

Broad, Robin. 2006. "Research, Knowledge, and the Art of 'Paradigm Maintenance': The World Bank's Development Economics Vice-Presidency (DEC)." *Review of International Political Economy 13*[3]: 387–419.

Brown, William Adams, Jr. 1950. *The United States and the Restoration of World Trade: An Analysis and Appraisal of the ITO Charter and the General Agreement on Tariffs and Trade.* Washington, DC: Brookings.

Bruton, Henry J. 1998. "A Reconsideration of Import Substitution." *Journal of Economic Literature 36*[2]: 903–36.

Burfisher, Mary E., Sherman Robinson, and Karen Thierfelder. 2001. "The Impact of NAFTA on the United States." *Journal of Economic Perspectives 15*[1]: 125–44.

Burgin, Angus. 2012. *The Great Persuasion: Reinventing Free Markets since the Depression.* Cambridge, MA: Harvard University Press.

Burney, Derek H. 2005. *Getting It Done: A Memoir.* Montreal: McGill-Queen's University Press.

Burns, John. F. 1987. "Canada Split on Drug Patents." *New York Times,* August 24. www.nytimes. com/1987/08/24/business/canada-split-on-drug-patents.html.

Burtless, Gary, Robert Z. Lawrence, Robert E. Litan, and Robert J. Shapiro. 1998. *Globaphobia: Confronting Fears about Open Trade.* Washington, DC: Brookings Institute.

Busby, Morris D. 1986. "Confidential Cable from the U.S. Embassy in Mexico to the Secretary of State." April. Latin American Affairs Directorate, NSC Records, Box 91740. Ronald Reagan Presidential Library.

Busch, Marc L., and Edward D. Mansfield. 2010. "Trade: Determinants of Policies." Pp. 7046–60 in Robert A. Denemark et al., eds., *The International Studies Encyclopedia.* Oxford: Wiley-Blackwell.

Bush, George. 1992. "Remarks and a Question-and-Answer Session with the National Governors' Association." February 3. *Public Papers of the Presidents of the United States: George H. W. Bush,* Book I, pp. 182–93. https://www.govinfo.gov/content/pkg/PPP-1992-book1/pdf/PPP-1992-book1-doc-pg182.pdf.

Business Roundtable. 1981. Pamphlet. June. Elizabeth Dole Records, Box 15. Ronald Reagan Presidential Library.

Business Week. 1983. "The Businessman Who Could Replace Trudeau." *Business Week,* July 11, p. 48.

Bustamante, Jorge A. 1994. "El Consejo Asesor del Tratado de Libre Comercio de América del Norte." Pp. 127–33 in Carlos Arriola, ed., *Testimonios sobre el TLC.* Mexico City: Diana-Miguel Ángel Porrúa.

Büthe, T., and H. V. Milner. 2008. "The Politics of Foreign Direct Investment into Developing Countries: Increasing FDI through International Trade Agreements?" *American Journal of Political Science 52:* 741–62.

Calder, Kent E. 1988. "Review: Japanese Foreign Economic Policy Formation: Explaining the Reactive State." *World Politics 40*[4]: 517–41.

Calderón Salazar, J. A., and A. Arroyo, eds. 1993. *Tratado de Libre Comercio de América del Norte: Análisis, Crítica, y Propuesta*. Mexico City: RMALC.

Caliendo, Lorenzo, and Fernando Parro. 2015. "Estimates of the Trade and Welfare Effects of NAFTA." *Review of Economic Studies* 82[1]: 1–44.

Cameron, Duncan, ed. 1986. *The Free Trade Papers*. Toronto: Lorimer.

Cameron, Maxwell A., and Brian W. Tomlin. 2000. *The Making of NAFTA: How the Deal Was Done*. Ithaca, NY: Cornell University Press.

Cameron, Maxwell A., and Carol Wise. 2004. "The Political Impact of NAFTA on Mexico: Reflections on the Political Economy of Democratization." *Canadian Journal of Political Science* 37[2]: 301–23.

Camp, Roderic Ai. 1989. *Entrepreneurs and Politics in Twentieth-Century Mexico*. New York: Oxford University Press.

Camp, Roderic Ai. 1995. *Mexican Political Biographies, 1935–1993*. 3rd ed. Austin: University of Texas Press.

Camp, Roderic Ai. 2002. *Mexico's Mandarins: Crafting a Power Elite for the Twenty-First Century*. Berkeley: University of California Press.

Campbell, John L. 2002. "Ideas, Politics, and Public Policy." *Annual Review of Sociology* 28: 21–38.

Campbell, John L., and Ove K. Pedersen. 2014. *The National Origins of Policy Ideas: Knowledge Regimes in the United States, France, Germany and Denmark*. Princeton, NJ: Princeton University Press.

Canadian Chamber of Commerce. 1984. "Canadian Trade Policy for the 1980's: Response to Minister for International Trade." March. Department of Foreign Affairs and International Trade Library.

Canadian Egg Producers Council. 1987. Minutes of Proceedings and Evidence of the Standing Committee on External Affairs and International Trade. Respecting to consideration of the Canada-U.S. Free Trade. House of Commons. Second Session of the Thirty-Third Parliament, 1986–87. November 26. Witness No. 49.

Canadian Manufacturers' Association. 1920. "Submission—1920, Official Statement Submitted by the Canadian Manufacturers' Association to the Committee of Ministers of the Crown Appointed by the Government of Canada to Hear Representations in Regard to the Canadian Customs Tariff, Winnipeg, September 14th, 1920." Canadian Manufacturers' Association fonds, MG28 I 230, vol. 1. Library and Archives Canada.

Canadian Manufacturers' Association. 1948. "Minutes of the Meeting of the Tariff Committee, Toronto, September 15 1948." Canadian Manufacturers' Association fonds, MG28 I 230, vol. 17. Library and Archives Canada.

Canadian Manufacturers' Association. 1955a. "Royal Commission on Canada's Economic Prospects—1955, Representations of the Canadian Manufacturers' Association, to the Royal Commission on Canada's Economic Prospects, December 1955." Canadian Manufacturers' Association fonds, MG28 I 230, vol. 23. Library and Archives Canada.

Canadian Manufacturers' Association. 1955b. "Appendix II, Statement of Tariff Policy for Canada. Eighty-Fourth Annual General Meeting, held in Montreal, P.Q., on May 25th, 26th and 27th, 1955, approved of the following Statement of Tariff Policy for Canada." Canadian Manufacturers' Association fonds, MG28 I 230, vol. 23. Library and Archives Canada.

Canadian Manufacturers' Association. 1974. "Submission of the Canadian Manufacturers' Association to the Canadian Trade and Tariffs Committee with Respect to the GATT Negotiations, August, 1974." Canadian Manufacturers' Association fonds, MG28 I 230, vol. 7. Library and Archives Canada.

Canadian Manufacturers' Association. 1977. "The Multilateral Trade Negotiations and Canadian Manufacturing." December. Canadian Manufacturers' Association fonds, MG28 I 230, vol. 7. Library and Archives Canada.

Canadian Manufacturers' Association. 1984. "A Future That Works: The Canadian Manufacturers' Association Outlines a Possible Future and How to Get There." September. AMICUS No. 4894340, HD9734 C2 F98. Library and Archives Canada.

Canadian Textiles Institute. 1983. "Submission to the Royal Commission on Economic Union and Development Prospects for Canada." October 14. Macdonald Commission fonds, RG 33/137, vol. 91. Library and Archives Canada.

Caplan, Bryan. 2007. *The Myth of the Rational Voter: Why Democracies Choose Bad Policies.* Princeton, NJ: Princeton University Press.

Capling, Ann. 2001. *Australia and the Global Trade System: From Havana to Seattle.* Cambridge: Cambridge University Press.

Capling, Ann, and Brian Galligan. 1992. *Beyond the Protective State: The Political Economy of Australia's Manufacturing Industry Policy.* Cambridge: Cambridge University Press.

Carroll, William K. 2004. *Corporate Power in a Globalizing World: A Study in Elite Social Organization.* Don Mills, ON: Oxford University Press.

Carroll, William K. 2010. *The Making of a Transnational Capitalist Class: Corporate Power in the 21st Century.* New York: Zed Books.

Carroll, William K., and Murray Shaw. 2001. "Consolidating a Neoliberal Policy Bloc in Canada, 1976–1996." *Canadian Public Policy* 27[2]: 195–217.

Centeno, Miguel Ángel. 1993. "The New Leviathan: The Dynamics and Limits of Technocracy." *Theory and Society* 22[3]: 307–35.

Centeno, Miguel Ángel. 1997. *Democracy within Reason: Technocratic Revolution in Mexico.* 2nd ed. University Park: Pennsylvania State University Press.

Centeno, Miguel Ángel, and Joseph N. Cohen. 2012. "The Arc of Neoliberalism." *Annual Review of Sociology* 38: 317–40.

Centeno, Miguel Ángel, and Sylvia Maxfield. 1992. "The Marriage of Finance and Order: Changes in the Mexican Political Elite." *Journal of Latin American Studies* 24[1]: 57–85.

Centeno, Miguel Ángel, and Patricio Silva, eds. 1998. *The Politics of Expertise in Latin America.* New York: St. Martin's Press.

Center for Public Integrity. 1993. "The Trading Game: Inside Lobbying for the North American Free Trade Agreement." Unpublished study. Washington, DC.

Chang, Ha-Joon. 2002. *Kicking Away the Ladder: Development Strategy in Historical Perspective.* London: Anthem Press.

Chang, Ha-Joon. 2013. "Comments on 'Comparative Advantage: The Silver Bullet of Industrial Policy' by Justin Lin and Célestin Monga." Pp 39–42 in Joseph E. Stiglitz and Justin Yifu Lin, eds., *The Industrial Policy Revolution I: The Role of Government Beyond Ideology.* London: Palgrave Macmillan.

Chase, Kerry A. 2003. "Economic Interests and Regional Trading Arrangements: The Case of NAFTA." *International Organization* 57[1]: 137–74.

Chase, Kerry A. 2006. "Multilateralism Compromised: The Mysterious Origins of GATT Article XXIV." *World Trade Review* 5: 1–30.

Chavez, Rebecca Bill. 2017. "Nafta's Renegotiation Risks National Security." *New York Times,* November 20. https://www.nytimes.com/2017/11/20/opinion/nafta-national-security-mexico.html.

Chorev, N. 2007. *Remaking U.S. Trade Policy: From Protectionism to Globalization,* Ithaca, NY: Cornell University Press.

Chow, Frank. 1993. "Recent Trends in Canadian Direct Investment Abroad—the Rise of Canadian Multinationals, 1969–1992." Research Paper No. 8. Statistics Canada, Balance of Payments Division. As published in *Canadian Economic Observer,* December 1993, Catalogue no. 11-010.

Christensen, Johan. 2017. *The Power of Economists within the State.* Stanford, CA: Stanford University Press.

Chrysler Ford General Motors. 1991. "Letter to Robert A. Mosbacher, Secretary of Commerce." September 9. Wonnacott Box, OA/ID 41477. George H. W. Bush Presidential Library.

Chwieroth, Jeffrey. 2007. "Neoliberal Economists and Capital Account Liberalization in Emerging Markets." *International Organization* 61: 443–63.

Cipollina, Maria, and Luca Salvatici. 2010. "Reciprocal Trade Agreements in Gravity Models: A Meta-analysis." *Review of International Economics* 18[1]: 63–80.

Clarke, V. L. 1984. "Memo to File, Re: BCNI position on Free Trade with USA." February 21. Macdonald Commission fonds, RG33/137, vol. 10. Library and Archives Canada.

Clarkson, Stephen. 1993. "Economics: The New Hemispheric Fundamentalism." Pp. 61–69 in Ricardo Grinspun and Maxwell A. Cameron, eds., *The Political Economy of North American Free Trade*. New York: St. Martin's Press.

Clausing, Kimberly. 2001. "Trade Creation and Trade Diversion in the Canada–United States Free Trade Agreement," *Canadian Journal of Economics* 34[3]: 677–96.

Cleaves, Peter S., and Charles J. Stephens. 1991. "Business and Economic Policy in Mexico." *Latin American Research Review* 26[2]: 187–202.

Clement, W. 1977. "The Corporate Elite, the Capitalist Class, and the Canadian State." Pp. 225–48 in L. Panitch, ed., *The Canadian State: Political Economy and Political Power*. Toronto: University of Toronto Press.

Coats, A. W., ed. 1997. *The Post-1945 Internationalization of Economics*. Durham, NC: Duke University Press.

Coatsworth, J. H., and J. G. Williamson. 2004. "Always Protectionist? Latin American Tariffs from Independence to Great Depression." *Journal of Latin American Studies* 36: 205–32.

Cohen, Benjamin J. 2008. *International Political Economy: An Intellectual History*. Princeton, NJ: Princeton University Press.

Cohen, Bernard C. 1973. *The Public's Impact on Foreign Policy*. Boston: Little, Brown.

Colantone, Italo, and Piero Stanig. 2018. "The Trade Origins of Economic Nationalism: Import Competition and Voting Behavior in Western Europe." *American Journal of Political Science* 62[4]: 936–53.

Cole, Matthew A., Robert J. R. Elliott, and Liyun Zhang. 2017. "Foreign Direct Investment and the Environment." *Annual Review of Environment and Resources* 42: 465–87.

Conconi, Paola, Manuel García-Santana, Laura Puccio, and Roberto Venturini. 2018. "From Final Goods to Inputs: The Protectionist Effect of Rules of Origin." *American Economic Review* 108[8]: 2335–65.

Congressional Budget Office. 2000. "Causes and Consequences of the Trade Deficit: An Overview." CBO Memorandum. https://www.cbo.gov/publication/12139.

Congressional Budget Office. 2003. "The Effects of NAFTA on U.S.-Mexican Trade and GDP." https://www.cbo.gov/publication/14461.

Cook, P. 1981. "Executives Still Wary of Free Trade," *Globe & Mail*, June 15, B1.

Council of Economic Advisers. 1976. "U.S. International Economics Policy and Developing Country Relations." December 14. Staff Office—CEA Box 44. Jimmy Carter Presidential Library.

Cowal, Sally. 1991. "Secret Briefing Memorandum to the United States Secretary of State, Subject: Meeting with Mexican Foreign Relations Secretary Fernando Solana, March 26 1991." March 22. Charles A. Gillespie Files, OA/ID CF01379. George H. W. Bush Presidential Library.

Cox, Ronald W., ed. 2012. *Corporate Power and Globalization in US Foreign Policy*. New York: Routledge.

Cronin, Patrick. 2003. "Explaining Free Trade: Mexico 1985–1988." *Latin American Politics and Society* 45[4]: 63–95.

Crouch, Colin. 2011. *The Strange Non-death of Neoliberalism*. Cambridge: Polity Press.

Crouch, Colin. 2016. "The March towards Post-democracy, Ten Years On." *Political Quarterly* 87[1]: 71–75.

Cuevas, Alfredo, Miguel Messmacher, and Alejandro Werner. 2005. "Foreign Direct Investment in Mexico since the Approval of NAFTA." *World Bank Economic Review* 19[3]: 473–88.

Cuff, Robert, and J. L. Granatstein. 1977. "The Rise and Fall of Canadian-American Free Trade, 1947–8." *Canadian Historical Review* 58[4]: 459–82.

Dahl, Robert A. 1958. "A Critique of the Ruling Elite Model." *American Political Science Review* 52[2]: 463–69.

Daly, Herman E. 1993. "The Perils of Free Trade." *Scientific American* 269: 24–29.

Dam, Kenneth W. 2005. "Cordell Hull, the Reciprocal Trade Agreements Act, and the WTO: An Essay on the Concept of Rights in International Trade." *New York University Journal of Law and Business 1*: 709–30.

Dargent, Eduardo. 2014. *Technocracy and Democracy in Latin America: The Experts Running Government*. New York: Cambridge University Press.

Dasko, Donna. 1986. "Canadian Public Opinion: Sources of Support and Dissent." Pp. 26–32 in Duncan Cameron, ed., *The Free Trade Papers*. Toronto: James Lorimer.

Dattu, Riyaz. 2000. "A Journey from Havana to Paris: The Fifty-Year Quest for the Elusive Multilateral Agreement on Investment." *Fordham International Law Journal 24*[1]: 275–316.

Dell, Melissa. 2015. "Trafficking Networks and the Mexican Drug War." *American Economic Review 105*[6]: 1738–79.

Department of Commerce. 1977. "Confidential Nontariff Barrier Analysis." June 29. Domestic and International Business Administration, International Economic Policy and Research. USTR, 364/UD-UP 12 / Box 1. Jimmy Carter Presidential Library.

Department of Finance. 1986. "Can Canada Compete?" Pp. 107–11 in Duncan Cameron, ed., *The Free Trade Papers*. Toronto: James Lorimer.

Department of Foreign Affairs and Trade. 2014. "Australia's Foreign Investment—Historical Overview." Economic Diplomacy, Trade Advocacy and Statistics Section Economic Advocacy & Analysis Branch, Trade Investment & Economic Diplomacy Division. https://dfat.gov.au/about-us/publications/Documents/australias-foreign-investment-historical-overview.pdf.

Destler, I. M. 1995. *American Trade Politics*. 3rd ed. Washington, DC: Institute for International Economics.

Dezalay, Yves, and Bryant G. Garth. 2002. *The Internationalization of Palace Wars: Lawyers, Economists, and the Contest to Transform Latin American States*. Chicago: University of Chicago Press.

Diebold, William, Jr. 1952. "The End of the I.T.O." Essays in International Finance 16. Department of Economics and Social Institutions, Princeton University.

Docquier, Frédéric, Elisabetta Lodigiani, Hillel Rapoport, and Maurice Schiff. 2016. "Emigration and Democracy." *Journal of Development Economics 120*: 209–23.

Doern, G. Bruce, and Brian W. Tomlin. 1991. *Faith and Fear: The Free Trade Story*. Toronto: Stoddart.

Domhoff, G. William. 2010. *Who Rules America: Challenges to Corporate and Class Dominance*. 6th ed. New York: McGraw-Hill.

Domínguez, Jorge I., ed. 1997. "Technopols: Freeing Politics and Markets in Latin America in the 1990s." University Park, PA: Pennsylvania State University Press.

Domínguez, Jorge I., and James A. McCann. 1996. *Democratizing Mexico: Public Opinion and Electoral Choices*. Baltimore: Johns Hopkins University Press.

Drache, Daniel, and Duncan Cameron. 1985. "The Other Macdonald Report: The Consensus on Canada's Future That the Macdonald Commission Left Out." Toronto: James Lorimer.

Dreiling, Michael. 2001. *Solidarity and Contention: The Politics of Security and Sustainability in the NAFTA Conflict*. New York: Garland.

Dreiling, Michael, and Derek Darves. 2011. "Corporate Unity in American Trade Policy: A Network Analysis of Corporate-Dyad Political Action." *American Journal of Sociology 116*[5]: 1514–63.

Dreiling, Michael, and Derek Darves. 2016. *Neoliberal Globalization: Corporate Networks, State Structures and Trade Policy*. New York: Cambridge University Press.

Dresser, Denise. 1991. *Neopopulist Solutions to Neoliberal Problems: Mexico's National Solidarity Program*. San Diego: UCSD Center for U.S.-Mexican Studies.

Druckman, James N., and Lawrence R. Jacobs. 2015. "Who Governs? Presidents, Public Opinion, and Manipulation." Chicago: University of Chicago Press.

Duina, Francesco. 2006. *The Social Construction of Free Trade: The European Union, NAFTA, and Mercosur*. Princeton, NJ: Princeton University Press.

Duménil, Gérard, and Dominique Lévy. 2004. *Capital Resurgent: Roots of the Neoliberal Revolution*. Translated by Derek Jeffers. Cambridge, MA: Harvard University Press.

Dutt, P., and D. Mitra. 2002. "Endogenous Trade Policy through Majority Voting: An Empirical Investigation." *Journal of International Economics* 58: 107–33.

Dyck, H., and S. Greenfield. 1994. "A Survey Analysis of Free Trade Attitudes in Mexico: Implications for Global Strategic Investment Decisions." *Journal of Applied Business Research* 10[3]: 68–77.

Dye, Thomas R., Louis Schubert, and Harmon Zeigler. 2011. *The Irony of Democracy: An Uncommon Introduction to American Politics*. Boston: Wadsworth.

Dymond, William A., and Laura Ritchie Dawson. 2002. "The Consultative Process in the Formulation of Canadian Trade Policy." Pp. 23–33 in *The Trade Policy-Making Process: Level One of the Two Level Game. Country Studies in the Western Hemisphere*. Occasional Paper 13. New York: Inter-American Development Bank.

Ebenstein, Avraham, Ann Harrison, Margaret McMillan, and Shannon Phillips. 2014. "Estimating the Impact of Trade and Offshoring on American Workers Using the Current Population Surveys." *Review of Economics and Statistics* 96[4]: 581–95.

Eckes, Alfred E. 1992. "Trading American Interests." *Foreign Affairs* 71[4]: 135–54.

Economic Commission for Latin America. 1950. "The Economic Development of Latin America and Its Principal Problems." New York: United Nations. https://repositorio.cepal.org/bitstream/handle/11362/29973/002_en.pdf.

Economic Council of Canada. 1975. *Looking Outward: A New Trade Strategy for Canada*. Ottawa: Information Canada.

Economic Policy Group Task Force on International Investment. 1977. "U.S. Policy and Objectives for Direct International Investment." Staff Office—CEA Box 66. Jimmy Carter Presidential Library.

Edwards, Martin S. 2006. "Public Opinion Regarding Economic and Cultural Globalization: Evidence from a Cross-National Survey." *Review of International Political Economy* 13[4]: 587–608.

Eichengreen, B., and D. Leblang. 2008. "Democracy and Globalization." *Economics and Politics* 20: 289–334.

Eichengreen, Barry. 1984. "Keynes and Protection." *Journal of Economic History* 44[2]: 363–73.

Eisenstadt, Todd A. 1997. "The Rise of the Mexico Lobby in Washington: Even Further from God, and Even Closer to the United States." Pp. 89–124 in Rodolfo O. de la Garza and Jesús Velasco, eds., *Bridging the Border: Transforming Mexico-U.S. Relations*. New York: Rowman and Littlefield.

Ernst, Alan. 1992. "From Liberal Continentalism to Neoconservatism: North American Free Trade and the Politics of the C.D. Howe Institute." *Studies in Political Economy* 39: 109–40.

Espinosa Velasco, J. Enrique, and Jaime Serra Puche. 2004. "Diez años del Tratado de Libre Comercio de América del Norte." Pp. 163–205 in Pascual García Alba, Lucino Gutiérrez, and Gabriela Torres Ramírez, eds., *El Nuevo Milenio Mexicano*, vol. 1: *México y el Mundo*. Mexico City: Universidad Autónoma Metropolitana—Azcapotzalco and Ediciones y Gráficos Eón.

Esquivel, Gerardo, Nora Lustig, and John Scott. 2010. "A Decade of Falling Inequality: Market Forces or State Action?" Pp. 175–217 in Luis F. López-Calva and Nora Lustig, eds., *Declining Inequality in Latin America: A Decade of Progress?* Washington, DC: Brookings Institution Press.

Estévez, Dolia. 2012. "U.S. Ambassadors to Mexico: The Relationship through their Eyes." Woodrow Wilson International Center for Scholars. https://www.wilsoncenter.org/sites/default/files/Estevez_Amb_to_Mex.pdf.

Esty, Daniel C., and James Salzman. 2017. "Rethinking NAFTA: Deepening the Commitment to Sustainable Development." Pp. 125–39 in C. Fred Bergsten and Monica de Bolle, eds., *A Path Forward for NAFTA*. Washington, DC: Peterson Institute for International Economics.

Ethier, Wilfred J. 2004. "Political Externalities, Nondiscrimination, and a Multilateral World." *Review of International Economics* 12[3]: 303–20.

Ethier, Wilfred J. 2007. "The Theory of Trade Policy and Trade Agreements: A Critique." *European Journal of Political Economy* 23: 605–23.

Evans, Rhonda, and Tamara Kay. 2008. "How Environmentalists 'Greened' Trade Policy: Strategic Action and the Architecture of Field Overlap." *American Sociological Review* 73[6]: 970–91.

Fairbrother, Malcolm. 2007. "Making Neoliberalism Possible: The State's Organization of Business Support for NAFTA in Mexico." *Politics and Society* 35: 265–300.

Fairbrother, Malcolm. 2008. "How Countries Globalize: The Variable Roles of Political and Economic Elites." Forthcoming in Yildiz Atasoy, ed., *Hegemonic Transitions and the State.* New York: Routledge.

Fairbrother, Malcolm. 2010. "Trade Policymaking in the Real World: Elites' Conflicting Worldviews and North American Integration." *Review of International Political Economy* 17[2]: 319–47.

Fairbrother, Malcolm. 2014. "Economists, Capitalists, and the Making of Globalization: North American Free Trade in Comparative-Historical Perspective." *American Journal of Sociology* 119[5]: 1324–79.

Faux, Jeff, and Thea Lee. 1993. "Implications of NAFTA for the United States: Investment, Jobs, and Productivity." Pp. 235–49 in Ricardo Grinspun and Maxwell A. Cameron, eds., *The Political Economy of North American Free Trade.* New York: St. Martin's Press.

Feenstra, Robert C. 2016. *Advanced International Trade: Theory and Evidence.* 2nd ed. Princeton, NJ: Princeton University Press.

Fernández-Kelly, Patricia. 2007. "NAFTA and Beyond: Alternative Perspectives in the Study of Global Trade and Development." *Annals of the American Academy of Political and Social Science* 610: 6–19.

Fetter, Frank Whitson. 1942. "The Economists' Tariff Protest of 1930." *American Economic Review* 32[2]: 355–356.

Findlay, Ronald, and Kevin H. O'Rourke. 2009. *Power and Plenty: Trade, War, and the World Economy in the Second Millennium.* Princeton, NJ: Princeton University Press.

Finlayson, Jock A., and J. Christopher Thomas. 1986. "The Elements of a Canada–United States Comprehensive Trade Agreement." *International Lawyer* 20[4]: 1307–34.

Finlayson, Jock A., and Mark W. Zacher. 1981. "The GATT and the Regulation of Trade Barriers: Regime Dynamics and Functions." *International Organization* 35[4]: 561–602.

Finnemore, Martha. 1996. "Norms, Culture, and World Politics: Insights from Sociology's Institutionalism." *International Organization* 50[2]: 325–47.

Fligstein, Neil, and Frederic Merand. 2002. "Globalization or Europeanization? Evidence on the European Economy since 1980." *Acta Sociologica* 45: 7–22.

Flores Quiroga, A. R. 1998. *Proteccionismo versus Librecambio: La Economía Política de la Protección Comercial en México, 1970–1994.* Mexico City: Fondo de Cultura Económica.

Florida Fruit and Vegetable Association. 1992. "Florida Fruit and Vegetable Association Policy Statement on the North American Free Trade Agreement." September 10. Gary Blumenthal Files, OA/ID 05870. George H. W. Bush Presidential Library.

Forbes, Kristin J. 2001. "Skill Classification Does Matter: Estimating the Relationship between Trade Flows and Wage Inequality." *Journal of International Trade and Economic Development* 10[2]: 175–209.

Fourcade, Marion. 2006. "The Construction of a Global Profession: The Transnationalization of Economics." *American Journal of Sociology* 112[1]: 145–94.

Fourcade-Gourinchas, Marion, and Sarah Babb. 2002. "The Rebirth of the Liberal Creed: Paths to Neoliberalism in Four Countries." *American Journal of Sociology* 108: 533–79.

Frey, Bruno S., Werner W. Pommerehne, Friedrich Schneider, and Guy Gilbert. 1984. "Consensus and Dissension among Economists: An Empirical Inquiry." *American Economic Review* 74[5]: 986–94.

Friedman, Milton. 1953. *Essays in Positive Economics.* Chicago: University of Chicago Press.

Friedman, Thomas. 1999. *The Lexus and the Olive Tree*. New York: Farrar, Straus and Giroux.

Frye, Timothy, and Edward D. Mansfield. 2003. "Concentration of Government Authority and Trade Liberalization in Post-Communist Countries." *British Journal of Political Science* 33: 635–57.

Fukuyama, Francis. 1995. "Virtue and Prosperity." *National Interest* 40: 21–27.

Gabel, Matthew J. 1998. *Interests and Integration: Market Liberalization, Public Opinion, and European Union*. Ann Arbor: University of Michigan Press.

Gagné, Gilbert. 2000. "North American Free Trade, Canada, and US Trade Remedies: An Assessment after Ten Years." *World Economy* 23[1]: 77–91.

Gagné, Gilbert, and Michel Paulin. 2013. "The Softwood Lumber Dispute and US Allegations of Improper NAFTA Panel Review." *American Review of Canadian Studies* 43: 413–23.

Galbraith, John W. 1993. "Afterword." Pp. 269–72 in A. R. Riggs and Tom Velk, eds., *Beyond NAFTA: An Economic, Political and Sociological Perspective*. Vancouver: Fraser Institute.

Gallagher, Kevin P. 2004. *Free Trade and the Environment: Mexico, NAFTA, and Beyond*. Stanford, CA: Stanford University Press.

Gallardo, Juan. 1994. "La Coordinadora de Organismos Empresariales para el Comercio Exterior." Pp. 135–44 in Carlos Arriola, ed., *Testimonios sobre el TLC*. Mexico City: Diana-Miguel Ángel Porrúa.

García Rocha, Adalberto, and Timothy Kehoe. 1991. "Efectos del Tratado de Libre Comercio sobre la Economía Mexicana." Pp. 199–240 in *Hacia un Tratado de Libre Comercio en América del Norte*. Mexico City: SECOFI and Miguel Ángel Porrúa.

Gardner, Richard N. 1985-1986. "Sterling-Dollar Diplomacy in Current Perspective." *International Affairs* 62[1]: 21–33.

Garnaut, Ross. 2002. "Australia: A Case Study of Unilateral Trade Liberalization." Pp. 139–66 in Jagdish Bhagwati, ed., *Going Alone: The Case for Relaxed Reciprocity in Freeing Trade*. Cambridge, MA: MIT Press.

Garrett, Geoffrey. 2000. "The Causes of Globalization." *Comparative Political Studies* 33[6–7]: 941–91.

Gaston, Noel, and Daniel Trefler. 1997. "The Labour Market Consequences of the Canada-U.S. Free Trade Agreement." *Canadian Journal of Economics* 30[1]: 18–41.

Gauss, Susan M. 2010. *Made in Mexico: Regions, Nation, and the State in the Rise of Mexican Industrialism, 1920s–1940s*. University Park: Penn State University Press.

Geddes, Barbara. 1990. "How the Cases You Choose Affect the Answers You Get: Selection Bias in Comparative Politics." *Political Analysis* 2[1]: 131–50.

Geddes, Barbara. 1995. "The Politics of Economic Liberalization." *Latin American Research Review* 30[2]: 195–214.

George, Alexander L., and Andrew Bennett. 2005. *Case Studies and Theory Development in the Social Sciences*. Cambridge, MA: MIT Press.

Gerring, John. 2004. "What Is a Case Study and What Is It Good for?" *American Political Science Review* 98[2]: 341–54.

Gerschenkron, Alexander. 1962. "Economic Backwardness in Historical Perspective." Pp. 5–30 in A. Gerschenkron, ed., *Economic Backwardness in Historical Perspective: A Book of Essays*. Cambridge: Harvard University Press.

Gilens, Martin. 2009. "Preference Gaps and Inequality in Representation." *PS: Political Science & Politics* 42[2]: 335–41.

Gilens, Martin. 2012. *Affluence and Influence: Economic Inequality and Political Power in America*. Princeton, NJ: Princeton University Press.

Gilens, Martin, and Benjamin I. Page. 2014. "Testing Theories of American Politics: Elites, Interest Groups, and Average Citizens." *Perspectives on Politics* 12[3]: 564–81.

Gill, Stephen. 1995. "Globalisation, Market Civilisation, and Disciplinary Neoliberalism." *Millennium: Journal of International Studies* 24[3]: 399–423.

Gilson, Ronald J., and Curtis J. Milhaupt. 2011. "Economically Benevolent Dictators: Lessons for Developing Democracies." *American Journal of Comparative Law* 59[1]: 227–88.

Girling, John. 1994. "Thailand: Twin Peaks, Disturbing Shadows." *Southeast Asian Affairs* 21: 305–19.

Globe and Mail. 1980. "U.S. Governors Call for Forum on Common Market Possibility." *Globe and Mail*, February 27.

Goldberg, Pinelopi Koujianou, and Nina Pavcnik. 2007. "Distributional Effects of Globalization in Developing Countries." *Journal of Economic Literature* 45: 39–82.

Goldfinch, Shaun. 2000. *Remaking New Zealand and Australian Economic Policy: Ideas, Institutions and Policy Communities*. Wellington: Victoria University Press.

Goldstein, J. L., D. Rivers, and M. Tomz. 2007. "Institutions in International Relations: Understanding the Effects of the GATT and the WTO on World Trade." *International Organization* 61: 37–67.

Goldstein, Judith, and Robert O. Keohane. 1993. "Ideas and Foreign Policy: An Analytical Approach." Pp. 3–30 in Judith Goldstein and Robert O. Keohane, eds., *Ideas and Foreign Policy: Beliefs, Institutions, and Political Change*. Ithaca, NY: Cornell University Press.

Golob, S. R. 2003. "Beyond the Policy Frontier: Canada, Mexico, and the Ideological Origins of NAFTA." *World Politics* 55: 361–98.

Gonzalez-Barrera, Ana. 2015. "More Mexicans Leaving Than Coming to the U.S." Pew Research Center. http://www.pewhispanic.org/2015/11/19/more-mexicans-leaving-than-coming-to-the-u-s/.

Gordon, Roger, and Gordon B. Dahl. 2013. "Views among Economists: Professional Consensus or Point-Counterpoint?" *American Economic Review* 103[3]: 629–35.

Gordon, Sheldon E. 1983. "For a Free-Trade Pact between Canada and the US." *Christian Science Monitor*, May 20, 27.

Graefe, Peter. 2004. "The Quebec Patronat: Proposing a Neo-liberal Political Economy after All." *Canadian Review of Sociology and Anthropology* 41[2]: 171–93.

Granatstein, J. L. 1985. "Free Trade between Canada and the United States." Pp. 11–54 in Denis Stairs and Gilbert R. Winham, eds., *The Politics of Canada's Economic Relationship with the United States*. Toronto: University of Toronto Press.

Granatstein, J. L. 2015. *The Ottawa Men: The Civil Service Mandarins 1935–1957*. 2nd ed. Oakville, ON: Rock's Mills Press.

Graubart, Jonathan. 2008. *Legalizing Transnational Activism: The Struggle to Gain Social Change from NAFTA's Citizen Petitions*. University Park: Penn State University Press.

Grayson, George W. 1993. *The North American Free Trade Agreement*. New York: Foreign Policy Association.

Grayson, George W. 2007. *The Mexico-U.S. Business Committee: Catalyst for the North American Free Trade Agreement*. Rockville, MD: Montrose Press.

Greene, Kenneth F. 2007. *Why Dominant Parties Lose: Mexico's Democratization in Comparative Perspective*. New York: Cambridge University Press.

Greenwood, Scott. 2008. "Bad for Business? Entrepreneurs and Democracy in the Arab World." *Comparative Political Studies* 41[6]: 837–60.

Grossman, Gene M. 2016. "The Purpose of Trade Agreements." Pp. 379–434 in Kyle Bagwell and Robert W. Staiger, eds., *Handbook of Commercial Policy*, vol. 1, part A. Amsterdam: North-Holland.

Grossman, Gene M., and Elhanan Helpman. 1995. "The Politics of Free-Trade Agreements." *American Economic Review* 85[4]: 667–90.

Grossman, Gene M., and Alan B. Krueger. 1993. "Environmental Impacts of a North American Free Trade Agreement." Pp. 13–56 in Peter M. Garber, ed., *The Mexico-U.S. Free Trade Agreement*. Cambridge, MA: MIT Press.

Gruber, Lloyd. 2000. *Ruling the World: Power Politics and the Rise of Supranational Institutions*. Princeton, NJ: Princeton University Press.

Guisinger, Alexandra. 2009. "Determining Trade Policy: Do Voters Hold Politicians Accountable?" *International Organization* 63: 533–57.

Gutiérrez-Haces, María Teresa. 2015. *Lox Vecinos del Vecino: La continentalización de México y Canadá en América del Norte.* Mexico City: Universidad Nacional Autónoma de México.

Haggard, Stephan. 1988. "The Institutional Foundations of Hegemony: Explaining the Trade Agreements Act of 1934." *International Organization* 42[1]: 91–119.

Haggard, Stephan. 1995. *Developing Nations and the Politics of Global Integration.* Washington, DC: Brookings.

Haggard, Stephan, and Robert R. Kaufman. 1992. "Introduction: Institutions and Economic Adjustment." Pp. 3–37 in S. Haggard and R. R. Kaufman, eds., *The Politics of Economic Adjustment: International Constraints, Distributive Conflicts, and the State.* Princeton, NJ: Princeton University Press.

Hainmueller, Jens, and Michael J. Hiscox. 2006. "Learning to Love Globalization: Education and Individual Attitudes toward International Trade." *International Organization* 60: 469–98.

Hakobyan, Shushanik, and John McLaren. 2016. "Looking for Local Labor Market Effects of NAFTA." *Review of Economics and Statistics* 98[4]: 728–41.

Hall, Gillette, and Harry Anthony Patrinos. 2005. "Latin America's Indigenous Peoples." *Finance and Development* 42[4]. http://www.imf.org/external/pubs/ft/fandd/2005/12/hall.htm.

Haller, Max. 2008. *European Integration as an Elite Process: The Failure of a Dream?* London: Routledge.

Hanson, Brian T. 1998. "What Happened to Fortress Europe? External Trade Policy Liberalization in the European Union." *International Organization* 52[1]: 55–85.

Hanson, Gordon H. 2004. "What Has Happened to Wages in Mexico since NAFTA?" Pp. 505–38 in Antoni Estevadeordal, Dani Rodrik, Alan Taylor, and Andres Velasco, eds., *Integrating the Americas: FTAA and Beyond.* Cambridge, MA: Harvard University Press.

Hanson, Gordon H. 2006. "Illegal Migration from Mexico to the United States." *Journal of Economic Literature* 44[4]: 869–924.

Hanson, Gordon H. 2007. "Globalization, Labor Income, and Poverty in Mexico." Pp. 417–56 in Ann Harrison, ed., *Globalization and Poverty.* Chicago: University of Chicago Press.

Harberger, Arnold C. 1993. "Secrets of Success: A Handful of Heroes." *American Economic Review* 83[2]: 343–50.

Harberger, Arnold C. 1996. "Good Economics Comes to Latin America, 1955–95." Pp. 301–11 in A. W. Coats, ed., *The Post-1945 Internationalization of Economics.* Durham, NC: Duke University Press.

Harris, Richard, and David Cox. 1984. "Trade, Industrial Policy, and Canadian Manufacturing." Toronto: Ontario Economic Council.

Hart, David M. 2004. "'Business' Is Not an Interest Group: On the Study of Companies in American National Politics." *Annual Review of Political Science* 7: 47–69.

Hart, Michael. 2002. *A Trading Nation: Canadian Trade Policy from Colonialism to Globalization.* Vancouver: University of British Columbia Press.

Hart, Michael. 2008. *From Pride to Influence: Towards a New Canadian Foreign Policy.* Vancouver: University of British Columbia Press.

Hart, Michael, with Bill Dymond and Colin Robertson. 1994. *Decision at Midnight: Inside the Canada-US Free-Trade Negotiations.* Vancouver: University of British Columbia Press.

Harvey, David. 2005. *A Brief History of Neoliberalism.* Oxford: Oxford University Press.

Harvey, David. 2007. "Neoliberalism as Creative Destruction." *Annals of the American Academy of Political and Social Science.* 610[1]: 21–44.

Haydu, Jeffrey. 1998. "Making Use of the Past: Time Periods as Cases to Compare and as Sequences of Problem Solving." *American Journal of Sociology* 104[2]: 339–71.

Helgadóttir, Oddný. 2016. "The Bocconi Boys go to Brussels: Italian Economic Ideas, Professional Networks and European Austerity." *Journal of European Public Policy* 23[3]: 392–409.

Helleiner, Eric. 2003. "Economic Liberalism and Its Critics: The Past as Prologue?" *Review of International Political Economy* 10[4]: 685–96.

Helliwell, John F. 1998. *How Much Do National Borders Matter?* Washington, DC: Brookings Institution Press.

Hellman, Judith Adler. 1983. *Mexico in Crisis.* 2nd ed. New York: Holmes & Meier.

Hellman, Judith Adler. 1993. "Mexican Perceptions of Free Trade: Support and Opposition to NAFTA." Pp. 193–204 in Ricardo Grinspun and Maxwell A. Cameron, eds., *The Political Economy of North American Free Trade.* New York: St. Martin's Press.

Henderson, David. 1986. *Innocence and Design: The Influence of Economic Ideas on Policy.* Oxford: Basil Blackwell.

Henderson, David. 2001. *The Changing Fortunes of Economic Liberalism: Yesterday, Today and Tomorrow.* London: Institute of Economic Affairs.

Henisz, Witold J., and Edward D. Mansfield. 2006. "Votes and Vetoes: The Political Determinants of Commercial Openness." *International Studies Quarterly* 50[1]: 189–212.

Hicks, Raymond, Helen V. Milner, and Dustin Tingley. 2014. "Trade Policy, Economic Interests, and Party Politics in a Developing Country: The Political Economy of CAFTA-DR." *International Studies Quarterly* 58: 106–17.

Hiebert, Janet. 1991. "Interest Groups and Canadian Federal Elections." Pp. 3–76 in F. Leslie Seidle, ed., *Interest Groups and Elections in Canada.* Toronto: Dundorn Press.

Hills, Carla A. 1990. "Memorandum for the President from the U.S. Trade Representative, Subject: U.S.-Mexico Free Trade Agreement." August 2. OA/ID 17410. George H. W. Bush Presidential Library.

Hilts, Philip J. 1991. "At Heart of Debate on Quayle Council: Who Controls Federal Regulations?" *New York Times,* December 16, B11. https://www.nytimes.com/1991/12/16/us/at-heart-of-debate-on-quayle-council-who-controls-federal-regulations.html.

Hirschman, Daniel, and Elizabeth Popp Berman. 2014. "Do Economists Make Policies? On the Political Effects of Economics." *Socio-economic Review* 12[4]: 779–811.

Hiscox, Michael J. 2001. "Class versus Industry Cleavages: Inter-industry Factor Mobility and the Politics of Trade." *International Organization* 55[1]: 1–46.

Hiscox, Michael J. 2002. "Commerce, Coalitions, and Factor Mobility: Evidence from Congressional Votes on Trade Legislation." *American Political Science Review* 96[3]: 593–608.

Hiscox, Michael J. 2006. "Through a Glass and Darkly: Attitudes towards International Trade and the Curious Effects of Issue Framing." *International Organization* 60: 755–80.

Hogenboom, Barbara. 1998. *Mexico and the NAFTA Environmental Debate: The Transnational Politics of Economic Integration.* Utrecht: International Books.

Holding, William Frederick. 1950. "Trade and Tariff Problems, Letter to Prime Minister Louis St. Laurent." June 28. Canadian Manufacturers' Association fonds, MG28 I 230, vol. 109. Library and Archives Canada.

Holding, William Frederick. 1952. "Canada's Century If . . ." Speech given January 17 at the Empire Club of Canada. Pp. 185–98 in *The Empire Club of Canada Speeches 1951–1952.* Toronto: Empire Club Foundation.

Holsti, Ole R. 1996. *Public Opinion and American Foreign Policy.* Ann Arbor: University of Michigan Press.

Howse, Robert. 2017. "Economics for Progressive International Lawyers: A Review Essay." *London Review of International Law* 5[1]: 187–96.

Hrinak, Donna. 1992. Memo to Bernard Aronson, RE: Industry Advisory Group Reports on NAFTA. Not dated. National Security Council, Charles A. Gillespie files, Subject Files, OA/ID CF01377 through OA/ID CF01378, Mexico-General-October 1992 (OA/ID CF01377) (1 of 4). 5 pages, TAB B.

Huenemann, Jon E. 2002. "On the Trade Policy-Making Process in the United States." Pp. 67–73 in *The Trade Policy-Making Process: Level One of the Two Level Game. Country Studies in the Western Hemisphere.* Occasional Paper 13. New York: Inter-American Development Bank.

Hufbauer, Gary Clyde, Cathleen Cimino, and Tyler Moran. 2014. "NAFTA at 20: Misleading Charges and Positive Achievements." Pp. 6–29 in NAFTA: 20 Years Later. Washington,

DC: Peterson Institute for International Economics. https://piie.com/sites/default/files/publications/briefings/piieb14-3.pdf.

Hufbauer, Gary Clyde, and Jeffrey J. Schott. 1993. "*NAFTA: An Assessment.*" Rev. ed. Washington, DC: Institute for International Economics.

Hufbauer, Gary Clyde, and Jeffrey J. Schott. 2005. "NAFTA Revisited: Achievements and Challenges." Washington, DC: Peterson Institute for International Economics. https://piie.com/bookstore/nafta-revisited-achievements-and-challenges.

Hunter, Iain. 1985. "PM Urges 'Prudence' on Free Trade." *Ottawa Citizen*, February 16, A1.

Ikenberry, G. John. 1993. "Creating Yesterday's New World Order: Keynesian 'New Thinking' and the Anglo-American Postwar Settlement." Pp. 57–86 in Judith Goldstein and Robert Owen Keohane, eds., *Ideas and Foreign Policy: Beliefs, Institutions, and Political Change.* Ithaca, NY: Cornell University Press.

Ikeo, Aiko. 2014. *A History of Economic Science in Japan: The Internationalization of Economics in the Twentieth Century.* New York: Routledge.

International Intellectual Property Alliance. 1991. "Letter to George P. Bush." Signed by the presidents of RIAA, BSA, ADAPSO, NMPA, AAP, MPAA, AFMA, CBEMA. April 11. TA005, WHORM, 230260. George H. W. Bush Presidential Library.

International Labour Organization. 2015. *World Employment and Social Outlook: Trends 2015.* Geneva: International Labour Office. http://www.ilo.org/global/research/global-reports/weso/2015/lang--en/index.htm.

International Trade Commission. 1981. "Background Study of the Economies and International Trade Patterns of the Countries of North America, Central America, and the Caribbean." Report on Investigation No. 332-119. USITC Publication 1176. Washington, DC: US International Trade Commission.

International Trade Commission. 1992. "Economy-Wide Modeling of the Economic Implications of a FTA with Mexico and a NAFTA with Canada and Mexico." Report on Investigation No. 332-317. USITC Publication 2516. Washington, DC: US International Trade Commission.

International Trade Commission. 2016. "Economic Impact of Trade Agreements Implemented under Trade Authorities Procedures." Report on Investigation No. 332-555. USITC Publication 4614. Washington, DC: US International Trade Commission. www.usitc.gov/publications/332/pub4614.pdf.

Inwood, Gregory J. 2005. *Continentalizing Canada: The Politics and Legacy of the Macdonald Royal Commission.* Toronto: University of Toronto Press.

Ipsos. 2017. "Views from Mexico, Canada & the US: Trade & NAFTA." https://www.ipsos.com/en-us/news-polls/mexico-canada-us-trade-nafta-2017-09.

Irwin, Douglas A. 1998. *Against the Tide: An Intellectual History of Free Trade.* Princeton, NJ: Princeton University Press.

Irwin, Douglas A., and Randall S. Kroszner. 1999. "Interests, Institutions, and Ideology in Securing Policy Change: The Republican Conversion to Trade Liberalization after Smoot-Hawley." *Journal of Law and Economics* 42[2]: 643–74.

Jacobs, Alan M. 2015. "Process-Tracing the Effects of Ideas." Pp. 41–73 in Andrew Bennett and Jeffrey T. Checkel, eds., *Process Tracing in the Social Sciences: From Metaphor to Analytic Tool.* New York: Cambridge University Press.

James, Harold. 2001. *The End of Globalization: Lessons from the Great Depression.* Cambridge, MA: Harvard University Press.

Jensen, Nathan M., and Guillermo Rosas. 2007. "Foreign Direct Investment and Income Inequality in Mexico, 1990–2000." *International Organization* 61: 467–87.

Johnson, C. Donald. 2018. *The Wealth of a Nation: A History of Trade Politics in America.* New York: Oxford University Press.

Johnson, Harry G. 1960. "The Cost of Protection and the Scientific Tariff." *Journal of Political Economy* 68[4]: 327–45.

Johnson, Harry G. 1968. "Canadian Contributions to the Discipline of Economics since 1945." *Canadian Journal of Economics* 1[1]: 129–46.

Johnson Ceva, Kristin. 1998 "Business-Government Relations in Mexico since 1990." Pp. 125–57 in Riordan Roett, ed., *Mexico's Private Sector: Recent History, Future Challenges.* Boulder, CO: Lynne Rienner.

Johnston, Richard. 1986. *Public Opinion and Public Policy in Canada: Questions of Confidence.* Vol. 35, Research Report, Royal Commission on the Economic Union and Development Prospects for Canada. Toronto: University of Toronto Press.

Jones, Daniel Stedman. 2012. *Masters of the Universe: Hayek, Friedman, and the Birth of Neoliberal Politics.* Princeton, NJ: Princeton University Press.

Kabeer, Naila, and Hugh Waddington. 2015. "Economic Impacts of Conditional Cash Transfer Programmes: A Systematic Review and Meta-analysis." *Journal of Development Effectiveness* 7[3]: 290–303.

Kaplan, Edward S. 1996. *American Trade Policy, 1923–1995.* Westport, CT: Greenwood.

Kaufman, Robert R., and Leo Zuckermann. 1998. "Attitudes toward Economic Reform in Mexico: The Role of Political Orientations." *American Political Science Review* 92[2]: 359–75.

Kay, John. 2004. *Everlasting Light Bulbs: How Economics Illuminates the World.* London: Erasmus Press.

Kay, Tamara. 2005. "Labor Transnationalism and Global Governance: The Impact of NAFTA on Transnational Labor Relationships in North America." *American Journal of Sociology* 111[3]: 715–56.

Kay, Tamara. 2011. *NAFTA and the Politics of Labor Transnationalism.* New York: Cambridge University Press.

Kay, Tamara, and R. L. Evans. 2018. *Trade Battles: Activism and the Politicization of International Trade Policy.* New York: Oxford University Press.

Kearl, J. R., Clayne L. Pope, Gordon C. Whiting, and Larry T. Wimmer. 1979. "A Confusion of Economists?" *American Economic Review* 69[2]: 28–37.

Kelleher, James F. 1985. *How to Secure and Enhance Canadian Access to Export Markets.* Ottawa: Office of the Minister for International Trade / Department of External Affairs.

Khedouri, Frederick N. 1986. "Memorandum for the Vice President." June 9. Tyrus Cobb Files, Box 91097. Ronald Reagan Presidential Library.

King, J. E. 1974. "Canadian Chamber of Commerce, 1969–1974; Presentation to the Prime Minister and Cabinet By J.E. King, President." February 18. Mitchell Sharp fonds, MG 32 B 41, vol. 56. Library and Archives Canada.

King, John. 1983. "Business Council Recommends Canada-U.S. Free Trade Pact." *Globe and Mail,* April 19, B7.

Kingstone, Peter E. 2001. "Why Free Trade 'Losers' Support Free Trade: Industrialists and the Surprising Politics of Trade Reform in Brazil." *Comparative Political Studies* 34[9]: 986–1010.

Klamer, Arjo, and Jennifer Meehan. 1999. "The Crowding Out of Academic Economics: The Case of NAFTA." Pp. 65–85 in Robert F. Garnett, Jr., ed., *What Do Economists Know? New Economics of Knowledge.* London: Routledge.

Klein, Daniel B., and Charlotta Stern. 2007. "Is There a Free-Market Economist in the House? The Policy Views of American Economic Association Members." *American Journal of Economics and Sociology* 66[2]: 309–34.

Kleinberg, Katja B., and Benjamin O. Fordham. 2010. "Trade and Foreign Policy Attitudes." *Journal of Conflict Resolution* 54[5]: 687–714.

Kliesen, Kevin L. 1995. "The Fixation on International Competitiveness." *Regional Economist* (Federal Reserve Bank of St. Louis), January, 4–9. https://www.stlouisfed.org/publications/regional-economist/january-1995/the-fixation-on-international-competitiveness.

Knight, Alan. 2001. "The Modern Mexican State: Theory and Practice." Pp. 177–218 in Miguel Angel Centeno and Fernando López-Alves, eds., *The Other Mirror: Grand Theory through the Lens of Latin America.* Princeton, NJ: Princeton University Press.

Kono, D. Y. 2006. "Optimal Obfuscation: Democracy and Trade Policy Transparency." *American Political Science Review* 100: 369–84.

Kose, M. Ayhan, Guy M. Meredith, and Christopher M. Towe. 2005. "How Has NAFTA Affected the Mexican Economy? Review and Evidence." Pp. 35–81 in R. J. Langhammer and L. V. de Souza, eds., *Monetary Policy and Macroeconomic Stabilization in Latin America*. Berlin: Springer.

Kotz, David. 2015. *The Rise and Fall of Neoliberal Capitalism*. Cambridge, MA: Harvard University Press.

Krasner, Stephen D. 1985. *Structural Conflict: The Third World against Global Liberalism*. Berkeley: University of California Press.

Krueger, Anne O. 1990. "Asymmetries in Policy between Exportables and Import-Competing Goods." Pp. 161–78 in Ronald W. Jones and Anne O. Krueger, eds., *The Political Economy of International Trade*. Oxford: Basil Blackwell.

Krueger, Anne O. 1995. *American Trade Policy: A Tragedy in the Making*. Washington, DC: AEI Press.

Krugman, Paul R. 1991. "The Move toward Free Trade Zones." Pp. 7–41 in *Policy Implications of Trade and Currency Zones: A Symposium Sponsored by the Federal Reserve Bank of Kansas City*. Kansas City, MO: Federal Reserve Bank of Kansas City.

Krugman, Paul R. 1993. "What Do Undergrads Need to Know about Trade?" *American Economic Review* 83[2]: 23–26.

Krugman, Paul R. 1994. "Competitiveness: A Dangerous Obsession." *Foreign Affairs* 73[2]: 28–44.

Krugman, Paul R. 1996. *Pop Internationalism*. Cambridge, MA: MIT Press.

Krugman, Paul R. 1997. "What Should Trade Negotiators Negotiate About?" *Journal of Economic Literature* 35: 113–20.

Krugman, Paul R. 1998. "Ricardo's Difficult Idea: Why Intellectuals Can't Understand Comparative Advantage." Pp. 22–36 in Gary Cook, ed., *Freedom and Trade: The Economics and Politics of International Trade, vol. 2*. New York: Routledge.

Krugman, Paul R. 2008. "Trade and Wages, Reconsidered." *Brookings Papers on Economic Activity* 39[1]: 103–54.

Krugman, Paul R. 2018. "Paul Krugman Explains Trade and Tariffs." *New York Times*, March 15. https://www.nytimes.com/2018/03/15/opinion/paul-krugman-aluminum-steel-trade-tariffs.html.

Kuttner, Robert. 2017. "The Man from Red Vienna." Review of Gareth Dale, *Karl Polanyi: A Life on the Left* (Columbia University Press). New York Review of Books, December 21. http://www.nybooks.com/articles/2017/12/21/karl-polanyi-man-from-red-vienna/.

Lake, David A. 2006. "International Political Economy: A Maturing Interdiscipline." Pp. 757–77 in Barry R. Weingast and Donald A. Wittman, eds., *The Oxford Handbook of Political Economy*. Oxford: Oxford University Press.

Lal, Deepak. 2005. "The Threat to Liberty from International Organizations." *Cato Journal* 25[3]: 503–20.

Langille, David. 1987. "The Business Council on National Issues and the Canadian State." *Studies in Political Economy* 24: 41–85.

Langston, Joy. 2001. "Why Rules Matter: Changes in Candidate Selection in Mexico's PRI, 1988–2000." *Journal of Latin American Studies* 33[3]: 485–511.

Lao, Rattana. 2015. *A Critical Study of Thailand's Higher Education Reforms: The Culture of Borrowing*. New York: Routledge.

Laothamatas, Anek. 1988. "Business and Politics in Thailand: New Patterns of Influence." *Asian Survey* 28[4]: 451–70.

Laothamatas, Anek. 1992. "The Politics of Structural Adjustment in Thailand: A Political Explanation of Economic Success." Pp. 32–49 in Andrew J. MacIntyre and Kanishka Jayasuriya, eds., *The Dynamics of Economic Policy Reform in South-East Asia and the South-West Pacific*. New York: Oxford University Press.

Larue, Bruno. 2018. "Economic Integration Reconsidered." *Canadian Journal of Agricultural Economics* 66: 5–25.

Laux, Jeanne Kirk, and Maureen Appel Molot. 1988. *State Capitalism: Public Enterprise in Canada*. Ithaca NY: Cornell University Press.

Laver, Ross. 1985. "Free Trade." *Maclean's*, September 16, 24–28. https://archive.macleans.ca/article/1985/9/16/free-trade.

Lawrence, Robert Z. 2008. *Blue-Collar Blues: Is Trade to Blame for Rising US Income Inequality?* Policy Analyses in International Economics. Washington, DC: Peterson Institute for International Economics.

Lawson, C. H. 2002. *Building the Fourth Estate: Democratization and the Rise of a Free Press in Mexico*. Berkeley: University of California Press.

Leamer, Edward E. 2012. *The Craft of Economics: Lessons from the Heckscher-Ohlin Framework*. Cambridge, MA: MIT Press.

Lechner, Lisa. 2016. "The Domestic Battle over the Design of Non-trade Issues in Preferential Trade Agreements." *Review of International Political Economy* 23[5]: 840–71.

Lederman, Daniel. 2005. *The Political Economy of Protection: Theory and the Chilean Experience*. Stanford, CA: Stanford University Press.

LeDuc, Lawrence. 1989. "The Canadian Federal Election of 1988." *Electoral Studies* 8[2]: 163–67.

Leigh, Andrew. 2002. "Trade Liberalisation and the Australian Labor Party." *Australian Journal of Politics and History* 48[4]: 487–508.

Lemieux, Thomas. 2008. "The Changing Nature of Wage Inequality." *Journal of Population Economics* 21: 21–48.

Levin, Doron P. 1992. "Honda Cut from U.S. Auto Group." *New York Times*, November 26. http://www.nytimes.com/1992/11/26/business/honda-cut-from-us-auto-group.html.

Levitsky, Melvyn. 1988. "Memorandum for Colin L. Powell and Mr. Robert H. Tuttle." November 18. Robert S. Pastorino Files, Box 92429. Ronald Reagan Presidential Library.

Levitt, Kari. 1970. *Silent Surrender: The Multinational Corporation in Canada*. Toronto: Macmillan of Canada.

Levitt, Kari Polanyi. 2006. "Keynes and Polanyi: The 1920s and the 1990s." *Review of International Political Economy* 13[1]: 152–77.

Lewis, W. Arthur. 1954. "Economic Development with Unlimited Supplies of Labour." *Manchester School of Economic and Social Studies* 22: 139–91.

Li, Quan, and Rafael Reuveny. 2003. "Economic Globalization and Democracy: An Empirical Analysis." *British Journal of Political Science* 33: 29–54.

Lieberman, Evan S. 2001. "Causal Inference in Historical Institutional Analysis: A Specification of Periodization Strategies." *Comparative Political Studies* 34[9]: 1011–35.

Lieberman, Evan S. 2005. "Nested Analysis as a Mixed-Method Strategy for Comparative Research." *American Political Science Review* 99[3]: 435–52.

Lightman, Ryla Snider. 1983. "Letter to Mrs. Theresa Bruneau, Macdonald Royal Commission, Ottawa, from the Canadian Federation of Independent Business." November 16. Macdonald Commission fonds, RG 33/137, vol. 38. Library and Archives Canada.

Lindberg, Staffan I., Michael Coppedge, John Gerring, Jan Teorell, et al. 2014. "V-Dem: A New Way to Measure Democracy." *Journal of Democracy* 25[3]: 159–69.

Lindvall, Johannes. 2009. "The Real but Limited Influence of Expert Ideas." *World Politics* 61[4]: 703–30.

Lipsey, Richard G. 1990. "Canada at the U.S.-Mexico Free Trade Dance: Wallflower or Partner?" *C.D. Howe Institute Commentary* 20: 1–15.

Lipsey, Richard G., and Murray Smith. 1985. *Taking the Initiative: Canada's Trade Options in a Turbulent World*. Toronto: CDHI.

Litvak, Isaiah A. 1986. "Freer Trade with Canada: The Conflicting Views of U.S. Business." *Business Quarterly* 51[3]: 44–51.

Litvak, Isaiah A., and Christopher J. Maule. 1975-6. "Canadian Investment Abroad: In Search of a Policy." *International Journal* 31[1]: 159–79.

Litvak, Isaiah A., and Christopher J. Maule. 1981. *The Canadian Multinationals*. Toronto: Butterworths.

Liu, Xuepeng, and Emanuel Ornelas. 2014. "Free Trade Agreements and the Consolidation of Democracy." *American Economic Journal: Macroeconomics* 6[2]: 29–70.

Lloyd, Peter. 2008. "100 Years of Tariff Protection in Australia." *Australian Economic History Review* 48[2]: 99–145.

Logan, Jennifer. 2008. "Belted by NAFTA? A Look at Trade's Effect on the US Manufacturing Belt." *Regional Studies* 42[5]: 675–687.

Long, Tom. 2015. *Latin America Confronts the United States: Asymmetry and Influence.* New York: Cambridge University Press.

Los Angeles Times. 1992. "Clinton May Oppose Bush on Trade Pact." *Los Angeles Times*, August 1. http://articles.latimes.com/1992-08-01/news/mn-4291_1_free-trade-agreement.

Love, Joseph L. 1996. "Economic Ideas and Ideologies in Latin America Since 1930." Pp. 207–74 in Leslie Bethell, ed., *Ideas and Ideologies in Twentieth Century Latin America.* New York: Cambridge University Press.

Lucardi, Adrián. 2016. "Building Support from Below? Subnational Elections, Diffusion Effects, and the Growth of the Opposition in Mexico, 1984–2000." *Comparative Political Studies* 49[14]: 1855–95.

Lumley, Elizabeth, ed. 2005. *Canadian Who's Who. Vol. 40.* Toronto: University of Toronto Press.

Lustig, Nora. 1998. *Mexico: The Remaking of an Economy.* 2nd ed. Washington, DC: Brookings.

Lusztig, Michael. 1998. "The Limits of Rent Seeking: Why Protectionists Become Free Traders." *Review of International Political Economy* 5[1]: 38–63.

Lynch, Daniel. 2006. *Rising China and Asian Democratization: Socialization to "Global Culture" in the Political Transformations of Thailand, China, and Taiwan.* Stanford, CA: Stanford University Press.

Lyon, Peyton V., and David Leyton-Brown. 1977. "Image and Policy Preference: Canadian Élite Views on Relations with the United States." *International Journal* 32[3]: 640–71.

MacArthur, John R. 2000. *The Selling of "Free Trade": NAFTA, Washington, and the Subversion of American Democracy.* Berkeley: University of California Press.

MacIntyre, Andrew J., and Kanishka Jayasuriya, eds. 1992. *The Dynamics of Economic Policy Reform in South-East Asia and the South-West Pacific.* New York: Oxford University Press.

MacMillan, Whitney. 1992. "Letter to President George H.W. Bush, from the Chairman of the Investment Policy Advisory Committee, Accompanying Its Report to the U.S. Congress Concerning the Investment Chapter of the North American Free Trade Agreement." September 14. TA005, WHORM, 351076. George H. W. Bush Presidential Library.

Magee, Christopher Sean Patrick. 2010. "Would NAFTA Have Been Approved by the House of Representatives under President Bush? Presidents, Parties, and Trade Policy." *Review of International Economics* 18[2]: 382–95.

Mahoney, James. 1999. "Nominal, Ordinal, and Narrative Appraisal in Macrocausal Analysis." *American Journal of Sociology* 104[4]: 1154–96.

Mahoney, James. 2010. "After KKV: The New Methodology of Qualitative Research." *World Politics* 62[1]: 120–47.

Manger, Mark. 2005. "Competition and Bilateralism in Trade Policy: The Case of Japan's Free Trade Agreements." *Review of International Political Economy* 12[5]: 804–28.

Mansfield, Edward D., and Helen V. Milner. 2012. *Votes, Vetoes, and the Political Economy of International Trade Agreements.* Princeton, NJ: Princeton University Press.

Mansfield, Edward D., Helen V. Milner, and B. Peter Rosendorff. 2002. "Why Democracies Cooperate More: Electoral Control and International Trade Agreements." *International Organization* 56: 477–513.

Mansfield, Edward D., and Diana C. Mutz. 2009. "Support for Free Trade: Self-Interest, Sociotropic Politics, and Out-Group Anxiety." *International Organization* 63[3]: 425–57.

Mansfield, Edward D., and Diana C. Mutz. 2013. "US vs. Them: Mass Attitudes toward Offshore Outsourcing." *World Politics* 65[4]: 571–608.

Mansfield, Edward, Diana C. Mutz, and Laura Silver. 2015. "Men, Women, Trade and Free Markets." *International Studies Quarterly* 59: 303–15.

Margalit, Y. 2012. "Lost in Globalization: International Economic Integration and the Sources of Popular Discontent." *International Studies Quarterly* 56: 484–500.

Markoff, John, and Verónica Montecinos. 1993. "The Ubiquitous Rise of Economists." *Journal of Public Policy* 13[1]: 37–68.

Martínez, Leonardo, and Ben Ross Schneider. 2001. "Gatekeeper of Influence: The Mexican State and Agro-Industry in the NAFTA Negotiations." *Canadian Journal of Latin American and Caribbean Studies* 26[51]: 83–119.

Martínez, Salvador. 1990. "Fortalecemos la Economía con el TLC o Perdemos Fuentes de Empleo: CSG." *Excelsior*, September 7, 1 and 26.

Massey, Douglas S., Jorge Durand, and Karen A. Pren. 2014. "Explaining Undocumented Migration to the U.S." *International Migration Review* 48[4]: 1028–61.

Massicotte, Marie-Josée. 2001. "Construyendo Puentes en América del Norte: La Emergencia de la Alianza Social Continental y sus Redes Transnacionales." *Las Relaciones de México con Estados Unidos y Canadá: Una Mirada al Nuevo Milenio*. Mexico City: UNAM and CISAN.

Mastanduno, Michael. 2009. "System Maker and Privilege Taker U.S. Power and the International Political Economy." *World Politics* 61[1]: 121–54.

Maxfield, Sylvia, and Adam Shapiro. 1998. "Assessing the NAFTA Negotiations." Pp. 82–118 in Carol Wise, ed., *The Post-NAFTA Political Economy: Mexico and the Western Hemisphere*. University Park: Pennsylvania State University Press.

Mayda, Anna Maria, and Dani Rodrik. 2005. "Why Are Some People (and Countries) More Protectionist than Others?" *European Economic Review* 49: 1393–430.

Mayer, Frederick W. 1998. *Interpreting NAFTA: The Science and Art of Political Analysis*. New York: Columbia University Press.

McBride, Stephen. 2001. *Paradigm Shift: Globalization and the Canadian State*. Halifax: Fernwood.

McBride, Stephen. 2006. "Reconfiguring Sovereignty: NAFTA Chapter 11 Dispute Settlement Procedures and the Issue of Public-Private Authority." *Canadian Journal of Political Science* 39: 755–75.

McCabe, Michael J. 1963. "Letter from the Executive Assistant to the Minister to Mr. Richard O'Hagan, Special Assistant to the Prime Minister of Canada." May 7. Mitchell Sharp fonds, MG 32 B 41, vol. 5. Library and Archives Canada.

McLagan, T. R. 1961. "President's Address, the Ninetieth Annual General Meeting of the Canadian Manufacturers' Association." June 5. Canadian Manufacturers' Association fonds, MG28 I 230, vol. 17. Library and Archives Canada.

Mead, Kullada Kesboonchoon. 2004. *The Rise and Decline of Thai Absolutism*. New York: Routledge.

Medrano, J. D. and M. Braun. 2012. "Uninformed Citizens and Support for Free Trade." *Review of International Political Economy* 19[3]: 448–76.

Medvetz, Thomas. 2012. *Think Tanks in America*. Chicago: University of Chicago Press.

Mendelsohn, Matthew, and Robert Wolfe. 2001. "Probing the Aftermyth of Seattle: Canadian Public Opinion on International Trade, 1980–2000." *International Journal* 56[2]: 234–60.

Mendelsohn, Matthew, Robert Wolfe, and Andrew Parkin. 2002. "Globalization, Trade Policy and the Permissive Consensus in Canada." *Canadian Public Policy* 28[3]: 351–71.

Micklethwait, John, and Adrian Wooldridge. 2000. *A Future Perfect: The Essentials of Globalization*. New York: Crown Business.

Middlebrook, Kevin J. 1995. *The Paradox of Revolution: Labor, the State, and Authoritarianism in Mexico*. Baltimore: Johns Hopkins University Press.

Miller, Stephen C. 2009. "Economic Bias and Ideology: Evidence from the General Social Survey." *Journal of Private Enterprise* 25[1]: 31–49.

Millmow, Alex. 2005. "Australian Economics in the Twentieth Century." *Cambridge Journal of Economics* 29[6]: 1011–26.

Mills, C. Wright. 1956. *The Power Elite*. New York: Oxford University Press.

Milner, Helen V. 1997. "Industries, Governments, and Regional Trade Blocs." Pp. 77–106 in Edward D. Mansfield and Helen V. Milner, eds., *The Political Economy of Regionalism*. New York: Columbia University Press.

Milner, Helen V. 1999. "The Political Economy of International Trade." *Annual Review of Political Science 2*: 91–114.

Milner, Helen V., and Keiko Kubota. 2005. "Why the Move to Free Trade? Democracy and Trade Policy in the Developing Countries." *International Organization 59*: 107–43.

Milner, Helen V., and Bumba Mukherjee. 2009. "Democratization and Economic Globalization." *Annual Review of Political Science 12*: 163–81.

Mirowski, Philip. 2013. *Never Let a Serious Crisis Go to Waste: How Neoliberalism Survived the Financial Meltdown*. London: Verso.

Mirowski, Philip, and Dieter Plehwe, eds. 2009. *The Road from Mont Pèlerin: The Making of the Neoliberal Thought Collective*. Cambridge, MA: Harvard University Press.

Mizrahi, Yemile. 1992. "La Nueva Oposición Conservadora en México: La Radicalización Política de los Empresarios Norteños." *Foro Internacional 32*[5]: 744–71.

Mizruchi, Mark S., and Deborah M. Bey. 2005. "Corporate Control, Interfirm Relations, and Corporate Power." Pp. 310–30 in Thomas Janoski, Robert R. Alford, Alexander M. Hicks, and Mildred A. Schwartz, eds., *The Handbook of Political Sociology: States, Civil Societies, and Globalization*. New York: Cambridge University Press.

Montecinos, Verónica, and John Markoff. 2001. "From the Power of Economic Ideas to the Power of Economists." Pp. 105–50 in Miguel Angel Centeno and Fernando López-Alves, eds., *The Other Mirror: Grand Theory through the Lens of Latin America*. Princeton, NJ: Princeton University Press.

Montecinos, Verónica, and John Markoff, eds. 2009. *Economists in the Americas*. Northampton, MA: Edward Elgar.

Montgomery, D. W. 1986. "Issues." Canadian Manufacturers' Association fonds, MG28 I 230, vol. 1. Library and Archives Canada.

Moore, Mike. 1999. Statement by the WTO Director-General at President Bill Clinton's Lunch. Seattle. December 1. https://www.wto.org/english/thewto_e/minist_e/min99_e/english/press_e/dgclint_e.htm.

Mudge, Stephanie Lee. 2008. "What Is Neo-liberalism?" *Socio-Economic Review 4*: 703–31.

Muirhead, B. W. 1992. *The Development of Postwar Canadian Trade Policy: The Failure of the Anglo-European Option*. Montreal: McGill-Queen's University Press.

Mukherjee, Bumba. 2016. *Democracy and Trade Policy in Developing Countries*. Chicago: University of Chicago Press.

Mukherji, Rahul. 2013. "Ideas, Interests, and the Tipping Point: Economic Change in India." *Review of International Political Economy 20*[2]: 363–89.

Munck, Ronaldo. 2002. "Globalization and Democracy: A New 'Great Transformation'?" *Annals of the American Academy of Political and Social Science 581*: 10–21.

Murray, Joshua. 2017. "Interlock Globally, Act Domestically: Corporate Political Unity in the 21st Century." *American Journal of Sociology 122*[6]: 1617–63.

National Security Council. 1990. "From Amembassy Ottawa to the Secretary of State, Washington DC, Subject: Canadian Role in U.S./Mexico FTA Talks." September 5. SCS 7/19/13. 2008-1138-MR. George H. W. Bush Presidential Library.

Nelson, Stephen C. 2014. "Playing Favorites: How Shared Beliefs Shape the IMF's Lending Decisions." *International Organization 68*: 297–328.

Nelson, Stephen C. 2017. *The Currency of Confidence: How Economic Beliefs Shape the IMF's Relationship with Its Borrowers*. Ithaca, NY: Cornell University Press.

Neumayer, Eric. 2001. "Pollution Havens: An Analysis of Policy Options for Dealing with an Elusive Phenomenon." *Journal of Environment & Development 10*[2]: 147–77.

Neumayer, Eric, and Indra De Soysa. 2006. "Globalization and the Right to Free Association and Collective Bargaining: An Empirical Analysis." *World Development 34*[1]: 31–49.

Neumayer, Eric, and Laura Spess. 2005. "Do Bilateral Investment Treaties Increase Foreign Direct Investment to Developing Countries?" *World Development 33*[10]: 1567–85.

New York Times. 1930. "1,028 Economists Ask Hoover to Veto Pending Tariff Bill: Professors in 179 Colleges and Other Leaders Assail Rise in Rates as Harmful to Country and Sure to Bring Reprisals." *New York Times*, May 5, 1 and 4.

Newport, Frank. 2016. "American Public Opinion on Foreign Trade." Gallup Polling Matters. April 1. https://news.gallup.com/opinion/polling-matters/190427/american-public-opinion-foreign-trade.aspx.

Niosi, J. 1981. *Canadian Capitalism: A Study of Power in the Canadian Business Establishment.* Toronto: Lorimer.

Nordhaus, William D. 2006. "Geography and Macroeconomics: New Data and New Findings." *PNAS 103*[10]: 3510–17.

Nye, Joseph S., Jr. 2001. "Globalization's Democratic Deficit: How to Make International Institutions More Accountable." *Foreign Affairs 80*[4]: 2–6.

O'Rourke, Kevin H., and Richard Sinnott. 2001. "The Determinants of Individual Trade Policy Preferences: International Survey Evidence." *Brookings Trade Forum*: 157–206.

Organization for Economic Cooperation and Development (OECD) 1985. *The Role of the Public Sector: Causes and Consequences of the Growth of Government.* Paris: OECD.

Organization for Economic Cooperation and Development (OECD). 2011. *Divided We Stand: Why Inequality Keeps Rising.* Paris: OECD. http://dx.doi.org/10.1787/9789264119536-en.

Organization for Economic Cooperation and Development (OECD). 2018. GDP per hour worked (indicator). doi: 10.1787/1439e590-en. Total, US Dollars, 1978–2016.

Orden, David. 1996. "Agricultural Interest Groups and the North American Free Trade Agreement." Pp. 335–82 in Anne O. Krueger, ed., *The Political Economy of American Trade Policy.* Chicago: University of Chicago Press.

Ortiz Mena, Antonio. 2004. "Mexico's Trade Policy: Improvisation and Vision." Pp. 213–31 in Vinod K. Aggarwal, Ralph Espach, and Joseph S. Tulchin, eds., *The Strategic Dynamics of Latin American Trade.* Washington, DC: Woodrow Wilson Center Press.

Ortiz Mena, Antonio. 2017. "Toward a Positive NAFTA Renegotiation: A Mexican Perspective." Pp. 24–35 in C. Fred Bergsten and Monica de Bolle, eds., *A Path Forward for NAFTA.* PIIE Briefing 17–12. Washington, DC: Peterson Institute for International Economics. https://piie.com/system/files/documents/piieb17-2.pdf.

Ostroff, Jim. 1991. "ATMI, AAMA to Back NAFTA, with Limits." *Daily News Record,* October 25, 5.

Ostrom, Elinor. 2003. "Toward a Behavioral Theory Linking Trust, Reciprocity, and Reputation." Pp. 19–79 in Elinor Ostrom and James Walker, eds., *Trust and Reciprocity: Interdisciplinary Lessons for Experimental Research.* New York: Russell Sage.

Ostry, Jonathan D., Prakash Loungani, and Davide Furceri. 2016. "Neoliberalism: Oversold?" *Finance and Development 53*[2]: 38–41.

Ostry, Sylvia. 1997. *The Post–Cold War Trading System: Who's on First?* Chicago: University of Chicago Press.

Ostry, Sylvia. 2002. "Preface." Pp. i–iv in *The Trade Policy-Making Process: Level One of the Two Level Game. Country Studies in the Western Hemisphere.* Occasional Paper 13. New York: Inter-American Development Bank.

Page, Benjamin I., and Marshall M. Bouton. 2007. *The Foreign Policy Disconnect: What Americans Want from Our Leaders but Don't Get.* Chicago: University of Chicago Press.

Page, John M., Jr. 1992. "Trade Policies in Mexico." Pp. 361–79 in Dominick Salvatore, ed., *National Trade Policies: Handbook of Comparative Economic Policies, vol. 2.* New York: Greenwood.

Pandya, Sonal S. 2014. "Democratization and Foreign Direct Investment Liberalization, 1970–2000." *International Studies Quarterly 58*[3]: 475–88.

Panitch, Leo, and Sam Gindin. 2012. *The Making of Global Capitalism: The Political Economy of American Empire.* London: Verso.

Park, G. S., Y. S. Jang, and H. Y. Lee 2007. "The Interplay between Globalness and Localness: Korea's Globalization Revisited." *International Journal of Comparative Sociology 48*[4]: 337–53.

Parsons, Talcott. 1957. "The Distribution of Power in American Society." Review of *The Power Elite,* by C. Wright Mills (1956). *World Politics 10*[1]: 123–43.

Passel, Jeffrey, D'Vera Cohn, and Ana Gonzalez-Barrera. 2012. "Net Migration from Mexico Falls to Zero—and Perhaps Less." Washington, DC: Pew Research Center. http://www.pewhispanic.org/files/2012/04/Mexican-migrants-report_final.pdf.

Pastor, Manuel, and Carol Wise. 1994. "The Origins and Sustainability of Mexico's Free Trade Policy." *International Organization* 48[3]: 459–89.

Pastor, Robert A. 2011. *The North American Idea: A Vision of a Continental Future*. New York: Oxford University Press.

Peet, Richard. 2007. *Geography of Power: Making Global Economic Policy*. London: Zed.

Pemstein, Daniel, Stephen A. Meserve, and James Melton. 2010. "Democratic Compromise: A Latent Variable Analysis of Ten Measures of Regime Type." *Political Analysis* 18[4]: 426–49.

Petry, François, and Matthew Mendelsohn. 2004. "Public Opinion and Policy Making in Canada 1994–2001." *Canadian Journal of Political Science* 37: 505–29.

Phongpaichit, Pasuk. 1992. "Technocrats, Businessmen, and Generals: Democracy and Economic Policy-Making in Thailand." Pp. 10–31 in Andrew J. MacIntyre and Kanishka Jayasuriya, eds., *The Dynamics of Economic Policy Reform in South-East Asia and the South-West Pacific*. New York: Oxford University Press.

Phongpaichit, Pasuk, and Chris Baker. 1997. "Power in Transition: Thailand in the 1990s." Pp. 21–41 in Kevin Hewison, ed., *Political Change in Thailand: Democracy and Participation*. London: Routledge.

Phongpaichit, Pasuk, and Chris Baker. 2014. "A Short Account of the Rise and Fall of the Thai Technocracy." *Southeast Asian Studies* 3[2]: 283–98.

Pilliod, Charles J. 1988. Pastorino, Box 92429, Mexico 1987 3 of 10, November 21, 1988, Fax to "Dan Gregg or Sam Watson." From Charles J Pilliod, U.S. ambassador to Mexico, Subject: Trade & Debt.

Pincus, Jonathan. 1995. "Evolution and Political Economy of Australian Trade Policies." Pp. 53–73 in Richard Pomfret, ed., *Australia's Trade Policies*. Melbourne: Oxford University Press.

Pizarro, Fernando Ortega. 1990. "Mientras Publicamente Se Decía 'No' al Convenio con Washington, Ya Se Negociaba por la redacción." *Proceso*, March 31. https://www.proceso.com.mx/154686/mientras-publicamente-se-decia-no-al-convenio-con-washington-ya-se-negociaba.

Plehwe, Dieter, Bernhard Walpen, and Gisela Neunhöffer. 2006. "Introduction: Reconsidering Neoliberal Hegemony." Pp. 1–24 in Dieter Plehwe, Bernhard Walpen, and Gisela Neunhöffer, eds., *Neoliberal Hegemony: A Global Critique*. London: Routledge.

Poitras, Guy, and Raymond Robinson. 1994. "The Politics of NAFTA in Mexico." *Journal of Interamerican Studies and World Affairs* 36[1]: 1–35.

Pokarier, Christopher. 2017. "Australia's Foreign Investment Policy: An Historical Perspective." *International Journal of Public Policy* 13[3–5]: 212–31.

Polanyi, Karl. 1944. *The Great Transformation: The Political and Economic Origins of Our Time*. Boston: Beacon.

Polanyi-Levitt, Kari. 2012. "The Power of Ideas: Keynes, Hayek, and Polanyi." *International Journal of Political Economy* 41:[4]: 5–15.

Pomfret, Richard, ed. 1995. Preface. *Australia's Trade Policies*. Melbourne: Oxford University Press.

Pomfret, Richard. 2000. "Trade Policy in Canada and Australia in the Twentieth Century." *Australian Economic History Review* 40[2]: 114–26.

Pop-Eleches, Grigore. 2009. *From Economic Crisis to Reform: IMF Programs in Latin America and Eastern Europe*. Princeton, NJ: Princeton University Press.

Porter, John. 1958. "Higher Public Servants and the Bureaucratic Elite in Canada." *Canadian Journal of Economics and Political Science* 24[4]: 483–501.

Posner, Richard A. 1997. "Rational Choice, Behavioral Economics, and the Law." *Stanford Law Review* 50: 1551–75.

Prasad, Monica. 2006. *The Politics of Free Markets: The Rise of Neoliberal Economic Policies in Britain, France, Germany, and the United States*. Chicago: University of Chicago Press.

Prebisch, Raul. 1959. "Commercial Policy in Underdeveloped Countries." *American Economic Review* 49[2]: 251–73.

Presidencia de la República, Unidad de la Crónica Presidencial. 1992. *Diccionario Biográfico del Gobierno Mexicano 1992*. Mexico City: Fondo de Cultura Económica.

Przeworski, A., M. E. Alvarez, J. A. Cheibub, and F. Limongi. 2000. *Democracy and Development: Political Institutions and Well-Being in the World, 1950–1990.* New York: Cambridge University Press.

Puga, Cristina. 1994. "Las Organizaciones Empresariales en la Negociación del TLC." Pp. 171–93 in Ricardo Tirado, ed., *Los Empresarios ante la Globalización.* Mexico City: Cámara de Diputados del H. Congreso de la Unión, LV Legislatura, Instituto de Investigaciones Legislativas.

Pusey, Michael. 1991. *Economic Rationalism in Canberra: A Nation-Building State Changes Its Mind.* Cambridge: Cambridge University Press.

Putnam, Robert D. 1988. "Diplomacy and Domestic Politics: The Logic of Two-Level Games." *International Organization* 42[3]: 427–60.

Rabe, Stephen G. 1978. "The Elusive Conference: United States Economic Relations with Latin America, 1945–1952." *Diplomatic History* 2: 279–94.

Raby, Jean. 1990. "The Investment Provisions of the Canada-United States Free Trade Agreement: A Canadian Perspective." *American Journal of International Law* 84[2]: 394–443.

Rankin, David M. 2004. "Borderline Interest or Identity? American and Canadian Opinion on the North American Free Trade Agreement." *Comparative Politics* 36[3]: 331–51.

Rea, Kenneth J., and Jack T. MacLeod. 1976. *Business and Government in Canada: Selected Readings.* 2nd ed. Toronto: Methuen.

Regan, Donald H. 2015. "Explaining Trade Agreements: The Practitioners' Story and the Standard Model." *World Trade Review* 14[3]: 391–417.

Reisman, Simon. 1986. "The Issue of Free Trade." Pp. 33–40 in Duncan Cameron, ed., *The Free Trade Papers.* Toronto: James Lorimer.

Remes, Jaana. 2014. "A Tale of Two Mexicos: Growth and Prosperity in a Two-Speed Economy." Pp. 30–36 in *NAFTA: 20 Years Later.* Washington, DC: Peterson Institute for International Economics. https://piie.com/sites/default/files/publications/briefings/piieb14-3.pdf.

Reuber, Grant L. 1978. "Canadian Economic Policy: Some Perspectives Suggested by the Work of Harry Johnson." *Canadian Journal of Economics* 11: S121–S140.

Richardson, R. Jack. 1992. "Free Trade: Why Did It Happen?" *Canadian Review of Sociology and Anthropology* 29[3]: 307–28.

Riding, Alan. 1984. *Distant Neighbors: A Portrait of the Mexicans.* New York: Alfred A. Knopf.

Riley, Russell L. 2016. *Inside the Clinton White House: An Oral History.* New York: Oxford University Press.

Robert, Maryse. 2000. *Negotiating NAFTA: Explaining the Outcome in Culture, Textiles, Autos, and Pharmaceuticals.* Toronto: University of Toronto Press.

Robertson, Raymond. 2004. "Relative Prices and Wage Inequality: Evidence from Mexico." *Journal of International Economics* 64[2]: 387–409.

Robinson, Ian. 1994. "The Canadian Labor Movement Against 'Free Trade': An Assessment of Strategies and Outcomes." Latin American Labor Occasional Paper #15. Presented to the conference "Labor, Free Trade, and Economic Integration in the Americas: National Labor Union Responses to a Transnational World." Durham, NC, August 25–27.

Robinson, Ian. 2015. "What the NAFTA Fight Teaches about Trade Policy Politicization and Legitimation." Pp. 209–28 in Achim Hurrelmann and Steffen Schneider, eds., *The Legitimacy of Regional Integration in Europe and the Americas.* New York: Palgrave Macmillan.

Robinson, William I. 2014. *Global Capitalism and the Crisis of Humanity.* New York: Cambridge University Press.

Rodrik, Dani. 1994. "The Rush to Free Trade in the Developing World: Why So Late? Why Now? Will It Last?" Pp. 61–88 in Stephan Haggard and Steven B. Webb, eds., *Voting for Reform: Democracy, Political Liberalization, and Economic Adjustment.* New York: Oxford University Press.

Rodrik, Dani. 1997. *Has Globalization Gone Too Far?* Washington, DC: Institute for International Economics.

Rodrik, Dani. 2011. *The Globalization Paradox: Democracy and the Future of the World Economy.* New York: Norton.

Rodrik, Dani. 2018a. "Populism and the Economics of Globalization." *Journal of International Business Policy 1*[1-2]: 12–33.

Rodrik, Dani. 2018b. *Straight Talk on Trade: Ideas for a Sane World Economy.* Princeton, NJ: Princeton University Press.

Romalis, John. 2007. "NAFTA's and CUSFTA's Impact on International Trade." *Review of Economics and Statistics 89*(3): 416–35.

Ros, Jaime. 1992. "Free Trade Area or Common Capital Market? Notes on Mexico-US Economic Integration and Current Negotiations." *Journal of Interamerican Studies and World Affairs 34*[2]: 53–91.

Ross, Michael. 1993. "Clinton Sends NAFTA to Congress after Reaching Deals: Trade: The Administration's Last-Minute Side Accords with Mexico Are Considered Crucial to Passage of The Pact." *Los Angeles Times,* November 4. http://articles.latimes.com/1993-11-04/business/fi-52933_1_side-deal.

Rudra, Nita. 2005. "Globalization and the Strengthening of Democracy in the Developing World." *American Journal of Political Science 49*: 704–30.

Rudra, Nita, and Jennifer Tobin. 2017. "When Does Globalization Help the Poor?" *Annual Review of Political Science 20*: 287–307.

Ruggie, John G. 1982. "International Regimes, Transactions, and Change: Embedded Liberalism in the Postwar Economic System." *International Organization 36*[2]: 379–415.

Rupert, Mark. 2000. *Ideologies of Globalization: Contending Visions of a New World Order.* New York: Routledge.

Saad-Filho, Alfredo, and Deborah Johnston, eds. 2005. *Neoliberalism: A Critical Reader.* London: Pluto Press.

Sachs, Jeffrey D., and Andrew Warner. 1995. "Economic Reform and the Process of Global Integration." *Brookings Papers on Economic Activity 1*: 1–118.

Salinas de Gortari, C. 2000. *México: Un Paso Difícil a la Modernidad.* Barcelona: Plaza & Janés Editores.

Samuelson, Paul A. 1939. "The Gains from International Trade." *Canadian Journal of Economics and Political Science 5*[2]: 195–205.

Samuelson, Paul A. 1969. "The Way of an Economist." Pp. 1–11 in Paul Samuelson, ed., *International Economic Relations: Proceedings of the Third Congress of the International Economic Association.* London: Macmillan.

Sandholtz, Wayne, and John Zysman. 1989. "1992: Recasting the European Bargain." *World Politics 42*[1]: 95–128.

Schamis, Hector E. 1999. "Distributional Coalitions and the Politics of Economic Reform in Latin America." *World Politics 51*[2]: 236–68.

Schattschneider, E. E. 1935. *Politics, Pressures, and the Tariff.* New York: Prentice-Hall.

Scheve, K. F., and M. J. Slaughter. 2001. *Globalization and the Perceptions of American Workers.* Washington, DC: Institute for International Economics.

Schneider, Ben Ross. 1997. "Big Business and the Politics of Economic Reform: Confidence and Concertation in Brazil and Mexico." Pp. 191–215 in Sylvia Maxfield and Ben Schneider, eds., *Business and the State in Developing Countries.* Ithaca, NY: Cornell University Press.

Schneider, Ben Ross. 1998. "The Material Bases of Technocracy: Investor Confidence and Neoliberalism in Latin America." Pp. 77–95 in Miguel A. Centeno and Patricio Silva, eds., *The Politics of Expertise in Latin America.* New York: St. Martin's Press.

Schneider, Ben Ross. 2002. "Why Is Mexican Business So Organized?" *Latin American Research Review 37*: 77–118.

Schneider, Ben Ross. 2004. "Market Reform in Latin America." *World Politics 56*[3]: 456–79.

Schneider, Christina J. 2017. "The Political Economy of Regional Integration." *Annual Review of Political Science 20*[12]: 1–20.

Schnietz, Karen E. 2003. "The Reaction of Private Interests to the 1934 Reciprocal Trade Agreements Act." *International Organization* 57: 213–33.

Scholte, Jan Aart. 2005. "The Sources of Neoliberal Globalization." UNRISD Overarching Concerns Programme Paper 8. Geneva: United Nations Research Institute for Social Development.

Schultze, Charlie. 1979. "Memorandum for the President, McIntyre memo re: Reorganizing the Trade Functions of the Government." May 3. Jimmy Carter Presidential Library.

Sell, Susan K. 1995. "Intellectual Property Protection and Antitrust in the Developing World: Crisis, Coercion, and Choice." *International Organization* 49[2]: 315–49.

Serra Puche, Jaime. 1991. "La Competitividad, Punto Esencial del TLC." Pp. i–iv in *El Mercado de Valores* 19. October 1. Informe #6 de SECOFI. Intervención de Jaime Serra Puche realizó el 19 de septiembre 1991, en el Foro México Joven, organizado por la Universidad Iberoamericana.

Serrano, Mónica. 1993. "Comercio Internacional e Integración Económica: Las Perspectivas Mexicana y Estadounidense." Pp. 327–78 in Gustavo Vega Cánovas, ed., *México–Estados Unidos–Canadá, 1991–1992*. Mexico City: El Colegio de México.

Shadlen, Kenneth C. 2000. "Neoliberalism, Corporatism, and Small Business Political Activism in Contemporary Mexico." *Latin American Research Review* 35[2]: 73–106.

Shadlen, Kenneth C. 2004. *Democratization without Representation: The Politics of Small Industry in Mexico*. University Park: Pennsylvania State University Press.

Shadlen, Kenneth C. 2005. "Exchanging Development for Market Access? Deep Integration and Industrial Policy under Multilateral and Regional-Bilateral Trade Agreements." *Review of International Political Economy* 12: 750–75.

Shearer, Ronald A. 1986. "The New Face of Canadian Mercantilism: The Macdonald Commission and the Case for Free Trade." *Canadian Public Policy* 12: 51–58.

Sheils, G. K. 1953. "Testimony of the President of the CMA, Proceedings of the Senate Standing Committee on Canadian Trade Relations." April 28. Canadian Manufacturers' Association fonds, MG28 I 230, vol 109. Library and Archives Canada.

Sheppard, Eric. 2005. "Constructing Free Trade: From Manchester Boosterism to Global Management." *Transactions of the Institute of British Geographers* 30[2]: 151–72.

Shoch, James. 2000. "Contesting Globalization: Organized Labor, NAFTA, and the 1997 and 1998 Fast-Track Fights." *Politics & Society* 28[1]: 119–50.

Shoe Manufacturers' Association of Canada. 1983. "Submission to the Royal Commission on Economic Union and Development Prospects for Canada, by Jean-Guy Maheu, C.A., President." October. Macdonald Commission fonds, RG 33/137, vol. 91. Library and Archives Canada.

Sigler, John H., and Dennis Goresky. 1974. "Public Opinion on United States–Canadian Relations." *International Organization* 28[4]: 637–68.

Silva, Eduardo. 1998. "Organized Business, Neoliberal Economic Restructuring, and Redemocratization in Chile." Pp. 217–52 in Francisco Durand and Eduardo Silva, eds., *Organized Business, Economic Change, and Democracy in Latin America*. Coral Gables, FL: North-South Center Press.

Simeon, Richard. 1987. "Inside the Macdonald Commission." *Studies in Political Economy* 22: 167–79.

Simmons, Beth A. 2014. "Bargaining over BITs, Arbitrating Awards: The Regime for Protection and Promotion of International Investment." *World Politics* 66[1]: 12–46.

Simmons, Beth A., Frank Dobbin, and Geoffrey Garrett. 2006. "Introduction: The International Diffusion of Liberalism." *International Organization* 60: 781–810.

Simmons, Beth A., and Zachary. Elkins. 2004. "The Globalization of Liberalization: Policy Diffusion in the International Political Economy." *American Political Science Review* 98: 171–89.

Simon, Herbert A. 1995. "Rationality in Political Behavior." *Political Psychology* 16[1]: 45–61.

Sklair, Leslie. 2001. *The Transnational Capitalist Class*. Oxford: Blackwell.

Sklair, Leslie. 2002. *Globalization: Capitalism and Its Alternatives.* Oxford: Oxford University Press.

Slater, Dan, and Daniel Ziblatt. 2013. "The Enduring Indispensability of the Controlled Comparison." *Comparative Political Studies* 46[10]: 1301–27.

Slobodian, Quinn. 2018. *Globalists: The End of Empire and the Birth of Neoliberalism.* Cambridge, MA: Harvard University Press.

Smith, Mark A. 2000. *American Business and Political Power.* Chicago: University of Chicago Press.

Smith, Peter H. 1979. *Labyrinths of Power: Political Recruitment in Twentieth-Century Mexico.* Princeton, NJ: Princeton University Press.

Soares, Sergei, Rafael Guerreiro Osório, Fábio Veras Soares, Marcelo Medeiros, and Eduardo Zepeda. 2009. "Conditional Cash Transfers in Brazil, Chile and Mexico: Impacts upon Inequality." *Estudios Económicos:* 207–24.

Sobarzo, Horacio E. 1994. "The Gains for Mexico from a North American Free Trade Agreement— an Applied General Equilibrium Assessment." Pp. 83–99 in Joseph F. Francois and Clinton R. Shiells, eds., *Modeling Trade Policy: Applied General Equilibrium Assessments of North American Free Trade.* New York: Cambridge University Press.

Sorzano, Jose S. 1987. "Memo for Frank C. Carlucci." October 5. Confidential National Security Council. Robert S. Pastorino Files, Box 92329. Ronald Reagan Presidential Library.

Sousa, David J. 2002. "Converging on Competitiveness: Garbage Cans and the New Global Economy." *Environment and Planning C: Government and Policy* 20[1]: 1–18.

Spilimbergo, Antonio. 2009. "Democracy and Foreign Education." *American Economic Review* 99[1]: 528–43.

Spilker, Gabriele. 2012. "Helpful Organizations: Membership in Inter-governmental Organizations and Environmental Quality in Developing Countries." *British Journal of Political Science* 42[2]: 345–70.

Stallings, Barbara, and Philip Brock. 1993. "The Political Economy of Economic Adjustment: Chile, 1973–1990." Pp. 78–122 in Robert H. Bates and Anne O. Krueger, eds., *Political and Economic Interactions in Economic Policy Reform: Evidence from Eight Countries.* Cambridge, MA: Blackwell.

Stevens, J. Hugh. 1977. "'Agenda for Action': A Submission by the Canadian Manufacturers' Association." Macdonald Commission fonds, RG 33/137, vol. 29. Library and Archives Canada.

Stiglitz, Joseph E. 2004. "The Broken Promise of Nafta." *New York Times,* January 6. www.nytimes. com/2004/01/06/opinion/the-broken-promise-of-nafta.html.

Stiglitz, Joseph E., and Andrew Charlton. 2005. *Fair Trade for All: How Trade Can Promote Development.* New York: Oxford University Press.

Stokes, Bruce. 2018. "Americans, Like Many in Other Advanced Economies, Not Convinced of Trade's Benefits." September 26. http://www.pewglobal.org/2018/09/26/americans-like-many-in-other-advanced-economies-not-convinced-of-trades-benefits/.

Story, Dale. 1982. "Trade Politics in the Third World: A Case Study of the Mexican GATT Decision." *International Organization* 36[4]: 767–94.

Story, Dale. 1986. *Industry, the State, and Public Policy in Mexico.* Austin: University of Texas Press.

Streeck, Wolfgang. 2014. *Buying Time: The Delayed Crisis of Democratic Capitalism.* New York: Verso.

Streeck, Wolfgang. 2017. "The Return of the Repressed." *New Left Review* 104: 5–18.

Summers, Lawrence. 2016. "Global Trade Should Be Remade from the Bottom Up." *Financial Times,* April 10. https://www.ft.com/content/5e9f4a5e-ff09-11e5-99cb-83242733f755.

Tabb, William K. 1995. *The Postwar Japanese System: Cultural Economy and Economic Transformation.* New York: Oxford University Press.

Task Force on the Structure of Canadian Industry. 1968. *Foreign Ownership and the Structure of Canadian Industry: Report of the Task Force on the Structure of Canadian Industry.* Ottawa: Queen's Printer.

Taussig, Frank W. 1905. "The Present Position and the Doctrine of Free Trade—Presidential Address." *American Economic Association, Publications Third Series* 6[1]: 29–65.

Tavares, J. A. 2008. "Trade, Factor Proportions and Politics." *Review of Economics and Statistics* 90: 163–68.

Teichman, Judith A. 2001. *The Politics of Freeing Markets in Latin America: Chile, Argentina, and Mexico*, Chapel Hill: University of North Carolina Press.

Teichman, Judith A. 2004. "The World Bank and Policy Reform in Mexico and Argentina." *Latin American Politics and Society* 46[1]: 39–74.

Thacker, Strom C. 2000. *Big Business, the State, and Free Trade: Constructing Coalitions in Mexico*, New York: Cambridge University Press.

Thacker, Strom C. 1999. "NAFTA Coalitions and the Political Viability of Neoliberalism in Mexico." *Journal of Interamerican Studies and World Affairs* 41[2]: 57–89.

Thibault, Laurent. 1980. Comments to the Senate Standing Committee on Foreign Affairs. December 9. Proceedings on Canadian Relations with the United States. Issue No. 14. First Session, Thirty-Second Parliament, 1980–81.

Thibault, Laurent. 1985–86. The Canadian Manufacturers' Association, 1985–86 President's Report. Amicus 3777699. Library and Archives Canada.

Thorup, Cathryn L. 1991. "The Politics of Free Trade and the Dynamics of Cross-Border Coalitions in U.S.-Mexican Relations." *Columbia Journal of World Business* 26[2]: 12–26.

Torfason, Magnus Thor, and Paul Ingram. 2010. "The Global Rise of Democracy: A Network Account." *American Sociological Review* 75[3]: 355–77.

Townsend, James. 2007. "Do Tariff Reductions Affect the Wages of Workers in Protected Industries? Evidence from the Canada-U.S. Free Trade Agreement." *Canadian Journal of Economics* 40[1]: 69–92.

Transformación. 1993. *Transformación* 37[1]: 28.

Trefler, Daniel. 2004. "The Long and Short of the Canada-U.S. Free Trade Agreement." *American Economic Review* 94[4]: 870–95.

Truell, Peter. 1990. "U.S. and Mexico Agree to Seek Free-Trade Pact." *Wall Street Journal*, March 27, A3.

United Nations Conference on Trade and Development (UNCTAD). N.d. *FDI On-line.* New York: United Nations Conference on Trade and Development. http://stats.unctad.org/fdi.

Urzúa, Carlos M. 1997. "Five Decades of Relations between the World Bank and Mexico." Pp. 49–108 in Devesh Kapur, John P. Lewis, and Richard Webb, eds., The World Bank: Its First Half Century, *vol.* 2: Perspectives. Washington, DC: Brookings Institution Press.

Uslaner, Eric. M. 1998. "Let the Chits Fall Where They May? Executive and Constituency Influences on Congressional Voting on NAFTA." *Legislative Studies Quarterly* 23[3]: 347–71.

Valle, Henry. 1966. "Policy Presentation to Cabinet, Statement by Mr. Henry Valle—Chairman, Trade Committee." February 11. Canadian Manufacturers' Association fonds, MG28 I 230, vol. 68. Library and Archives Canada.

Van Apeldoorn, Bastiaan. 2000. "Transnational Class Agency and European Governance: The Case of the European Round Table of Industrialists." *New Political Economy* 5[2]: 157–81.

Van Apeldoorn, Bastiaan. 2002. *Transnational Capitalism and the Struggle over European Integration*. London: Routledge.

Velasco, Jesús. 1997. "Selling Ideas, Buying Influence: Mexico and American Think Tanks in the Promotion of NAFTA." Pp. 125–47 in Rodolfo O. de la Garza and Jesús Velasco, eds., *Bridging the Border: Transforming Mexico-U.S. Relations*. New York: Rowman and Littlefield.

Vice, David G. 1989. "The Aggressive Economy: Daring to Compete." Chairman of the Board, Canadian Manufacturers' Association, June. Department of Foreign Affairs and International Trade Library.

Vickery, William. 1964. *Microeconomics*. New York: Harcourt, Brace, and World.

Villarreal, Andrés. 2014. "Explaining the Decline in Mexico-U.S. Migration: The Effect of the Great Recession." *Demography* 51: 2203–28.

Villarreal, M. Angeles. 2010. *NAFTA and the Mexican Economy*. Congressional Research Service. CRS Report for Congress. 7-5700. RL34733.

Villarreal, M. Angeles, and Ian F. Fergusson. 2017. *The North American Free Trade Agreement (NAFTA)*. Congressional Research Service. R42965.

Ville, Simon, and Glenn Withers. 2014. *Cambridge Economic History of Australia*. New York: Cambridge University Press.

Vogel, David. 1983. "The Power of Business in America: A Re-appraisal." *British Journal of Political Science 13*[1]: 19–43.

Vogel, Steven K. 1999. "When Interests Are Not Preferences: The Cautionary Tale of Japanese Consumers." *Comparative Politics 31*[2]: 187–207.

Von Bertrab, Hermann. 1997. *Negotiating NAFTA: A Mexican Envoy's Account*. Westport, CT: Praeger and CSIS.

Wacquant, Loïc J. D. 1996. "Reading Bourdieu's 'Capital.'" *International Journal of Contemporary Sociology 33*[2]: 151–70.

Wacziarg, R., and K. H. Welch. 2008. "Trade Liberalization and Growth: New Evidence." *World Bank Economic Review 22*: 187–231.

Wade, Robert Hunter. 2003. "What Strategies ARE Viable for Developing Countries Today? The World Trade Organization and the Shrinking of 'Development Space.'" *Review of International Political Economy 10*[4]: 621–44.

Waldkirch, Andreas. 2003. "The 'New Regionalism' and Foreign Direct Investment: The Case of Mexico." *Journal of International Trade & Economic Development 12*[2]: 151–84.

Waterbury, John. 1999. "The Long Gestation and Brief Triumph of Import-Substituting Industrialization." *World Development 27*[2]: 323–41.

Watson, William G. 1987. "Canada-US Free Trade: Why Now?" *Canadian Public Policy 13*[3]: 337–49.

Watson, William G. 1993. "The Economics of NAFTA: How Much Zero-Sum?" Pp. 159–66 in A. R. Riggs and Tom Velk, eds., *Beyond NAFTA: An Economic, Political and Sociological Perspective*. Vancouver: Fraser Institute.

Weihs, Frederick H. 1974. "Canadian Trade Policy, 1945–1953." MA thesis, Department of History, University of British Columbia.

Weir, Margaret, and Theda Skocpol. 1985. "State Structures and the Possibilities for 'Keynesian' Responses to the Great Depression in Sweden, Britain, and the United States." Pp. 107–63 in Peter B. Evans, Dietrich Rueschemeyer, and Theda Skocpol, eds., *Bringing the State Back In*. New York: Cambridge University Press.

Wejnert, Barbara. 2005. "Diffusion, Development, and Democracy, 1800–1999." *American Sociological Review 70*: 53–81.

Weymouth, Stephen, and J. Muir Macpherson. 2012. "The Social Construction of Policy Reform: Economists and Trade Liberalization around the World." *International Interactions 38*[5]: 670–702.

Whalley, John, and Roderick Hill, eds. 1985. *Canada-United States Free Trade*. Vol. 11 of the Research Papers for the Royal Commission on the Economic Union and Development Prospects for Canada. Toronto: University of Toronto Press.

Whitehead, Laurence. 2006. *Latin America: A New Interpretation*. New York: Palgrave Macmillan.

Wike, Richard, Katie Simmons, Bruce Stokes, and Janell Fetterolf. 2017. "Globally, Broad Support for Representative and Direct Democracy." Pew Research Center. http://www.pewglobal.org/2017/10/16/globally-broad-support-for-representative-and-direct-democracy/.

Wilson, Carole Jeanne. 2001. "Understanding NAFTA in Mexico: Political Attitude Formation in a Changing Political and Economic Environment." PhD dissertation. Department of Political Science. University of North Carolina at Chapel Hill.

Winham, Gilbert. 1994. "NAFTA and the Trade Policy Revolution of the 1980s: A Canadian Perspective." *International Journal 49*: 472–508.

Woll, Cornelia. 2008. *Firm Interests: How Governments Shape Business Lobbying on Global Trade*. Ithaca, NY: Cornell University Press.

Wonnacott, Paul, and Ronald J. Wonnacott. 1982. "Free Trade between the United States and Canada: Fifteen Years Later." *Canadian Public Policy 8*: 412–27.

Wonnacott, Ronald J. 1981. Comments to the Senate Standing Committee on Foreign Affairs. February 3. Proceedings on Canadian Relations with the United States. Issue No. 18. First Session, Thirty-Second Parliament, 1980–81.

Wonnacott, Ronald J. 1993. "Trade Liberalization: Canadian Contributions since the 1960s." *Canadian Journal of Economics* 26[1]: 14–25.

Wonnacott, Ronald J., and Paul Wonnacott. 1967. *Free Trade between the United States and Canada: The Potential Economic Effects.* Cambridge, MA: Harvard University Press.

Woods, Ngaire. 1995. "Economic Ideas and International Relations." *International Studies Quarterly* 39[2]: 161–80.

Woods, Ngaire. 2006. *The Globalizers: The IMF, the World Bank, and Their Borrowers.* Ithaca: Cornell University Press.

Woods, Tim. 2003. "Capitalist Class Relations, the State, and New Deal Foreign Trade Policy." *Critical Sociology* 29[3]: 393–418.

World Bank. 1995. *Bureaucrats in Business: The Economics and Politics of Government Ownership.* New York: Oxford University Press.

World Bank. N.d. *World Development Indicators Online.* Washington, DC: World Bank. http://devdata.worldbank.org/dataonline.

World Trade Organization. 2013. *World Trade Report: Factors Shaping the Future of World Trade.* Geneva: World Trade Organization. https://www.wto.org/english/res_e/publications_e/wtr13_e.htm.

Yoshimatsu, Hidetaka. 1998a. "Economic Interdependence and the Making of Trade Policy: Industrial Demand for an Open Market in Japan." *Pacific Review* 11: 28–50.

Yoshimatsu, Hidetaka. 1998b. "Japan's Keidanren and Political Influence on Market Liberalization." *Asian Survey* 38[3]: 328–45.

Yoshimatsu, Hidetaka. 2000. *Internationalization, Corporate Preferences and Commercial Policy in Japan.* Houndmills, Hampshire: Macmillan Business.

Yoshimatsu, Hidetaka. 2002. "Preferences, Interests, and Regional Integration: The Development of the ASEAN Industrial Cooperation Arrangement." *Review of International Political Economy* 9: 123–49.

Zhang, Dong Dong. 1998. "Negotiating for a Liberal Economic Regime: The Case of Japanese FDI in China." *Pacific Review* 11: 51–78.

INDEX

Note: For the benefit of digital users, indexed terms that span two pages (e.g., 52–53) may, on occasion, appear on only one of those pages.